The Atlas of Shipwreck & Treasure
The Legacy of the Tek Sing
Lost Treasure Ships of the Twentieth Century
Lost Treasure Ships of the Northern Seas
Lady Bette and the Murder of Mr Thynn

SAMUEL
PEPYS
and the
STRANGE
WRECKING
of the
GLOUCESTER

SAMUEL PEPYS

and the

STRANGE

WRECKING

of the

GLOUCESTER

A True Restoration Tragedy

NIGEL PICKFORD

For Rosamund

First published 2021

The History Press
97 St George's Place, Cheltenham,
Gloucestershire, GL50 3QB
www.thehistorypress.co.uk

British Library Cataloguing in Publication Data.
A catalogue record for this book is available from the British Library.

ISBN 978 0 7509 9753 9

Typesetting and origination by The History Press
Printed and bound in Great Britain by TJ Books Limited, Padstow, Cornwall.

Trees for Life

CONTENTS

LIST OF ILLUSTRATIONS

ACKNOWLEDGEMENTS

It is always an immense pleasure and privilege to study original manuscript material whether in the form of letters, diaries, log books, ledgers, petitions, wills, charts, maps, or just shopping lists and bills. They all possess an immediacy and power, however ephemeral their origin, that transports the reader straight back into the past. For this reason, I feel a great debt of gratitude to all those archivists, conservationists and support staff in Manuscripts at the British Library, the National Archives at Kew, the Scottish National Archives in Edinburgh, the Lincolnshire Archives, the National Maritime Museum in Greenwich, the Guildhall Library in London, the Pepys Library at Magdalene College Cambridge, as well as the Roxburghe, Seton and Jarvis family archives. The printed word is, of course, equally vital to any study and I am again particularly grateful to the librarians and their support staff at the Caird Library in Greenwich, the University Library in Cambridge, the British Library in London and the Guildhall Library in London.

A very special thank you must go to my agent Barbara Levy for her continued encouragement and support, and to my editor Simon Wright for his commitment and enthusiasm. I would also like to thank all those at The History Press who have helped with the editing and design of this book, in particular Alex Boulton and Alex Waite.

I would like to thank all my diving and shipwreck colleagues whose persistence led to the discovery of the *Gloucester* wreck, and also my family and friends for their patience in listening to my many stories of the past.

Above all, I would like to thank my wife for her wonderful critical perspicacity when reading early drafts and unstinting generosity with her time.

1

THE NORFOLK COAST

At first the bodies sank to the seabed. Then, after only a few days of submersion, once the internal organs had begun to putrefy and the flesh had swelled with noxious gases, they rose again to the surface like inflated balloons. Later that same week they came ashore one by one and at different locations, as if in death they disdained each other's company. They fetched up all along the bleak and empty coastline that stretches from Yarmouth to Caister, Winterton and Happisburgh. There were even some that drifted as far north as Foulness and the estuary of the Humber.[1]

They were deposited on the sands as the tide ebbed. In some, the softer parts, the cheeks and the lips, had been eaten away by lampreys and hag fish. But there were no obvious signs of human violence, no gaping wounds. The waves nudged and licked at their ankles, alternately fawning and spurning.

It was the middle of May 1682. The weather was thick and often raining with blustering easterly winds that kept the temperatures unseasonably low. The wind moaned through the grey hair grass that grew luxuriantly over the sand dunes. The booming call of the bitterns was like the sound of distant cannon fire, both a warning and a requiem.

Shipwreck was common in these waters, and Newarp and Scroby Sands were both notorious graveyards for sailors. But usually there was some evidence of the ship itself, a standing mast or a floating spar, and the number of victims was not so numerous. On this occasion the absence of wreckage and the wide dispersal of corpses suggested that a great ship had gone down far out to sea. But there was no war raging and there had been no storm, so there was no obvious reason for a ship to have perished.

It was the scavengers of the coastline, the cockle pickers and the samphire gatherers, peering into the grey light of dawn, who first spotted this strange invasion of the dead. Most of the bodies still had strips of coarse blue cloth attached to them. There was even the odd telltale red hat washing back and forth in the slack water. It all spoke of a Royal Navy ship. The bodies were hurriedly searched for valuables. Shipwreck was looked on as part of God's beneficence by those who lived along this forlorn coast, far from the eye of the magistrates. Daniel Defoe in his *Tour thro' the Whole Island of Great Britain* remarked on how:

> As I went by land from Yarmouth northward, along the shoar towards Cromer … I was surprised to see, in all the way from Winterton, that the farmers, and country people had scarce a barn, or a shed, or a stable; nay, not the pales of their yards, and gardens, not a hogstye, not a necessary-house, but what was built of old planks, beams, wales and timbers, &c. the wrecks of ships, and ruins of mariners and merchants' fortunes.[2]

One or two of the corpses were sumptuously dressed, suggesting members of the gentry were among the drowned. They offered rich pickings for those who found them. The quickest and surest way to obtain a gold ring was to sever the finger on which it had become embedded.[3]

For the most part the dead could not be identified. They were wrapped in a simple shroud, placed on the backs of carts and buried in a common grave in the nearest churchyard. There was no bell, no book, no prayer, no distribution of ale and cheese to mourn their passing. It was important to keep the cost to the parish to a minimum. But in certain cases the names of the missing can be traced through the letters of survivors, the evidence of wills or the *ex gratia* payments made to widows.

Rowland Rowleson was one of the ordinary sailors who lost their lives when the *Gloucester* frigate sank, for that was the name of the Royal Navy ship that had foundered some 30 miles from the nearest land. He had made his will just two weeks before he sailed:

Know all men by these words that I, Rowland Rowleson belonging to his Majestie's Ship called the *Glocester* Sir John Berrie Commander have made … Hercules Browne of Wapping Whitechappell … slop seller my true and lawful attorney … and further considering the dangers and perils of the Seas and the uncertainty of my returne for the avoidance of variance and strife which may happen about that small estate which I shall leave at the time of my decease … do give unto Hercules Browne my said attorney all my wages debts moneys … goods chattels and estate whatsoever and do make the said Hercules Browne sole executor … whereof I have hereunto set my hand and seale the 19th day of April in the 34th year of Charles the second King of England Scotland France and Ireland in the year of our Lord God one thousand six hundred and eighty two, Rowland Rowleson, his mark …[4]

His use of the phrase, 'considering the dangers and perils of the Seas and the uncertainty of my returne', has, in the circumstances, a grim poignancy. Did he make this will because he had a premonition of his own death? Was there talk among the sailors of Whitechapel and Wapping, Stepney and Shadwell that the *Gloucester* was a cursed ship? It is not out of the question. There were already rumours that James, Duke of York, would be sailing on the *Gloucester* to fetch back his pregnant wife, Mary of Modena, from Scotland with the intention of then settling in Westminster, where he was expected to take over much of the running of the state. The old king, Charles II, was sick and the duke was his named heir. But James was a Catholic, as was his wife, and both of them were deeply unpopular in many quarters. There was a large constituency who wished James dead. Only a few weeks before his departure for Edinburgh, his portrait in the City of London had been slashed viciously with a knife. 'A vile indignity' had been 'offered to the picture of His Royal Highness the Duke of York standing in the Guildhall'.[5] The symbolism of this act of violence was not lost on the populace and not all sailors were loyal to the throne. There may well have been loose talk in the taverns along Ratcliffe Highway about how the voyage north was fated to be troublesome.

Certainly, no sooner was it known that the ship had sunk than there were those who were saying that the wrecking was all part of a plot carried out by the Fanatick Party, with the explicit aim of drowning James. It was claimed that at the centre of this supposed plot was Captain Ayres, the *Gloucester*'s pilot. A Mr Ridley wrote excitedly to Sir Francis Radcliffe of Dilston, 'I must inform you that the pilot is a known Republican ... it's not only suspicious but evident he designed his [James, Duke of York's] ruin with the whole ship, having made a provision for his own escape, but he is taken and will be tried for his life.'[6]

But there is another equally compelling explanation as to why Rowleson felt it necessary to make his will. It is an intriguing document, as much for what it doesn't say as for what it does. Rowleson was obviously a man very much alone in the world. He makes no mention of a mother or a wife, a child or a lover, or even a friend. Instead he makes Hercules Browne, simply referred to as a slop seller in Whitechapel, both his attorney and his sole beneficiary. He may have been an orphan or simply old, indigent and solitary. What is very strange is that a man in Rowleson's situation, a man with only a 'small estate' to dispose of, as he himself frankly described it, should bother to make a will in the first place. The most probable explanation for this meticulous ordering of his affairs before he set sail is that he owed Hercules Browne money and that it was Browne who had insisted on the will being made before he agreed to advance him any further credit. Slop sellers sold sailors their clothing, their canvas jackets and trousers, along with other small necessaries, quids of tobacco for a clay pipe, or dice carved from bone for playing backgammon.

2

YORK BUILDINGS

On the morning of 7 March 1682 Samuel Pepys rose long before the city was properly awake. He summoned a young female servant to perform her usual duties; the lighting of fires, the setting out of clothes. He was used to early starts, and relished the sense of purpose and excitement that they brought. There was a pronounced hush in the street below his windows and a strange luminosity as if the moon was shining upwards off the smart new paving stones. When the shutters were folded back it was evident that a fresh thin scattering of snow had fallen overnight. It had been much the same for several days.

These were not ideal weather conditions for making a long journey. A probing wind blew from the north-east, searching out the body's weakest points, the arthritic joint, the congested lung. Pepys was not without his aches and pains these days. Nor was the Newmarket coach known for its personal comforts. It was a draughty, jolting, incommodious form of transport, a far cry from the plush yellow carriage that Pepys used to own. But he was determined to be one of the first to welcome His Royal Highness the Duke of York back on to English soil, and for this privilege he was prepared to make some small personal sacrifices.

The maid laid out his fresh linen, helped him to dress and brushed his long curling wig. It was the usual morning ritual that he was still wealthy enough to indulge in. In the old days, when his wife was alive and he had lived in his own property in Seething Lane, he had enjoyed the attentions of a very pretty young maid called Mercer. When she dressed him in the mornings Pepys took the opportunity of fondling her breasts, 'they being the finest that I ever saw in my life; that is the truth of it'.[1] With another house maid called Debbie Willet he allowed himself a little more licence. 'And so by the fireside to have my head combed, as I do now often do, by Deb, whom I love should be fiddling about me.'[2] On one occasion, while Debbie was brushing his hair and he had his hand up her skirt, his wife came in and caught him. She was not pleased. Pepys was penitent, but these bouts of remorse never lasted very long. As for the girls, they put up with his gropings with quiet resignation. He was generally a good employer, generous with his presents, and he did not force the issue to actual coition – not with the housemaids and not beneath his own roof.

This particular morning, he was not exactly beneath his own roof. He was at 12 York Buildings, Buckingham Street, just south of the Strand. The street is still there today, as is the house. Pepys was living with his good friend William Hewer. He had been there for nearly three years, ever since he had been let out of prison. The last few years had been difficult ones. In 1679, after the so-called Popish Plot had led to a wave of anti-Catholic feeling, King Charles had considered it expedient to send his younger brother and heir, James, into temporary exile while passions calmed. Pepys's closeness to James left him very exposed. It was only a matter of a few weeks before Pepys found himself brought up before a Parliamentary Committee and accused of 'Piracy, Popery and Treachery'. Parliament was dominated by the Earl of Shaftesbury, considered by many as the leader of the anti-Catholic Whig faction, and so the end result of the enquiry was a foregone conclusion. Pepys was committed to the Tower, along with his long-time friend and business colleague Sir Anthony Deane. In the event, the case for the prosecution crumbled rapidly and Pepys and Deane were soon released. The main witness against Pepys was the poisonous John Scott, who disappeared abroad at a critical moment.[3] Scott's accusations were soon exposed by the detective work in Paris of Pepys's brother-in-law, 'Balty' St Michel, as being little more than a wild concoction of malice and fantasy. The other main witness against him was John James, Pepys's ex-butler, who had a grudge to settle over his dismissal. When John James realised he was terminally ill, he changed his testimony, most probably out of contrition. The altar that Pepys had supposedly worshipped at was no more than a painting of his late wife, above a dressing table, on which two candles had been placed. It was a sign of the troubled times the country had been going through that such preposterous accusations could ever have been taken seriously.

The danger for Pepys passed, but the humiliating memory of being incarcerated in a bare cell did not fade. Imprisonment had been a deeply unsettling and transforming experience that had left him with a residue of suspicion and bitterness against all those who espoused the cause of the puritans, the 'Fanaticks' as they were called in the loyalist press. Besides which, he was still without a job, having been rudely removed from his position at the Admiralty, where he had been working for more than twenty years. Before his departure he had been the secretary, responsible for running the country's largest administrative department. He oversaw the manning of the navy, the building of new ships, the wages and the victualling. His knowledge, his energy and his abilities were incomparable. He was only 49 years old. He was still hungry for power and prestige, and scathing about the way the Royal Navy was now being managed.

But all was not lost. There were signs that the winds of fortune were changing. Pepys had not met with the duke for two years, but if James was coming south again, possibly for good, then Pepys was anxious to take the first opportunity of reminding him that he was still alive and anxious to be of service. He was feeling optimistic and energetic, more so than he had done for many months past.

York Buildings was one of those bold and brash housing developments aimed at the new rich that were springing up all over central London in the late 1670s. The venal Duke of Buckingham had sold off the sprawling medieval mansion, York House, in 1672 for the colossal sum of £30,000. The enterprising Nicholas Barbon was part of the syndicate that made the purchase. The ancient palace of the archbishops was promptly demolished, only the Watergate and an avenue of ash trees along by the river being saved. Barbon, who had a lucrative finger in most of the big new construction schemes that were taking place, subdivided the grounds and then sold on small plots to individual builders. In the space of the next few years fashionable brick terraced houses, with large sash windows that let in lots of light, rose up on both sides of the newly created Buckingham Street. Externally they were almost identical; four storeys high with spacious attics for the servants and a basement – sensible, airy and easy to run.

Buckingham Street was a good address. It was close to the grand houses of the old aristocracy. Somerset House lay to the east, Northumberland House to the west. The handy shopping centre of the New Exchange was just at the top of the street on the Strand, and London's main thoroughfare, the Thames, was just at the bottom, with the beautiful York Gate providing a convenient embarkation point for taking a wherry down to Westminster. The new houses attracted a mix of successful merchants and minor gentry: Anne, the widowed Countess of Newburgh, was living at No. 9; James Richards, the ironmonger, was at No. 10; Robert Nott, Deputy Master of the King's Wardrobe, inhabited No. 11; and No. 12 was owned by Will Hewer, one-time clerk at the Admiralty and now a successful businessman, but best remembered for his lifelong friendship with Samuel Pepys, his early mentor. Hewer was a career bachelor; Pepys was a widower who never remarried. The two men eventually lived companionably together for nearly ten years.[4]

It was just about possible to ride from London to Newmarket by horse in one day, a distance of 54 miles, and, when younger, Pepys was known to do so. But these days he was more corpulent and the coach was more convenient. The journey took two days by coach, an overnight stop being required. The Bull in Bishopsgate was a favourite posting house for coaches going north. It was a huge timber-framed building with balconies and balustrades, constructed around a central yard where horses stamped and steamed and ostlers cursed. It was most probably from the Bull that Pepys left early on the morning of 7 March. After Bishopsgate the road led to Woodford, Epping, Harlow and Bishop's Stortford. In Bishop's Stortford, Pepys was fond of staying in the Reindeer Tavern, where Mrs Aynsworth, a renowned prostitute, had once been resident. 'All the good fellows of the country come hither,' was Pepys's glowing recommendation.[5] He knew Mrs Aynsworth well from when she used to live in Cambridge. She had taught him to sing 'Full forty times over', a 'very lewd song'.[6] Whether she was still at the Reindeer Tavern in 1682 is not known, but it seems unlikely. Mrs Aynsworth had had aspirations to move to London, an ambition Pepys disapproved of, 'for it will be found better for her to be chief where she is then to have little to do at London, there being many finer than she there'.[7] She might have been good value in Bishop's Stortford, but Pepys clearly felt she didn't have the necessary glamour to compete in the London market.

After Bishop's Stortford the road wound its way to Stansted, Ugley Street, Quendon Street, Newport, Audley End House, Littlebury, Great Chesterford, Bourn Bridge, the First Ditch, the White Post, Devil's Ditch and finally Newmarket Town. The weather did not improve. It was a long and tedious journey.

3

LEITH HARBOUR

At first light on the morning of 7 March, the same morning that Pepys set out from Buckingham Street in London, there was much commotion and bustle between Holyrood Castle and what was called the Shore, a cobbled causeway that forms the southern side of Leith Harbour, Edinburgh's gateway to the sea. The royal yacht, *Henrietta*, which had been tied up to the jetty for many weeks past, on constant standby for James's exclusive use, was at last being prepared to set sail as soon as the tide permitted.

James had wasted no time. William Legge, groom to the bedchamber and Charles's personal envoy, had just ridden non-stop from London with a letter in Charles's hand, inviting James to meet him in Newmarket. The exhausted messenger, flushed with the excitement of having completed his epic ride in under four days, had no sooner handed over the sealed letter than James was busy ordering his servants to prepare for his immediate departure.

This was the summons that James had been agitating for, for the best part of the last year. Now that it had finally arrived, he was impatient to set sail. The plan was for the brothers to meet in Newmarket, enjoy a little horse racing and gambling together, and progress from there to London. If all went well, James would shortly afterwards return to Edinburgh and bring back his family and entire retinue of servants on a permanent basis. James was very anxious to resume his place within the heart of government, from which position of strength he would be better able to ensure his eventual succession to the throne, in the event of Charles predeceasing him. This last was not an improbable eventuality. Charles's health had already given grave cause for concern. Furthermore, he had no legitimate children nor much likelihood of producing any.

For the past three years James had been living in virtual exile, firstly in Brussels and then in Scotland. The reason for his removal had been the mood of extreme hostility to Catholicism and all things Popish that had swept through the nation in the late 1670s. James was a devout Catholic and, still worse, he made no effort to conceal his religious allegiances. In the circumstances, Charles had thought it advisable to remove his younger brother from centre stage until the nation calmed down. With characteristic even-handedness he had also removed the Duke of Monmouth, his illegitimate son by a long since discarded and notoriously dissolute mistress, Lucy Walter. Monmouth was the main alternative contender for the succession, and the darling of the more extreme Protestant faction. He provided a rallying point for those who wished to exclude James from the throne.

James's transfer to Scotland was an improvement on Brussels, for at least while there he had had an opportunity to exercise his administrative skills. He had been appointed Charles's direct representative and head of the executive. His tenure of power was relatively successful, but it still did not endear him to the draughty hallways of Holyrood Castle. He was itching for London and the opportunities it would provide him.

The glistening and ornate gilt work of the *Henrietta* yacht can never have looked more alluring to James's eyes than it did that slow grey dawn, but the weather was hardly propitious. It was proving to be yet another filthy day, with a bitter wind gusting from the north bringing flurries of snow and hail. Hardly the ideal conditions for a cruise on the North Sea, but James had never been a man to allow a little physical hardship to get in the way of what he perceived as his divine destiny.

The royal yachts were the private jets of their age, luxuriously fitted out and horrendously expensive to run, but the Stuart brothers were not shy when it came to spending money from the public purse on their private peccadilloes. The attractions of the yachts were obvious. Of the various forms of transport available they were the most comfortable and the most discreet, providing the brothers with a welcome place of retreat from their official duties. They were also useful as something to be lent to court favourites and those whom one might wish to influence. They were used on diplomatic missions and sometimes on more nefarious activities. William Fazeby, the Captain of the *Henrietta*, had recently received a £400 bonus from the secret service fund for activities unnamed. And while the *Henrietta* was moored in Leith Harbour, James's personal favourite yacht, called the *Mary* after his wife, was anchored in Holland, having just whisked Karl Johann von Königsmarck across the Channel, shortly after this foreign count had murdered Thomas Thynn, a great supporter of Monmouth and a thorn in the flesh of the Stuart brothers. The royal yachts were an integral part of court life and dear to the hearts of both James and Charles. Hardly surprising then that they should name them after their mistresses and loved ones: as well as the *Mary* there was the *Fubbs* (Charles's pet name for his mistress the Duchess of Portsmouth) and the *Cleveland* (named after the title Charles gave his mistress Barbara Palmer).

The *Henrietta*, 162 tons burthen and about 80ft long, had been recently built in the yards of Woolwich on the Thames by Jonas Shish – 'Old Shish', as Pepys somewhat dismissively described him, adding that he was 'illiterate' and 'a great drinker'. Pepys, as he approached 50 years of age himself, was increasingly curmudgeonly in his opinions. By contrast, the writer John Evelyn was more generous in his assessment of the shipbuilder, calling him 'a plain honest carpenter, hardly capable of reading, yet of great ability'.[1]

Whatever the shortcomings of Jonas Shish, the *Henrietta* was a sumptuous creation, with an ornately carved stern of exotic writhing sea creatures and scantily draped nymphs, surmounted by the royal arms of the lion and the unicorn in rampant pose. The elaborate gilt work was continued all around the portholes and the prow. Inside, the state rooms were furnished with damask-covered couches, and the walls were panelled and painted with the usual classical sylvan scenes of banquets and reclining maidens, hanging bunches of grapes competing with pendulous breasts.

William Fazeby, the captain, was a loyal and trusted seaman with more than twenty years' continuous service to his credit. He had fought in the Dutch wars alongside James, and lost a leg in action, which did not seem to hinder his ability to clamber up and down ships' ladders, even in rough weather. He was just the sort of Royal Navy man that James liked to spend time with. The only slight blemish on James's good humour that morning, as he gave instructions to his stewards for the stowing of his baggage, was the attitude adopted by his wife, Mary of Modena, towards his imminent departure.

Mary had been very reluctant to marry him in the first place, but once she was wed she proved to be fiercely loyal. She had chosen to share his bed and she chose also to share his exile, staying resolutely by his side throughout all the political turmoil. Now James was returning to England, Mary, unsurprisingly, wanted to travel with him. James refused to allow it. It wasn't simply that Charles had not explicitly sanctioned her return; James himself did not think it a good idea. He had already made his views clear on this subject the previous August, when writing to George Legge, elder brother of William, and one of his most steadfast retainers:'If I have leave to go up, I intend to leave the Duchess and my daughter behind, which they will be very well contented with, it not being proper for women to make such a voyage for so short a stay.'[2] On this occasion, as on others, James had misread the political runes. He had to wait eight more months before he finally got the official nod for coming south. He was also quite wrong about Mary being content to stay behind. She had no more liking for life in Scotland than her husband, but she had put up with it stoically for his sake.

Though unhappy about the decision, Mary had little choice in the matter, particularly as she was pregnant with her fifth child. Of the previous four, only one had survived infancy, and she was a girl, not the longed for male heir. Perhaps the fifth would prove to be a boy. Mary's pregnancy was James's trump card when it came to convincing his elder brother that it was time for him to return to centre stage. But it was a card that needed to be played with care.

It was perhaps understandable that James did not want her to make the long and dangerous journey in her delicate condition, with the strong possibility that it would turn out to be pointless and he would have to return into exile again almost immediately. Far better for Mary to remain in Edinburgh while he checked out the lay of the land. Besides which, he had a small private purpose of his own that he did not confide to her, but for which her absence would be a decided advantage. So James persuaded her that a yacht would be too violent in its movement. It would not be a safe mode of transport for her in her pregnant state; instead he would send a larger ship to fetch her as soon as it was possible. On 21 April, Mary wrote from Edinburgh to her brother, the Duke of Modena, 'in three weeks time the Duke will come and fetch me in a big vessel, which will be safer and have less motion than the yachts'.[3] It is evident from her letter that her brother was of the opinion that she should remain in Scotland until the baby was born, but this was something that Mary was not prepared to consider. She wrote:

> I am sorry you disapprove of my going, for it is certainly the best thing for our interests, for now the Duke is so popular and well thought of by all that they would never allow him to leave the country, and if he remain there, I certainly can not remain here. He has only been away a month and already it seems more than I can bear.[4]

James's departure from Holyrood may have been rushed, but he still took care to orchestrate it with an appropriate flourish. This was a period when the visual iconography surrounding kingship was all important in establishing power and authority in the popular imagination. So, he had insisted that he was accompanied from Holyrood House to Leith Harbour by the trumpets, bagpipes and drums of the officially trained military bands. As soon as he was on board his yacht, 'All the great guns from the Castle, pier and ships were fired and thousands of people from the shore never ceas'd crying, God preserve his Royal Highness.' The reference to thousands of well-wishers crowding the narrow pier may have been something of a journalistic exaggeration but all the same the warmth of his send-off was sweet music to his ears. He must have been hoping that his reception in England would be equally fulsome, for he had received some very frosty treatment when he had last exposed himself to the whims of the English populace.

4

MODENA

Mary of Modena had been a controversial figure from the moment she first set foot on British soil, at Dover on 21 November 1673. She was very beautiful, on that simple fact everyone was agreed. All the famous painters of the time – Lely, Wissing, Kneller, Verelst – celebrated her good looks in a series of glamorous if highly stylised portraits. Exactly how you viewed such beauty was rather more problematic. If you were loyal to the crown, as Aphra Behn was, then Mary's handsome looks were no more than a reflection of her inner goodness. In her 1682 poem, Behn acknowledges that the nation is divided in its opinions but believes Mary's self-evident purity will act as a healing agent:

> How e're they differ, this they all must grant,
> Your form and Mind, no One perfection want,
> Without all Angel and within all Saint.

But not everyone was convinced. The militant Protestants and Parliamentarians saw in Mary's beauty nothing but a seductive snare sent by the Pope to betray the English court into the hands of Rome and the devil. They regarded Mary herself as little better than a hired Catholic whore, the latest in a long line who had infiltrated their way into the corrupt beds of the Stuart brothers. Amid talk of her imminent arrival, Clerk of the Privy Council Sir Joseph Williamson received intelligence of heightened tensions in the build-up to Guy Fawkes Night. 'Should she arrive tonight', wrote a Mr Denham, 'she would certainly be martyred.' He continued, 'The common people here and even those of quality in the country, believe she is the Pope's eldest daughter'.[1]

Some commentators blamed the increase in ill-founded gossip on the growth in the number of coffee houses:

> Wee have had various reports about the Duchess of Modena ... But the common people talk anything, for every carman and porter is now a statesman; and indeed the coffee houses are good for nothing else. It was not thus when we dranke nothing but sacke and claret, or English beer and ale. These sober clubs produce nothing but scandalous and censorious discourses.[2]

The evil of coffee houses aside, if the people of England had known of the bizarre truth that lay behind the marriage of the Duke of York to Mary, the young princess of d'Este, their suspicions about her would have been inflamed still further.

On 23 February 1673, Henry Mordaunt, 2nd Earl of Peterborough, had set off across the Channel on a very secret mission. At 52 he was a man of mature years, a little paunchy around the stomach, a little tired around the eyes, but he was the consummate diplomat and both his discretion and his loyalty to the crown were unquestioned. His instructions were straightforward in their goal but potentially fraught with difficulty in their accomplishment. He was to find a new wife for James and this time there were to be no slip-ups. James's first wife, Anne Hyde, had been a 'commoner'. Although she had conducted herself well, she was never fully approved of as consort for the future king. Her early death, in excruciating pain from breast cancer, provided the monarchy with a second chance. This time around it was thought vital that a more suitable replacement be found at the earliest opportunity. There was some worry within government circles that if left too long to his own devices, James, who was something of a loose

cannon where women were concerned, might well make another inappropriate commitment.

A shortlist of eleven princesses was drawn up and Mordaunt set off to view them. Five were rejected out of hand. Of the remainder, the Duchess of Guise was seriously considered for a while, but then she too was dismissed. Mordaunt decided she was, after all, too short, with an 'ill shape'. Mademoiselle de Rais was put forward with enthusiasm by her relations but Mordaunt didn't like her picture. He knew very well that she was not the sort of woman who would please the tastes of his fickle master. Princess Mary Ann of Würtemberg was next on his hit list. Mordaunt did not rule her out. Her appearance was not entirely ravishing but nor was it unpleasant. He wrote back to England that she had a 'fair complexion with brown hair, the figure of her face turned very agreeably, her eyes grey, her looks grave, but sweet'.[3] But with the Würtemberg princess, Mordaunt ran into a different kind of problem. Louis XIV did not approve on political grounds, and as Louis was Charles's private paymaster, Charles did not approve. So Mordaunt wearily left Paris and travelled incognito to Dusseldorf to take a look at the daughter of the Duke of Neuburg. Once again, he was disappointed. 'At those years she was inclined to be fat.'[4] Unforgiveable. Mordaunt knew his master's inclinations well and he knew that unlike his elder brother, who had been quite prepared to marry Catherine of Braganza, despite her dumpy physique, for the benefit of the kingdom, James was not one to compromise when it came to either his religion or his bed partners. James liked his women slim and he liked them young.

Mordaunt now turned southwards and headed for Italy. He had been pursuing princesses for the best part of four months, and was getting a little desperate. The weather had turned warm and sultry. It was not the ideal time of year to be travelling down through Provence and across the foothills of the Apennines. Eventually he arrived in the broiling town of Modena with its shimmering piazzas of pale yellow flagstones and its dazzling palaces of pink brick. He was conducted to the Palazzo Conti, where he was shown the portrait of the young Mary d'Este. He was instantly enchanted. 'It bore the appearance of a young creature about 14 years of age; but such a light of beauty, such Character of Ingenuity and Goodness,' he later recorded in his memoirs. He was convinced he had at last found 'the fortune of England'.[5] He pressed for an interview but Mary's mother, the Duchess Laura, was not keen to oblige him. Her daughter was very young. She knew little but the convent. Her entire wish was to become a nun and devote herself to God. James was already 41. Wouldn't the Duke of York perhaps prefer a woman nearer his own age? The Duchess suggested Mary's aunt Leonara, aged 30, also a princess of the noble house of d'Este. Surely she would be more suitable? But Mordaunt was not interested in Aunt Leonara, whom he described as 'very ugly' and, even worse, 'redheaded'. Besides, she was almost an old woman, certainly past her best child-bearing years. Mordaunt wanted the 14-year-old Mary for his master. He was unsure whether the duchess was genuine in her objections or whether she was simply employing a time-honoured negotiating tactic in order to raise the price.

Eventually Mordaunt's persistence paid off and he was granted an audience with the girl herself in the ducal palace. He wrote back to England full of enthusiasm: 'she was tall and admirably shaped, her complexion was of the last fairness, her Hair black as Jet, so were her Eyebrows and her Eyes; but the latter so full of light and sweetness so they did dazzle and charm too'.[6] He wrote like a man intoxicated, but he was not so entirely carried away that he omitted to also make mention of that most vital attribute: 'she appears very healthful'.[7] He had not forgotten that her prime duty would be to give birth to a male heir, a boy who would survive the diseases of childhood and live long enough to inherit the crown of England. His appraisal had just that touch of the professional surveyor of horseflesh.

Mordaunt was full of charm but, even so, the going was not easy. Mary had been 'bred so simple' that she had never even heard of England. Even more problematic: she told Mordaunt that she had an 'invincible aversion to marriage'. She desperately wanted to be a nun. Besides, the Duke of York was over 40. Why should she want to marry an old man she had never even set eyes on? But powerful diplomatic wheels were being slowly and grindingly set in motion. Cardinal Altieri, adopted nephew of Pope Clement X, urged Mary's mother to support the marriage. The duchess yielded, as perhaps she had been planning to all along. The financial deal was hammered out. Louis XIV promised to chuck in some cash from his own coffers. The entire diplomatic force of the Catholic Church was mobilised. Everything possible was being done to pressure the 14-year-old Mary to marry James. But Mary was stubborn. She knew what she wanted. She wanted to devote her life to God and spend the rest of her days in the convent at Modena with her adored Mother Superior.

It was then that the Pope stepped in. He wrote directly to Mary. It is a most extraordinary letter. He bluntly told Mary that it was her religious duty to enter into this marriage in order to help re-establish Catholicism in England and end the persecution of her co-religionists. 'Dear daughter in Christ … consider the great profit which may accrue to the Catholic faith … through your marriage … we easily conceive a firm hope that an end might come to the persecution still smouldering in that Kingdom.'[8] Clement X did not pull his papal punches, and the letter achieved its aim. Indeed, it is difficult to conceive quite how a devout Catholic girl could have held out against the written command of the most Holy Father, who is, after all, the representative of God on earth. Mary might not exactly have been the Pope's daughter as her enemies suggested, but she was certainly his sacrificial lamb.

On 30 September 1673, Mordaunt left the house of Count Ugo Molza, where he had been staying, and processed to the ducal palace. He was dressed in a suit of English scarlet cloth. There, with Mordaunt acting as James's proxy, the marriage ceremony took place. Afterwards, elaborate *trionfi* created out of paste sugar and marzipan were devoured. Toasts of rich dark wine were drunk. And within a few days Mary was trundling her way in an impressive train of royal carriages towards England.

It was a slow business. They covered 20 to 30 miles a day, and Mary suffered from the usual traveller's ailments. In Paris she contracted dysentery and was really quite ill. As for the political nightmare that she was blindly heading towards, the situation was getting steadily worse. The French aristocrat and celebrated letter-writer Madame de Sévigné wrote, 'English affairs are not going well; the Parliament will not have the match and want to disunite England and France; this is at present the grand pétoffe of Europe.'[9]

Despite the discomfort and the perils of her journey, Mary's mood remained surprisingly upbeat and she even managed a little religious sightseeing. At the tomb of St Francis of Sales she marvelled at 'the mattress on which he died, his cassock, his cushion, his writing table'.[10] And when she finally reached the English Channel, she was enthralled by the voyage, even though it was her first time on the sea and the weather was quite rough. She wrote to her beloved Mother Superior back in the Convent at Modena that 'on board this boat ... everything goes on, reading, writing, playing, eating, sleeping, laughing' – quickly adding, in case the Mother Superior might think she was becoming too frivolous – 'and also saying our offices'.[11]

The mood in England was far from universally welcoming to the young princess and future queen, but Mary in her innocence was quite oblivious of the viper's nest that awaited her. She crossed the Channel in the royal yacht *Catherine*, escorted by four ships of war. It was an impressive show. The voyage from Calais to Dover took ten hours. Her husband, James – they were after all legally married, even though neither of them had yet set eyes on the other – was waiting to greet her. On sight of him Mary burst into tears, though whether with horror or relief was not recorded. Mordaunt was more sanguine in his description of their first meeting. 'Upon her landing she took possession of his heart as well as his arms and was thence conducted to her lodgings.'[12] So far as Mordaunt was concerned, after nearly a year of traipsing round the courts of Europe in search of a suitable bride, it was job done.

Mary was nothing if not intrepid and resourceful. She quickly adapted to her new existence. Within two months of her arrival in England she wrote back to her Mother Superior in the Modena convent, 'May it be a consolation to you, dear Mother, to know that the Duke is a very good man and wishes me well, and would do anything to prove it to me.'[13] She may have been mistaken in this last belief but her 100 per cent commitment to James throughout the remainder of her life never wavered. She threw herself wholeheartedly into court life and before long she was playing ombre and enjoying the putting on of plays.

It wasn't long before she became pregnant. Her first child, Charlotte, was born early in 1675. Mary was 16 years of age. But before the year was out Charlotte had died. Another girl, Isabella, was born the following September. Mary's spirits revived. The gossipy Lady Chaworth wrote:

> The Dutchesse is much delighted with making and throwing of snow balls, and pelted the Duke soundly with one the other day and ran away quick into her closet and he after her, but she durste not open the doore. She hath also much pleasure in one of those sledges which they call trainias and is pulled up and down the ponds in them every day.[14]

She was high spirited and playful, still only 17 years of age.

In 1677 Mary finally gave birth to the much longed for male heir. Mordaunt had been right about her fecundity – she had no problem producing babies. King Charles had no legitimate children of his own and he wasn't expected to have any now, so this baby boy was the heir to the throne. He was promptly christened Charles, but within a few weeks he too was dead, this time from smallpox.

Meanwhile, the political situation for James in England had taken a sharp turn for the worse. Hysteria about Catholic plots was whipped up daily by the likes of Titus Oates. Parliament, led by the Earl of Shaftesbury, was determined to have James excluded from the throne. Mary was keenly aware of what was happening around her, it would have been difficult for her not to be. Her own private secretary, Edward Coleman, had just been hanged, drawn and quartered as a result of some indiscreet letters he had written. In the festive season before Lent, Mary wrote to her brother: 'I hope you are having a merrier Carnival than we; for here no one is in good humour, and there are no diversions.'[15]

It was at this point that Charles decided that the best way of cooling the political temperature was to send James and his wife to Brussels. Mary wanted to take her only surviving child, Isobel, with her, but this was forbidden. Mary did not enjoy her banishment but put up with it with her usual stoicism. In June 1679 she wrote: 'I have no hope yet of going to my deare England again.'[16] It is noticeable that she now regarded England as her true home, not Modena. Her understanding of Charles's character was astute: 'The King always expresses great tenderness for his brother, and I really believe he wishes him well, but he allows himself to be persuaded by everybody.'[17] Her mother travelled up from Italy to visit her and wrote back to Mary's adored Uncle Rinaldo a letter full of concern for Mary's health and wellbeing: 'She is very tall but rather thin.'[18]

Later in the year, Charles fell ill, and James was hurriedly recalled to London. The illness proved to be a false alarm, but it was decided to transfer James to Edinburgh. Charles offered to Mary that she could stay in the Palace of Whitehall if she wished but Mary did not want to be separated from her husband, even though her one surviving child, Isabella, was required to stay in London. James and Mary made the journey to Scotland by road, because Mary had been so ill during her last two voyages across the North Sea. The decision was not altogether a happy one. The populace along the route made it quite clear to the Catholic couple that they were not wanted in England. James's impatience with his situation increased. He blamed his continued banishment on Charles's influential mistress, the Duchess of Portsmouth. He claimed, 'she has play'd me a dog trick, and is absolutely join'd with the Duke of Monmouth'.[19]

Then Isabel, Mary's only surviving child, succumbed to a fever. The small girl died without her mother near her on 2 February 1681. The following month, Mary gave birth a fourth time, but this baby was also soon dead. It was typical of Mary that she tried to see the positive in these repeated bereavements:

> I console myself with the thought that I have more angels to pray for me, and ought esteem myself honoured that while other women give their children to the world, I have given all mine to God ... in whose

mercy I still hope that he may some day comfort me by giving me a male child who shall live, and yet in the end gain heaven.[20]

James's youngest daughter by his first wife, called Anne like her mother, came to Scotland on a visit. Mary got on well with her step-daughter, whom she was nearer to in age than she was her husband. Anne enjoyed the country dancing. James passed the time playing golf. Mary took up horse riding. James liked to see his wife astride a horse, but in October Mary had a bad fall while riding on the beach. Her dress caught on the saddle and she was dragged for some distance, her face scraping along the sand and bruising her left side. She was already expecting her fifth child, so it was fortunate that she did not miscarry. Mary was not one for self-pity. She described sadness as 'the most cowardly and stupid, or to speak less injuriously, the weakest and laziest of all the passions'.[21]

And then at last the call came. James was asked to meet with Charles in Newmarket.

5

NEWMARKET

It was at the beginning of the seventeenth century, during the reign of James I, that horse racing first took off as a royal pastime on the bare heath just outside Newmarket. But it was not until the Restoration period and the patronage of Charles II that this small Suffolk town became a 'go-to' destination. Its popularity rapidly outgrew its capacity, but not everybody who visited appreciated the town's special attractions. It was certainly miserably cold, crowded and expensive during those early spring days of 1682. Old Sir Thomas Browne, physician, antiquarian, philosopher and naturalist, was glad not to be part of the racing circus that year. He wrote to his son Edward in London from his beloved house in Norwich close by the cathedral, 'The cold wether spoyls the field sports at Newmarkett, where some are content to drink very bad claret at 18 pence a bottle.'[1] Browne was a loyalist, but that didn't stop him thinking that many of the king's coterie were possessed of more money than sense. Nor was it just the claret that was overpriced. So many of London's glitterati had descended upon Newmarket to welcome the Duke of York on his long-awaited return from Scotland that the cost of a room in a cheap hostelry had gone through the roof. 'There is such a concourse of persons of quality at Newmarket that lodgings are at 10 pounds a week, a guinea a night being cheap for a lodging, several persons of quality (some say above 100) sitting up every night for want of room.'[2] Browne could be forgiven for not turning up for the great Newmarket jamboree. He was already 77 years of age and was to die later that same year.

Browne, like so many seventeenth-century intellectuals, was also a passionate experimental scientist, and it was this that led to his long friendship with Charles Scarborough, physician to both Charles and James, and one of those who very shortly was to find himself struggling for his life in the waters off Norfolk. Browne had once given Scarborough an 'aquila gesners', a rare breed of eagle, which Browne had been keeping in his house for the previous two years. During that time, Browne had been experimenting on it, feeding it cats, puppies and rats, but never giving it any water. It seemed to survive perfectly well without it. When Scarborough received the great bird, he housed it at the Royal College of Physicians, where it later died in the 'commone fire'. Browne also kept bitterns in his house. He was fascinated by the mournful, mugient noise they made and spent much effort dissecting them to try and discover how they produced such a forlorn sound.

Some of those who did attend the Newmarket frenzy were less than enamoured with the whole horse racing circus. The urbane Earl of Conway would much rather have been gracing a London salon with his witticisms than bellowing into the wind upon a barren stretch of heathland. But he was an impeccably faithful servant of the Stuart house, and as Secretary of State it was his duty to attend upon the king. So he contented himself with making laconic gossipy observations in his dispatches to his fellow Secretary of State, Sir Leoline Jenkins, about what a tedious time he was having, and passing on racing tips, 'the crack this day is 6 to 4 on Sir Robert Carr's horse, called the Postboy, against his Majesty's gelding called Mouse ... Pray don't acquaint Lord Halifax with this, for he will laugh at us secretaries for communicating such secrets which I assure you is all the place affords.'[3]

The intellectual Conway might have disdained the pleasures of Newmarket but the king couldn't get enough of them. In his diary, the bluff Yorkshireman Sir John Reresby describes Charles's typical day:

Waking in the morning til ten oclock; then he went to the cockpit til dinner time; about three he went to the horse races, at six to the cockpit for an hour, then to the play (though the comedians were indifferent), soe to supper, next to the Duchess of Portsmouth's till bedtime, and then to his own apartment to bed.[4]

There is no intention here to satirise. Reresby is a doggedly factual and faithful diarist. But the description he provides of Charles's leisure activities is remarkably similar to the round of inanities enjoyed by Prig in Thomas Shadwell's 1679 play, *A True Widow*:

Newmarket's a rare place, there a Man's never idle: We make Visits to Horses, and talk with Grooms, Riders, and Cock Keepers, and saunter in the heath all the forenoon; then we dine and never talk a word but of Dogs, Cocks, and Horses again, then we saunter into the Heath again; then to a Cock match; then to a Play in a Barn; then to Supper, and never speak a word but of Dogs, Cocks and Horses again; then to the Groom Porters where you may play all night. Oh tis a heavenly life. We are never idle.

Charles no longer rode his own racehorses as he had done as a younger man, but he still loved the smell and the thrill of the open fields, the thudding of hooves, the roar of the crowd. He was notoriously proud of his nickname 'Old Rowley', which was derived from a remarkably well-endowed stallion in the royal stable. It is not every king who would necessarily appreciate being called after his horse, but Charles considered it a compliment to his own sexual prowess.

So fond was Charles of the whole Newmarket experience that in 1668 he had bought his own house in the centre of the town. It was situated on the west side of the High Street close to where the United Reformed Church and a supermarket now stand. It was just a skip and a hop to Nell Gwynn's house on Palace Street, which, remarkably, is still there. The snobbish aesthete John Evelyn was very disparaging of the attractions of Charles's chosen abode. 'This house is plac'd in a dirty street without any courte or avenue, like a common Burgers,' was his damning verdict.[5]

But Evelyn was rather missing the point. The whole attraction of Newmarket for Charles was that it was a place he could forget about kingship, let his hair down and just be an ordinary citizen for once. Again, it is Reresby who puts it most succinctly. He describes how Charles would 'let himself down from Majesty to the very degree of a country gentleman … mixed himself amongst the crowd, allowed every man to speak to him that pleased'.[6] This mingling with the common people could be regarded as an admirably democratic quality in a king but there was a darker side to Charles's fondness for slumming it. It was during his stays in Newmarket that he used to adopt disguise and in the company of his pet jester, John Wilmot, Earl of Rochester, go whoring in the common brothels. Rochester would take care to procure for his master the choicest of the local young women.

The spring of 1682, however, did not find Charles in the best of form. According to Conway, the king was 'so much alone that for his diversion he was forced to play at bassett and, as I am informed, retires to his chamber every night at nine'.[7] This was hardly the fun-loving, party-going Charles of legend. But the truth was he had been suffering from poor health for some time and he was beginning to worry about who would succeed him on his death. It was this increasing concern that had finally prompted him to summon his younger brother, James, down south from Scotland. Charles was determined that the normal protocols should be followed despite the political complications of James's stubborn and open avowal of his Catholicism.

But where was he? James had been expected to arrive in time for dinner on Thursday, 9 March. But Thursday came and went and there was no sign of him. The racing started without His Royal Highness having arrived. The weather continued inclement. Conway wrote somewhat bitterly, 'This afternoon we began to have horse races which, considering the season, will be very cold sport.'[8]

By Friday morning there was still no word from James. Meanwhile, some of James's servants had already arrived, having come down from Scotland by post horse. The road was an alternative mode of travel that Conway for one regarded as far preferable to the hazards of a sea voyage and which he was 'of opinion, had been his best way'. Conway clearly took a landsman's view of physical comfort and the propriety of having something solid under one's feet. Not that the coach at such a period was without its problems as they did have a nasty habit of turning over. A contemporary newspaper records how:

> By reason of the great rain that has lately fallen, there is hardly any travelling in the country without great danger; for several passengers have lost their lives, and among them the York stage coach missing the road was turned over and all the passengers drowned, the coachman only escaping.[9]

The king himself had recently been upset when one of the supporting leather straps of his coach broke suddenly. At best, there was still the mud, the jolting and the tedium to endure.

James preferred the sea route. He was by personal inclination extremely enamoured of all maritime matters and he was not going to take any notice of Conway's opinion, or anyone else's for that matter. It was, after all, he and Charles who had first introduced the sport of yachting to England, and one of his fondest pastimes in happier days had been racing against his brother upon the River Thames. James was not by nature very literary or poetical in his voluminous writings, but on the subject of sea voyages he could wax quite lyrical. On his previous brief visit to London from Scotland in February 1681 he had also travelled by ship and he wrote then somewhat condescendingly to his brother, who had, like Conway, questioned the wisdom of his choice of transport:

> If you were a seaman, I could soon make you understand that it is better going from Scotland to London by sea, in winter … There will be a light moon at the time I name, and both the Duchess and I have a great mind to go back by sea, having been greatly tired by our land journey to Edinburgh.[10]

In the event, their passage had been extremely rough and taken an entire week, but clearly the experience had not altered James's prejudices on the relative merits of sea and land travel. James was nothing if not stubborn in his attachments.

There was also another very sound and more directly political reason why James wanted to make this latest voyage by ship rather than by carriage. He styled himself very much as a man of the navy. He had been Lord High Admiral during the Second and Third Dutch Wars and though he had later been removed from this post because of political pressure, he was in hopes of once again obtaining this influential position. He drew a large part of his support from the maritime interest and if he wished to impress upon his brother his renewed popularity in the country it was sensible to associate himself with those who were most likely to give him a warm welcome. James was an astute enough political operator to know that his support was likely to be much stronger in a naval port such as Yarmouth, than trekking down the great North Road via posting towns such as York, Doncaster, Newark, Stamford and Hatfield, along which route he had received some very rough treatment in 1679.

6

YARMOUTH

The voyage from Leith to Yarmouth was calculated to take about two days with favourable winds. However, a storm late on Wednesday night, with strong winds blowing from the south, had made landing impossible. James's yacht was driven out into the North Sea again and only finally dropped anchor in Yarmouth Roads around midday on Friday, 10 March, some thirty-six hours after it had been expected.

The duke was met there by his loyal friend Colonel George Legge, the elder brother of William, who had recently undertaken the arduous ride from London to Edinburgh to deliver the all-important message that James was at last permitted to come south. George was already a member of Charles's Privy Council and had recently been entrusted with heading up a special commission to review all the forts and garrisons of the kingdom. He came from a staunchly Royalist family and though only 34 years of age was widely regarded as one of the most distinguished and brilliant courtiers of his generation.

According to the newsletters, James's eventual arrival was a remarkable success:

> He was received at Yarmouth and Norwich with all imaginable demonstrations of joy. So eager were the sailors of the first place to have him on shore, that several went up to their necks in water and carried him out of the sea on their heads a great way into the land.[1]

James was 48 years old and, although a fanatic about taking exercise, he was beginning to put on weight, so such a display of devotion on the part of his supporters must have involved a considerable degree of physical effort. Perhaps the newsletter was a little exaggerated – but it was without doubt a triumphant homecoming.

Once safely on land, James was treated to a splendid dinner by the Corporation of Yarmouth. Among the local dignitaries present were Sir Thomas Medowe and a bailiff named Thomas Gooch. Both men were to play key roles in the search for survivors after the *Gloucester* wrecked. Medowe was a former MP for Yarmouth and one of the richest men in the town. He was a brewer whose beer had victualled many a Royal Navy ship. His income was said to exceed £2,000 a year. He was also a member of the Order of the Royal Oak, one of those semi-secret societies beloved by Royalists. Whether he ever wore the silver medallion depicting the fleeing Charles hiding in the oak tree at Boscobel is not recorded, but his loyalty to the Stuarts was never in question.

Not all the inhabitants of Yarmouth were Royalists. Far from it. James Johnson was the leader of the large community of Non-conformists that lived in the area and his views on Charles were representative and uncompromising. He remarked that at least 'the King of France could whore well and govern well, our King could whore well but not govern'.[2] According to local politician Paston, Yarmouth's inhabitants were the 'stubbornest most ill natured men in the world'.[3] Some of them perhaps, but on that particular Friday, 10 March, cordiality was uppermost and the wine flowed. After dinner was finished, James and Legge departed for Norwich, where they spent the night. Francis Gwyn, a clerk of Charles II's Privy Council, summed up James's arrival back in England in a letter to Secretary Jenkins. 'His Royal Highness is in very good health, looks very well and is grown much fatter. He has met with very ill weather in his voyage but was very well entertained at Yarmouth on his landing and most magnificently at Norwich, where he lay.'[4]

Pepys had been one of the first to arrive in Newmarket, which at least meant that he had secured accommodation at not too extortionate a rate and was not having to make do on someone else's floor. He was as impatient to see James arrive safely as anyone, being no more enamoured of horse racing than Secretary Conway. When James finally showed, Pepys was in agreement that the weight increase was a good thing. 'Plumper, fatter and all over in better liking than ever I knew him,' he wrote to his friend James Houblon.[5] All the omens appeared to be good.

Meanwhile, the king was feeling a little recovered. Pepys wrote to his friend Lord Brouncker in his characteristically gossipy style: 'I have not yet been at Mrs Nelly's, but I hear Mrs Knight is better, and the King takes his repose there once or twice daily.'[6] Mrs Knight was one of the most renowned singers of the period. Pepys had written glowingly of her abilities some fourteen years back, so she was by then not in the first flush of her youth. She was, however, one of Charles's closest and most longstanding confidantes and rumoured to have played a key role in the procuring of Nell Gwyn. But Pepys was not in Newmarket to observe the king; even less to have a flutter on the horses. It was the renewal of his friendship with James that was important to him and the ways in which, between them, they might shape the future of the Royal Navy.

Top of Pepys's agenda was to scupper the plan to build a new wet dock at Chatham. After conferring with James on the subject he immediately dashed off a very typical, forthright and entirely unasked for letter to the Admiralty commissioners, pointing out to them that their proposals were both ludicrously expensive and a security nightmare. One cannot imagine that his opinion was received with any great enthusiasm, but then popularity with the Admiralty commissioners was not Pepys's prime concern. He wanted to fire a warning shot over the commissioners' bows that he was on the way back to influence and power.

Despite Pepys's verbal pugnacity, and his closeness to James regarding naval matters, it is noticeable that he appears to be somewhat on the fringes of the great circus that surrounded the duke. The sense one gets of him being something of an outsider was no doubt in part to do with his humble social origins, his father being a tailor and his mother a wash maid. But there is more to it than that. Not only was he not a natural courtier, he was certainly never a warrior, unlike so many of James's closest friends. His office work may have been crucial to the success of the navy at battles such as Solebay, but he was not himself present amid the smoke and the blood. He was much too self-reflective to be an instinctive man of action. He was, by temperament, far more at home with his wealthy business friends in London such as Houblon and Hewer.

James's own rehabilitation into the innermost circles of the court progressed remarkably smoothly. As Pepys somewhat ponderously put it, 'his political state of body seems to be much mended too, since his nearer partakings of his brother's sunshine'.[7]

After a fortnight of such cordial fraternisation Charles gave James leave to send for his duchess, still languishing in Edinburgh. Charles, ever the gallant, but also with an eye to the ongoing line of succession, was concerned that she should 'lie in' in London, where she would receive the best medical care. The birth of a boy would be the ultimate coup in re-establishing James right at the very centre of British politics again. But James did not seem to be in any particular hurry to have her back by his side. Instead of immediately dispatching a yacht to fetch her, he decided he would defer her arrival for a couple of months. He had a much better plan for her eventual return. He himself would set sail from London at the head of a small but impressive fleet of Royal Navy ships, to bring her back in style. This way he would make far more of a grand statement.

Meanwhile, the racing and gambling continued apace. Conway describes the scene with his usual elegant flippancy:

Here happened yesterday a dispute on the greatest point of critical learning that was ever known at Newmarket. A match between a horse of Sir Robert Carr's and a gelding of Sir Robert Geere's for a mile and a half only had engaged all the court in many thousand pounds, much depending in so short a course to have them start fairly. Mr Griffin was appointed to start them. When he saw them equal he said, Go, and presently he cried out, Stay. One went off and ran through the course;

the other never stirred at all. You may say this was not a fair starting, but the critics say, after the word Go was out of his mouth, his commission was determined and it was illegal for him to say Stay. I suppose volumes will be written on this subject.[8]

You can almost hear Conway yawning.

This unfortunate Mr Griffin, who had failed to start the race according to the correct rules, was soon to find himself in much deeper water than a mere scandal at the racecourse. As James's equerry he was to travel back to Scotland with His Highness on the *Gloucester* frigate. He was one of the lucky ones who survived the sinking, although the exact manner of his rescue, like so much about the *Gloucester* wreck, was to become a matter of some historical debate. According to Sarah Churchill's memoirs, Mr Griffin was able to save his life by clutching hold of a hen coop that must have come off the poop deck and was floating nearby. Sarah had the story from her husband, John, another survivor of the disaster. By contrast, Thomas Bruce, the Earl of Ailesbury, reported that:

Colonel Griffin sat in a porthole his legs in the sea, and had soon suffered the same ill fate (drowning) but for an old servant of his, bottleman to the Duke, that had a rope tied about his waist, and bade his old master take hold of that, and he was thus preserved by that man that swam perfectly.

DORSET GARDENS

The road leading from Fleet Ditch to St Paul's Cathedral was one of the most crowded thoroughfares in London. The stretch from Blackfriars at the bottom to the Stone Gateway near the top was called Ludgate Hill. Beyond the gateway it became Ludgate Street. The gateway itself housed an old prison and through its barred windows the inmates begged alms off passers-by. It was calculated that more than 100,000 people passed through Ludgate each day – and that was not counting the cabs, the coaches, the carts and those on horseback.

On the evening of 8 April 1682, the narrow thoroughfare was even more packed than usual. Charles, together with his younger brother James, had just returned from Newmarket, and it seemed as if half the population of London had poured out on to the streets to welcome them back. One of the fiercest and most outspoken of the loyalists was a Captain Simons. He was the proprietor of the Dog-Wonder Tavern just beyond the gateway. He built an enormous bonfire in the road outside his inn and helped construct a network of ropes from St Martin's church all the way to St Paul's itself, to which firecrackers and squibs were attached for the amusement of the masses.

Similar demonstrations of support took place across London. At Will's Coffee House in Covent Garden a pole was erected over a bundle of faggots and the green ribbons of the perfidious Whigs that were attached to it went up in flames. Outside the Dog Tavern in Drury Lane an effigy of Lord Shaftesbury, the most prominent of the exclusionists, was burnt. His figure was described as a 'little meagre fac'd wither'd old conjuror'.[1] Shaftesbury famously suffered from a constantly weeping abscess in his side, the pus from which had to be drawn off, and his effigy had a tap and spigot attached to it in a mocking allusion to his medical condition.

In front of the Globe in Cornhill another great fire was lit and an effigy of 'Jack Presbyter', a composite figure representing the Puritans, was cremated. Church bells were rung by order of the Lord Mayor all across the city, creating a great cacophony, and on the streets the loyalists joined in with the new popular song:

> The glory of the British line,
> Old Jimmy's come again.

Of course, not everyone was so pleased to see James back. Even before he had set foot in England, someone had slipped into the Guildhall where his portrait hung and slashed it. The message was unambiguous. There were those who wanted James dead. The church bells might ring, but there were also plenty of anti-Pope demonstrations on the street, which continued unabated throughout the troubled early months of 1682. Windows in houses where Catholics were known to live were stoned, lanterns were smashed and constables attacked. For James it was far from a unanimously friendly reception.

Another annoyance, though of a rather different kind, was that he finally arrived back at Whitehall only to discover that his private quarters had been taken over by his brother in his absence. The king was having his own rooms refurbished and so had found it convenient to move into those that had been vacated by James. Now the two men found themselves sharing. James did not protest. In the circumstances it would hardly have been tactful.

The round of royal pleasures continued apace. On 20 April James was given a splendid entertainment by the Honourable Artillery Company of the City of London, a loyal powerbase where he had always been welcome. The following evening, which was a Friday, he was at the theatre watching a play by Thomas Otway entitled *Venice Preserv'd*, or

A Plot Discover'd. This was staged by the Duke's Company at the Dorset Garden Theatre. It was a new theatre, built in 1671 in the former grounds of Dorset House, which had been destroyed in the Great Fire. John Evelyn had been impressed when he had first stepped inside the theatre to take a look at the 'new machines' for changing the scenery, remarking that they 'were indeede very costly and magnificent'.[2] The building had three bays, a fine porch and an ogee dome. Outside it was adorned with the arms of the Duke of York and statues of the muses Melpomene and Thalia. It was best approached by river via Dorset Stairs, which was doubtless how James chose to arrive. The play was highly political and written to appeal to James. It was a thinly disguised attack on Shaftesbury, portrayed in the character of Antonio, a perverted Venetian senator.

It would be interesting to know whether John Churchill accompanied James on this occasion or whether he considered it more discreet to absent himself. Churchill was another of James's intimate circle. He had, however, recently disgraced himself at the Dorset Garden Theatre, more familiarly known as the Duke's Theatre, by beating up a young orange seller girl with whom he had fallen out. The cause of the disagreement goes unrecorded, though it would not be difficult to hazard a guess. Otway, the resident playwright, felt strongly enough about the injustice of what had occurred to challenge Churchill to a duel in which Churchill was defeated but uninjured. The incident might have ended there but Admiral John Holmes mentioned the affair in passing to Charles. Churchill got to hear that he had become the subject of royal gossip and the butt of jokes, and considered that John Holmes had slighted his reputation in his relation of the event and so challenged Holmes to a duel. Churchill again lost. It seems that the great general and future victor at Blenheim was not particularly handy with the épée. In view of these rather embarrassing episodes it seems probable that Churchill may have wished to absent himself from Otway's play.

None of this fracas, however, had done anything to tarnish Churchill's standing with James. He was still only 32 years old in 1682, but he was now a gentleman of James's bedchamber and firmly established as one of his favourites. Churchill's father had been poor but well-connected, and it was through these connections that he had been able to place his children Arabella and John in James's service in 1667. Arabella was a maid of honour, or lady in waiting, to James's first wife, Anne, and very shortly after her appointment she also became James's mistress, a frequent career move accomplished by maids of honour, not always to the liking of the royal wife that they were supposedly serving.

John Churchill started out as James's page but his sister's affair did his prospects no harm and he was very quickly making his way in the world on his own account. He was clearly something of an attraction in court circles, for by 1670, at the tender age of 20, he had the distinction of becoming Barbara Palmer's lover. Palmer, later Lady Castlemaine and finally, by 1670, Duchess of Cleveland, was one of Charles's earlier mistresses. She was 30 years old in 1670, and so, according to the standards of the time, was already well past her sell-by date. Women were 'at their prime at twenty, decayed at four and twenty, old and insupportable at thirty', according to Dorimant in George Etherege's comedy *The Man of Mode*. However, if the painting of Barbara at 30 by the artist John Michael Wright is anything to go by, she was still very attractive – especially for an ambitious young man like Churchill, for she retained considerable influence as well as beauty. Wright depicts her as a woman relishing both her own sensuality and the sumptuousness of her recently acquired wealth.

Samuel Pepys was famously besotted with her. In his diary he frequently comments on her attractions and wonders why it is, when he knows that she's a whore, that he feels such sympathy for her. He even records his dreams of her, 'the best that ever was dreamed – which was, that I had my Lady Castlemayne in my armes and was admitted to use all the dalliance I desired with her'.[3] But Pepys preferred to lust from afar, at any rate where the royal mistresses were concerned. When he wanted something more than dreaming, he chose women from the lower social orders to gratify his desires.

Churchill's liaison with Barbara Palmer lasted for five years. Shortly before he dropped her, he persuaded her to put up the money for his purchase of the position of Master of the Robes, a profitable sinecure. James might have seen in this piece of cynical opportunism a foretaste of his own eventual betrayal by Churchill, but the prevailing mores when it came to men's treatment of women no doubt prevented him from thinking anything of the kind. Cheating on one's mistress was fair play but cheating on one's king was an entirely different matter.

Churchill remained, throughout the 1670s, very much James's protégé. Like James, he had acquired the invaluable experience of fighting for the French army under the great marshal general the Viscount of Turenne during the period of their exile when Oliver Cromwell was in power. It was an experience that was to stand him in good stead in later years. Even more crucially, so far as cementing bonds of friendship with James was concerned, he fought at the Battle of Solebay in 1672, serving on the flagship *Prince*, until that vessel was so badly damaged James had been forced to remove himself and the royal standard to the *Michael*. By 1682 James was probably closer to Churchill than any other courtier, excepting perhaps George Legge.

The news that James was very shortly to return to Edinburgh to fetch back the pregnant duchess rapidly became common knowledge throughout the capital, and the versatile Mr Otway penned a few appropriate lines to wind him on his way, which were spoken in the epilogue to his play when James was in the audience:

An Infant Prince yet lab'ring in the womb,
Fated with wond'rous happiness to come,
He goes to fetch the mighty blessing home:
Send all your wishes with him, let the Ayre
With gentle breezes waft it safely here,
The Seas, like what they'l carry, calm and fair.[4]

Such well wishes on the eve of departure may have been a conventional piece of politesse but as an example of poetic prediction it could hardly have turned out to be more inaccurate. It would be interesting to know whether the reference to Ayre was a deliberate pun on Captain Ayres, the pilot who was to accompany James on the *Gloucester*, and who was shortly to be sentenced to a lifetime of imprisonment in the Marshalsea.

8

PORTSMOUTH

Towards the end of April the indefatigable George Legge was dispatched to Portsmouth to oversee the final preparations for the small fleet that was being hastily assembled to accompany James on his return to Scotland. This fleet was intended to be a piece of political showmanship, impressing the public with James's military prowess. It was to be a reminder of his naval triumphs over the Dutch in earlier years, and a celebration of his place at the very heart of the kingdom. James had a few outstanding business matters to complete in Edinburgh, some new appointments to the Scottish executive to formally ratify, and then it would be straight back to England with his pregnant duchess at his side in what was planned as a triumphant homecoming. It didn't quite work out like that.

Legge first went to sea at the age of 17 and two years later, in 1667, he was appointed captain of the *Pembroke*, with very little previous navigational experience. He was a good example of what was then called the 'gentleman captain' – that is, someone appointed through the exercise of patronage rather than on the basis of any proven merit or competence. It was a system that put the noses out of joint of many of the older Commonwealth captains who had risen through the ranks under Cromwell. It was also a practice that Pepys deplored, and during his time at the Admiralty he had done his best to abolish the more flagrant abuses of it. This had already caused some serious tensions between Legge and Pepys. Indeed, so bad had relations become between the two men that at one point Pepys accused Legge of 'uttering no small menaces against me as an enemy to gentlemen captains'.[1] More recently they had also clashed over the vacant position of provost of King's College, Cambridge, which Pepys had had a mind to apply for but which Legge had already promised to his own preferred candidate, a Dr John Coplestone.

Pepys had good reason to be critical of Legge's navigational skills. Legge had only been in command of the *Pembroke* about one month when it sank in Torbay, following a collision with the *Fairfax*. The loss of life was considerable. It was generally agreed that Legge's inexperience was largely responsible but James was characteristically quick to forgive and forget such youthful errors among his protégés.

By 1682, Legge had become James's general fixer, one of the most trusted of his inner circle. He was a devout Protestant but that never got in the way of his loyalty to the Crown. James regarded him as a safe pair of hands despite his accident with the *Pembroke*. He was someone whom James felt he could rely on in a moment of crisis.

During Legge's journey to Portsmouth the rain was torrential and there was widespread flooding. He entered the town through the dripping Landport Gate, headed up Hog Market Street past what was to become known as Legge's Demi-Bastion, turned down Church Lane and Little Penny Lane and sought shelter in the governor's house, Domus Dei. His stay there was no doubt more salubrious than it would have been at the Red Lion Inn at the top end of the High Street, where Pepys had once stayed with his wife and found the accommodation very unsatisfactory.

Portsmouth was a rapidly growing dockyard town, second only to Chatham on the Medway for the tonnage of new shipping that was being constructed on its slipways. It was entirely dependent on Royal Navy contracts rather than merchant shipping for its wealth, and it was this dominance of garrison soldiers and sailors on leave, a rootless and frequently mutinous population constantly clamouring for unpaid wages, that gave the town its peculiarly raw and hard-living edge. Charles II found it 'cold and unwholesome'. Clearly the fact that it was here where he had first welcomed his Portuguese bride, Catherine of Braganza, on to English soil held no sentimental memories for him. Pepys was more enthusiastic, describing it as 'a very pleasant and strong place'.[2] But then Pepys was obsessively interested in every last detail of the shipbuilding process, so the town was almost bound to be of particular fascination to him.

The most notorious district was called the Point, a cluster of low-built squalid houses, situated just outside the city walls, beyond what was shortly to be remodelled as King James's Gate. By virtue of being outside the walls, the Point considered itself to be also outside the law. Taverns here were open twenty-four hours a day, seven days a week, and brothels were present in abundance. Extracts from the Court Session Records give something of the flavour of the area: 'Certifies that Joan wife of Tho. Wilks, seaman, lives in a house on the Point generally accounted a bawdy-house and that she is reputed a notorious whore, an uncivil and ungodly woman, who curses and swears and is a great disturber to her neighbours.'[3]

Colonel Legge, in his role as surveyor of the nation's forts, was more interested in the new defensive walls and ramparts that the brilliant Dutch engineer Sir Bernard de Gomme was rapidly constructing than in the leisure activities of the mob. It is somewhat ironic that a Dutchman should have been used to fortify a town during a period when the Dutch were widely perceived as the main enemy, but war was in many ways much less of an all-consuming nationalistic enterprise at this period than it was to become in future centuries, and men with skills that were in short supply were free to sell to the highest bidder. Legge's main purpose, however, in coming to Portsmouth was to survey the state of readiness of the *Gloucester* frigate and those other naval ships that were to provide the escort for the voyage of the pregnant duchess from Scotland.

According to one of the Pepys manuscripts, today preserved in the darkly panelled and cloistered Pepys Library in Magdalene College, Cambridge, the *Gloucester* had a burden of 755 tons, was manned with 210 men in peacetime, carried fifty-two iron guns and was 117ft long in the keel and 34ft 10in wide in the beam. The hold was 14ft 6in deep and the draught was 17ft 6in.[4] This last statistic was to be of particular importance when it came to trying to establish exactly where the

Gloucester first struck the Leman and Ower sandbank. There were not many places on the outer sandbanks where the water was sufficiently shallow to cause a problem for a ship of that draught.

By 1682, the *Gloucester* was already an old ship. It had been built at Limehouse by a Mr Graves and launched in 1654. It first saw active service in the Caribbean under Admiral Sir William Penn. The West Indies station was notorious for its corrosive effect both on timbers and men, but the *Gloucester* survived the experience and returned to home waters to play an active role in both the Second and Third Dutch Wars. It was not considered necessary to change its name at the Restoration because *Gloucester*, unlike – say – *Naseby*, *Richard* or *Bridgewater*, was not regarded as politically unsuitable. Up until its disastrous end, the *Gloucester* was probably most famous for the destruction, in one-to-one combat, of the Dutch treasure ship *Klein Hollandia* off the Isle of Wight in 1672. The captain on that occasion had been John Holmes, the same John Holmes who was later to be challenged to a duel by Churchill over the orange seller.

The selection of a third rate, rather than a first or second rate, to transport James to Scotland, was not in any way a slight on his standing. The first rates were really showpieces, useful in set battles, but otherwise unwieldy and extremely expensive to operate. Much the same could also be said of the second rates. The third rates were the workhorses of the fleet, the handiest ships for speed and versatility, while still providing spaciousness and comfort for a full retinue of gentlemen and their servants.

The more customary mode of sea transport during this period for members of the royal family and high-ranking officials, if the voyage was to be relatively short and in home or western European waters, was by royal yacht. James, however, clearly considered that on this occasion nothing but a fleet of warships would be appropriate. He wanted to make a grand statement. The Duke of York was back and a force to be reckoned with. But there was much to be done to prepare a fleet of ships for sea.

A warship was a complex social organism and an intricate piece of engineering designed to function simultaneously as a weapon, a place to live, a storehouse and a means of transport. For this reason it was equipped with a vast array of different fittings: navigational, military and social. The *Gloucester*, for instance, carried 10½ tons of cordage for its rigging alone. There were twenty different sizes of rope varying in thickness from 1.25in to 14in and amounting to a total length of 41,454ft or nearly 8 miles. In addition, there were a further 16 tons of 22in cable for the six anchors. The ropes alone amounted to a formidable organisational problem, but the difficulties were increased by the fact that so much hemp was of such poor quality. Russian hemp was to be avoided at all costs, but even good Riga hemp was frequently damaged and rotten on the inside, though appearing sound on the outer surface. The situation was made still worse by the high levels of endemic corruption to be found in the Royal Dockyards, a problem compounded by poor and irregular wages.

Cordage was just one part of a ship's total gear. The *Gloucester* also carried twenty-four separate sails amounting to 6,558 yards of canvas, six anchors weighing on average over 1 ton each and 482 blocks and deadeyes for the working of the rigging, not to mention miscellaneous boatswain's, carpenter's and gunner's stores. The ordnance was comprised of fifty-six iron guns weighing a total of 104 tons, probably made up of twenty-four demi cannon on the lower deck, twenty-two culverin on the upper deck, and eight light sakers, plus two three-pounders on the quarter deck. Also stored in the gun room were 270 barrels of powder and 36 tons of shot, not to forget the ladles, the sponges, the rammers, the fuses and the matches all essential for loading and firing.

The *Gloucester*'s hull was badly in need of graving and paying. This involved scraping off all the weed and barnacles that had accumulated on the lower part of the hull, replacing any rotten or worm-eaten timbers, recaulking any defective seams with a mixture of oakum and tar, and then covering all the exposed timbers with a protective layer of 'white stuff'. The latter was a mixture of 9cwt of rosin, 24 gallons of oil (whale, seal or fish) and 108lb of sulphur. These quantities would have been sufficient for a ship of the *Gloucester*'s dimensions. White stuff was believed to be both poisonous to worm and protective of wood, though applying it must have been a fairly noxious business.

After the white stuff had gone on, an additional layer of tallow and soap, both derived from animal fats, might be applied on top. As well as providing a protective layer of grease, this helped the ship to slip faster through the water. Tallowing was particularly favoured for small, fast boats such as the royal yachts, but could also be used as a substitute for white stuff during times of war, when it might be difficult to obtain supplies of rosin from Scandinavia. It is evident from the letters of Richard Beach, the resident officer at Portsmouth in charge of fitting out, that the *Gloucester* was in need of the full treatment. On 10 March 1682 he wrote to the Admiralty commissioners that he needed 'pitch, tarr, tallow, rozen, oyle for caulking and repairing'.[5] A few days later he added, 'we are providing to grave the *Gloucester* the next spring [tide] if rozen and other materials come here enough'.[6] That the materials did eventually arrive is evident from the logbook of the fourth-rate warship *Happy Return*, for on Sunday, 23 April, Lieutenant Joseph Wetwang recorded that 'boatswain and 40 men went aboard the *Gloucester* to heave in her guns'.[7] The guns would never have been taken out if the *Gloucester* had not been put into dry dock for graving and paying.

It was not just the routine maintenance work that was being rushed at the last minute, it was all a mad scramble to get things done. There were no half-hour glasses to be found; these were the most popular size of sand glass for measuring time. Even more vital than half-hour glasses was the beer. 'The beere for those ships is not yet all brewed (but not a day or two more I hope it will) Mr Ridge not having had timely notice thereof,' wrote a frantic Richard Beach.[8]

There were numerous other requirements. There was no royal barge, for instance. It was too late to get one sent down from Chatham, so instead it was decided to use the barge that had previously belonged to the *Royal James*. The *Royal James* had been famously burnt and sunk during the Battle of Solebay but its barge was later salvaged and had been preserved at Portsmouth ever since. In the opinion of Richard Beach, 'she is the best barge here and shall be timely fitted'.[9] But the barge itself was not the end of it. There was also an absence of any oars for rowing it.

The root of the problems was, as always, money. Beach had written to the commissioners on 4 April, 'there being no oares, planke etc for supplying the ships ordered to sea, nor none to be had in these parts but what Mr Clemense hath ... he will part with no more before there be money to pay him'.[10] Somehow or other Mr Beach managed to lean on Mr Clemence, however, for by the 18th he writes, 'I had prevailed with Mr Clemence to send us in 30 dozen of barge and boats oares together with scoops, hand spikes, top hoops and plank, upon the cheapest terms'.[11]

Nor was it just a matter of equipping the *Gloucester*. It was even more vital that it should look like a royal ship. But here too there were problems. The painting of the ship's outside was delayed because of the wet weather. There was no painted canvas available for the protection of the glass windows should it prove rough. The royal standards could not be located (two were required). The suite of pendants was missing. Still worse, there were no crimson cloths, or kerseys as they were known, to be had anywhere. No royal procession could be considered complete without crimson kerseys. They were needed to drape the waist of the ship as well as for sprucing up the royal cabin. But where were they? The navy commissioners thought they were in store at Portsmouth, but Richard Beach thought otherwise. 'As for kerseys your honours know here is none in store; we did advise Sir John Berry that he might move the board for a supply for his accommodation as well as for the cabin as the barge,' wrote Beach testily.[12]

There was also no yawl, the small boat carried on the deck of larger ships, 'nor any stuff to build one with'.[13] As for awnings, Beach was fussing like an irritable, proud housewife:

I was confident there was an awning at Chatham but here was never any, neither for the Royal Charles, Royal James, or any other ship ... as to what can be done here for fitting or beautification of the ship (according to what the store can afford or can be had in these parts) shall be done, and all the care imaginable hitherto hath been and is taken for the doing thereof ...[14]

THE PORTSMOUTH ROAD

The *Gloucester* may have been berthed in Portsmouth, but more than 80 per cent of the men who went on the frigate came from the East End of London. During the second half of April a motley collection of these sailors straggled down the Portsmouth Road on the backs of carts and on foot in order to sign on under Captain John Berry. There was no need for press gangs or recruiting agents; word of mouth was all that was required.[1] Although officially still at war with the Algerines, England had been relatively at peace for nearly ten years and there was no shortage of unemployed sailors.

The journey from the Elephant and Castle Tavern in Southwark to Portsmouth Hard was a distance of 71 miles. It could take five days by foot or a couple of days by fast coach, and tramping sailors were a common sight. Pepys referred to a gang of them recently discharged from HMS *Cambridge* as 'the most debauched, damning, swearing rogues that ever were in the navy'.[2] There were plenty of inns along the route to relieve the tedium, such as the Flying Bull at Rake or the Castle at Petersfield, where King Charles had once stopped briefly and Pepys enjoyed a game of bowls. Pepys had liked to lie upon the same bed that Charles had previously slept in. It gave him a vicarious sense of being part of the royal circle.

There is a popular image of the sailor's life in earlier centuries as being one of unmitigated hardship and misery, enduring conditions little better than that of a slave in a galley ship until drowned, starved or killed in battle. Life was certainly harsh. Edward Barlow, who started out as a common seaman of the late seventeenth century and was one of the very few to leave a written account of his experiences, describes climbing the rigging during a storm in the following graphic terms:

> In stormy weather, when the ship rolled and tumbled, as though some great millstone were rolling up one hill and down another, we had much ado to hold ourselves fast by the small ropes from falling by the board; and being gotten up into the tops there we must haul and pull to make fast the sail, seeing nothing but air above us and water beneath us, and that so raging as though every wave would make a grave for us.[3]

But the lot of a sailor of this period was not altogether without its attractions. There is, of course, a great lack of first-hand evidence, but where accounts do exist the picture that emerges is rather more nuanced than might at first seem to be the case. Edward Barlow, for instance, for all his moaning and general grumpiness, served in both navy and merchant ships, and eventually rose to the position of master. He makes it clear that he first enlisted as a young boy because he was attracted by the idea of seeing something of the world, and life at sea seemed like a more exciting prospect than becoming an agricultural labourer. His successful career and painstaking acquisition of significant wealth proved him right. The sea offered a man the possibility of social mobility through the existence of a rudimentary career structure, which was not so readily available in other walks of life. The career of John Berry, captain of the *Gloucester*, is another example of progressing through the ranks. Berry was of a higher social standing than Barlow, being the son of a vicar, and he had had more in the way of an education, but he started out with very little in the way of possessions, and yet died a wealthy man.

It was not just the lure of novelty and money that prompted a man to sign on. The navy also offered a very rudimentary form of care in old age to certain deserving and long-serving sailors, security of a kind that was again not usually available to his land-based brothers. Some of the elderly mariners, who were too infirm to serve at sea, were given token positions on ships that were laid up in port. Those who had been injured during hostilities were also shared out among the ships. A vessel the size of the *Gloucester* would probably have carried four or five men who had lost legs, arms or suffered some similar incapacitating injury. There was also the Chatham Chest, an early form of social security, to be called upon by indigent but worthy sailors.[4]

The supply of food on board a naval ship was a further attraction. It was relatively plentiful and of reasonable quality if somewhat monotonous. According to the Swiss travel writer César-François de Saussure, who sailed on a naval ship a few decades after the *Gloucester* voyage:

> Each sailor eats one pound of boiled salted beef three days in the week for dinner, together with a pudding made of flour and suet. On two other days he eats boiled salted pork with a pudding of dried peas, and on the remaining two days, pea soup and salt fish or bargow, which is a nasty mixture of gruel as thick as mortar.[5]

No one seemed to have had a good word to say about bargow but Saussure was highly partial to ship's biscuit and describes them as being 'as large as a plate, white, and so hard that those sailors who have no teeth, or bad ones, must crush them or soften them with water. I found them, however, very much to my taste, and they reminded me of nuts.'[6]

Of even more importance than the supply of food was the ration of beer, a gallon per day per man. It sounds excessive but beer was far weaker than the modern-day equivalent and was a necessary item because it did not contaminate as quickly as the water that was carried. Tobacco was another vital part of life on board ship. The smoking of it was considered to be medicinal and the smell probably helped to disguise some of the more noxious odours of life below decks, where several hundred men were crowded into a very confined space. As well as tobacco, the other great recreational pursuits were cards and dice and, on occasion, musical entertainment. There were amateur fiddlers among most crews and the *Gloucester* would also have carried at least two official trumpeters, apart from James's own personal musicians.

The sailors on the *Gloucester* would not have been issued with a uniform as such, but it is probable that they would have all been similarly dressed in red caps, blue shirts and blue neck cloths, with canvas jackets and cotton drawers, Irish stockings and flat-heeled shoes with buckles. It is easy to see how this choice of clothes gradually mutated into the uniform of later years. If anyone was short of some necessary item they could acquire it from the slop seller on board, who carried a supply of clothing.

Issues of clothing and tobacco could both be set against future wages. An able seaman on the *Gloucester* was paid 24s a month, which was roughly equivalent to the average for a skilled manual worker of the period. To qualify as 'able' the seaman had to be competent with the helm and casting the lead, as well as skilled in rope work and furling and unfurling sails. This involved climbing into the tops and along the yard arms, dangerous work as well as physically demanding. Ordinary seamen who lacked the necessary experience were paid 19s a month. The wages of the warrant officers or petty officers on board varied according to their importance. The boatswain, the gunner, the carpenter and the purser on a third rate such as the *Gloucester* all received £3 per month. They were the most important among the crew and their wages were commensurate with their status. The surgeon got £2 10s, midshipmen £1 17s 6d and the quartermaster £1 12s. Below this there was a variety of other positions paying a few more shillings a month than the basic able-seaman rate, such as that of swabber, cook, coxswain or yeoman, but these roles did not necessarily carry officer status.

One of the main grouses of seamen was that wages were so often late in being paid. The treasury was perennially short of money and it was not uncommon for sailors to be owed many years in back wages. In 1682, the sailors on board the *Mary* yacht, under Captain Christopher Gunman, were already five years in arrears. This was to be an issue when Gunman was eventually court-martialled, because it was rumoured that creditors of the mate, William Sturgeon, offered inducements to ensure his freedom, with Gunman condemned in his place.

As soon as Sir John Berry had been appointed captain of the *Gloucester*, the word went out among the sailing community that there was work to be had for those who wanted it. A few of those who enlisted did come from Portsmouth or other well-established naval ports such as Plymouth, Tynemouth, Hull, Yarmouth and even the Channel Islands. A handful came from south of the river, Deptford and Greenwich. Still, the vast majority came from the East End parishes of Limehouse, Stepney, Whitechapel, Wapping, Aldgate, Shadwell and Ratcliffe. Partly this reflected the fact that the greatest numbers of sailors were concentrated in London Docklands, but it was also because Sir John Berry lived in Stepney, and many of his regular followers inhabited the neighbouring area. A lot of the men who enlisted were part of Sir John's personal entourage. This was particularly true, of course, of the more important officers. His first lieutenant, for example, was his younger brother Thomas, who already had ten years' experience as an officer, and it is highly probable that many of the other senior personnel, such as John Deane the purser, John Hull the boatswain and Benjamin Holmes the master, were also well known to him.

Over the space of two or three weeks, a motley collection of sailors straggled down the Portsmouth Road on the backs of carts in order to sign on the *Gloucester*'s books. Apart from the clothes they stood up in, their possessions would have been few. If they were lucky they would have had a 'watch coat' for the cold nights and a roll of bedding and perhaps woollen gloves and stockings. Personal items such as knives, razors, scissors, needles and thread, paper and ink were also carried. Some of the more established seamen would have had their own wooden chests. Sir John Berry was supplied with £60 of 'conduct money' to cover their travel costs. At the going rate of about one penny a mile, this would have been sufficient to transport about 120 men from London to Portsmouth by cart.

Cornelius Balling, a midshipman from Limehouse, was one of the first to be entered on to the *Gloucester*'s books on 15 April. He was probably around 40 years old, judging from the age of his children and his rank. The position of midshipman frequently indicated a valued and experienced sailor, as well as, on occasion, a very young officer from the gentry class. Balling was one of those who was drowned, leaving behind a widow, Frances, and two children, Francis, 5, and Thomas, 14, a child by a former husband of Frances.

Two days later, John Poor was entered. He was an able seaman from the precinct of St Katherine's near the Tower of London. He also drowned, leaving Anne, 'a poor desolate distressed widow' in the words of her minister, and two children, 18-year-old William and 12-year-old Thomas.[7]

A surprisingly large number of these mainly illiterate sailors with very limited possessions still took the trouble to formally draw up their wills and final testaments shortly before setting out for Portsmouth. In the light of what was shortly to take place, these formal and legalistic documents have a very poignant quality. Thomas Seaverne, for instance, who was one of those who drowned, rather touchingly begins his will, 'To all people to whom this present writing shall come I Thomas Seaverne of Limehouse in the Parish of Stepney Hebenheath in the County of Middlesex mariner now bound forth on a voyage to the seas do send greeting'. He left everything to his 'honnoured and loveing mother Susanna Mitchell … widow', including, 'estates, goods, debts, rights, credits, wages, adventures, wares, merchandises, sume or sumes of money or moneys, clothes, commodities and things whatsoever that I shall have or that shall be due oweing or belonging unto mee at the time of my death'.[8]

The prolixity of lawyers has changed little down the centuries.

10

DEAL

On 27 April Sir John Berry arrived in Portsmouth to oversee the final details of the fleet's fitting out. The following day, Sir George Legge returned to London to report to James on the progress made so far. Sir John travelled to Portsmouth in the company of his newly appointed second lieutenant, James Hyde. This young man wrote to his elder brother Lawrence in a letter dated 3 May, in tones that make clear both his enthusiasm for his new posting and his admiration for his senior officer:

> We found the Gloucester in a pretty good forwardness, but, for all that, stood in need of Sir John Berry's presence, who did three times more to her after he came, than was done before; I am sure the officers of the yard may say there was never ship of her bigness fitted out so soon.[1]

The relationship here between lieutenant and captain was, as so often, not entirely straightforward. Berry was the senior officer and much older man, but it was Hyde who came from the powerful aristocratic family. Berry was a lowly tarpaulin who had worked his way up through the ranks. Hyde, on the other hand, was very much the gentleman by right of birth. And so there was this anomalous situation in which the captain's own future career might depend on favourably impressing his junior officer.

Few men came from a family more powerful than James Hyde. His elder brother, Henry, was the Earl of Clarendon. The middle brother, Laurence, was King Charles's First Lord of the Treasury and was later created Earl of Rochester. Their sister Anne had been James's first wife. This odd confusion of roles becomes evident further on in James Hyde's letter:

> I write this to you, because you were not certain of coming with the Duke; but if you do, I hope this will not come to your hand; for I can give you a better account of Sir John Berryes' extreme diligence by word of mouth, who has desired me to present his most humble service to you.[2]

This is the junior officer commending the senior officer rather than the other way round. They were also the last words that James Hyde was to write, for he was one of several high-profile members of the gentry who were shortly to drown.

As well as the *Gloucester*, two fourth rates, the *Happy Return* and the *Ruby*, and a fifth rate, the *Dartmouth*, were being hurriedly prepared. A second fifth rate, the *Pearl*, already at sea, was ordered to go directly from Portland to the Downs to await the rest of the fleet. The *Ruby* was in particularly bad shape. On a recent cruise to the Americas it had encountered some rough weather, which had left it desperately short of sails. Richard Beach wrote to his superiors on 4 April, 'for the Ruby unless we can be permitted to cut up third rate sails we cannot fit her'.[3] Still more worrying from the point of view of her captain, Thomas Allin, son of the famous Admiral Sir Thomas Allin, was the sickness of his men. He wrote to the Admiralty on 2 April, 'pleased to send me down some more books and tickets for I shall be forced to discharge what men I have now sick ashore with scurvy for they will not be in a fit condition to go with me again to sea'.[4]

The ticket book mentioned here refers to the system by which the men received their pay. The Admiralty found it more efficient not to issue its sailors with money but with tickets of entitlement that they had to come to London to cash. The problem with this system from the sailors' point of view was that travel was expensive and time consuming. The net result was the wretched sailor would cash his ticket with a local money lender, with which species of person the ports were rife, usually at a 20 per cent discount to its face value.

Portsmouth was not the only place where James's forthcoming departure was creating a stir of activity. Christopher Gunman, captain of the royal yacht *Mary*, which had been on the ground at Deptford waiting to be graved for a month, wrote to the Admiralty on 26 April that as he had now received orders that he was 'to go for Scotland to attend his Royal Highness my humble request to the Honourable is that you would be pleased to give the order unto Mr Shish of Deptford to grave the said yacht and do such other repairs thereon as he shall find needful'.[5]

The captains of the *Charlotte*, *Kitchin* and *Katherine* yachts likewise received orders to prepare for the Scottish voyage, as did William Gifford, newly appointed to his first ever command as captain of the sixth-rate *Lark*. All these last-mentioned vessels were berthed in the Thames. Captain Gifford was particularly anxious about the state of his ship. On 28 April he wrote to the Admiralty that he had a 'want of materials for rebuilding his binnacle' and still more troubling, 'no oven to the cook room'.[6] He also made the unusual request of asking for an additional small boat to carry on board 'a small yawl that will store within my pinnace'. The reason he gave was somewhat prescient. He was not satisfied with 'having but one boat if any accident should happen by a man's falling overboard etc'. We do not know whether he was issued with a second boat but even if he was, it would have made no difference to the *Gloucester*'s sailors struggling in the water, for the *Lark* was to get hopelessly lost from the rest of the fleet.

On 1 May a letter from Sir John arrived at Windsor, informing James that the *Gloucester* was now ready for sea and stating that 'it will be convenient for him to have his Majesty's orders for the victualling of his Royal Highness, his servants and watermen and others that attach him in this voyage ... otherwise none can have any provisions but what belong to the ship'.[7] Clearly the sailor's staple fare of beer, biscuit and salt beef was not considered appropriate for the royal party. This was hardly surprising. The iniquities of victuallers and pursers have always been notorious in the navy. Pepys considered that the quality of food had deteriorated from what it was before, 'our victuals to our seamen were much better heretofore than now, and our seamen then better contented, though with less wages; an Englishman's satisfaction being always observed to lie most in his belly'.[8] Pepys was particularly scathing about Irish meat, which was considered 'very unwholesome, as well as lean, and rots our men'.[9] Unfortunately we do not know what delicacies James requested for himself and his chosen guests but it was more likely to have consisted of sturgeon and venison than Irish beef.

On that same Monday morning of 1 May, the small fleet finally edged out of Portsmouth Harbour on a flood tide, with the wind coming from the north-west and west. The ships departed around noon and anchored off Spithead at 2 p.m. At 6 p.m. the *Gloucester, Happy Return* and *Dartmouth* weighed anchor again and set sail for the Downs. The *Ruby* was left behind, presumably because of some last-minute hitch, and did not finally depart Spithead until 4 the following morning.

It was a fine evening with light winds now coming from the west-south-west. The fleet, as it made its way up the Channel, would have made an impressive sight. The *Gloucester* was a particularly beautiful ship. The most accurate portrait still in existence is probably the drawing by Willem van de Velde the Elder that is conserved in the Museum Boijmans Van Beuningen in Rotterdam. It is dated around 1680 and shows the newly fashionable decorative round wreaths circling the upper deck portholes, instead of the square portholes of the earlier Commonwealth style. The stern must also have been entirely remodelled when the *Gloucester* underwent its major refit. The large coat of arms of the Commonwealth ships had been replaced by a smaller coat of arms flanked by the usual rampant lion and unicorn. This allowed for a second tier of windows fitted with Muscovy glass to let light into the rear of the quarter deck, above the original tier that was on the level of the upper deck. The coat of arms was decorated in gilt, but the rest of the carved work was adorned with a mixture of yellow paint and tar. The taffrail was elaborately carved with a 'CR' at its centre, and the quarter galleries were wonderfully ornate creations resembling miniature overhanging glass and wood palaces, surmounted by intricately fluted cupolas.

This was the great age of Grinling Gibbons; woodcarving would never be more stylish or fanciful. The *Gloucester*, with its beautifully sculptured figures, mythical animals and wild baroque flourishes, was a splendid creation. Inside the roundhouse and the great cabin the artistry was continued. The walls were panelled with oak, 'very curiously wrought and gilded with divers histories, and very much other work in oil colours'.[10] The sailors' quarters were painted red, apparently so the blood stains of combat did not show. The officers were allowed more subtle hues of green and blue. Despite the frequently gory nature of its business, there can have been few more glorious sights in history than that of a seventeenth-century warship under sail.

An express letter was sent to James informing him of the fleet's departure. Steady progress was made up the Channel and Sir John Berry was able to anchor his ships in the Downs on 3 May at 9 in the morning, in clear sight of the staunch round towers of Deal Castle. There was the usual saluting and deafening exchange of gunfire between castle and ship. The *Ruby* came in only three hours afterwards, having made good time.

The Downs was a reasonably deep stretch of water in the lee of the Goodwin Sands. It was much used by the Royal Navy as an anchorage throughout the Age of Sail because of the protection it provided from both westerly and easterly winds. But it was not the safest of havens. During the Great Storm of 1702, thousands of sailors were to lose their lives as Royal Navy ships were driven on to the treacherous sucking sands. The local inhabitants of Deal were much criticised for failing to rescue more men and it was this that led Daniel Defoe to write his poem 'The Just Reproach':

If I had any satire left to write,
Could I with suited spleen indite,
My verse should blast that fatal town,
And drown'd sailors' widows pull it down;
No footsteps of it should appear,
And ships no more cast anchor there.
The barbarous hated name of Deal shou'd die,

Or be a term of infamy;
And till that's done, the town will stand
A just reproach to all the land.[11]

But even before the Great Storm, Deal had a bad reputation. Pepys described it as a 'pitiful' place, and was particularly disgusted by the poor quality of the beer that he was given in an inn called Fullers.[12] All their ales were what Pepys described as 'in the fat'.[13]

There was no pier or harbour wall at Deal, just a long, windswept, shingle beach with small boats drawn up on it and the odd broken-down shed or cottage. All communication between the land and the larger ships at anchor in the Roads was by rowing boat or barge. Hundreds of rich merchant ships passed through these waters every year on their way to London, bringing goods from the Far East, the Americas or the Mediterranean. Smuggling was rife and it was partly this and the usual squalor and immorality that came with navy towns that gave Deal its reputation.

It was also the place for the taking on of pilots. It is probable that the ill-fated Captain Ayres joined the *Gloucester* as its pilot at Deal. One man who definitely joined at this late stage was Thomas Smith, able seaman. He was entered on to the books on 3 May, listed as a swabber. His wife, Joan, was 50 years old and described as blind and indigent, so Smith was most probably also an old man, or old anyway for his class at this time. He had just recently been released from debtors' prison. It was a condition of his release that he should sign on as a seaman, an arrangement that relieved the local authority of the expense of prisoners who had no means of their own, while at the same time helping to solve any shortage of naval manpower.

An express was received on board the *Gloucester* from James almost the very moment it had dropped anchor, commanding the ships to proceed immediately for Margate Roads. Lieutenant Hyde expected to leave that same evening if it was possible, but in the event it proved impractical and they did not weigh anchor until 6 a.m the following day, Thursday, 4 May.

11

PUTNEY

James was bored. He was a man who bored easily. On 24 April the royal entourage had moved from Whitehall to Windsor, but the change of scene had done little to lift his mood. If anything, it had made it worse. He paced the terrace overlooking the deer park with restless energy. There had been more heavy rain, causing widespread flooding.

Later that same day, he wrote to his niece, Charlotte Lee, Countess of Lichfield, who was Barbara Palmer's second daughter by the king. She was half James's age, but he had a close and gossipy relationship with her. He vented his ill feeling about the weather:

> It keeps us prisoners, for there is no sturing out farther than the little Parke, the waters being still so much out, and the ways so durty that I have not been able to go farther, and this day has been so very rainy that I have not been able to walke abroad at all, but a little in the morning early upon the terasse.[1]

James's letter writing style was peculiarly clumsy and inept but often, because of this very lack of sophistication, highly revealing. When explaining to his niece that he would be travelling directly to Scotland without having the opportunity to call in again at London, he made an intriguing remark:

> I shall go straight to the yacht and not call in at London at all, and this I do by advice and not by inclination for I should have been very glad

to have stay'd there one night, but pray do not take notice that I have sayd this to you.[2]

It is the last part that gives pause for thought. Why was he counselling the countess to be silent regarding his casual comment that he would have been glad to stop the night in London if he had been able? If he hadn't drawn attention to it in this way, his remark would have been entirely forgettable. It is unlikely to be part of some surreptitious flirtation between the two of them. The countess was a regular correspondent, but she was also married with four young children, as well as being a blood relation. A more probable explanation is that he was thinking of a recent night spent with his mistress Catherine Sedley. The countess was a mutual confidante to this affair.

Catherine Sedley was described by John Evelyn as being 'none of the most virtuous, but a wit'. It is a somewhat prissy turn of phrase, but it pretty much sums her up. She had had little to do with her mother, who was declared mad and banished to a convent in France while Catherine was still a child. As for her father, he was the notoriously debauched Sir Charles Sedley, hardly a role model for a vulnerable young woman. In view of her parentage it is not surprising that she was unconventional in her behaviour. At 15 she became a maid of honour to Mary of Modena. The two women were of a similar age. And at the age of 20 she graduated to James's bed. By 1682 she had already been James's on–off mistress for four years and was to continue in this role for her six remaining years in England.

So far as her appearance was concerned, she has had a bad press. Partly this was a result of her own bluntness. When asked what the duke saw in her, she remarked that 'none of us are handsome and if we had wit he has not enough to discover it'.[3] From the evidence of her portraits she was pale, with dark eyes, dark curly hair and a long, rather pointed face. But female portraits of this period all tended to represent an ideal of female beauty rather than the individual, so that it is often difficult to tell one subject from another. The written word was hardly more reliable. Contemporaries variously described her as thin to the point of emaciation and suffering from a squint in her eye. Part of this was nothing more than the usual animadversions levelled against a royal mistress, but she also had the disadvantage of being naturally thin in an age when plumpness was regarded as a feminine virtue.

Whatever the truth about Catherine Sedley's looks, there was something about her that fascinated James, for he returned to her again and again, despite his wife's fury and his own religious scruples. Perhaps it was because she obliged the duke in her choice of garments. According to Philibert, Count de Grammont, a French nobleman at the English court, it was James's conviction that 'no woman's leg was worth anything without green stockings'.[4]

On 1 May, James at last received a message from Captain John Berry announcing that the *Gloucester* frigate was now ready and would shortly be off the South Foreland, where it was planned that James should embark. Early in the morning of Wednesday, 3 May, James set out by coach from Windsor for the small Thameside village of Putney. He was used to early starts and regarded himself as a man of action. He liked to be depicted in martial dress as a Roman general, his hamstrings taught with power, his muscles bulging and potent. He had relished his role as Lord High Admiral of the Seas until his enemies had plotted to have it snatched from him, but it seemed the tide was at long last turning in his favour. His patience, his loyalty and his sincere love for his brother must surely, finally, reap their just reward. And, as if by divine arrangement, that same morning there was at last a change in the weather. A brisk breeze began to blow from the south-west, bringing warmer air and blue skies. What surer proof could there be that the heavens smiled on him? At Putney he was cheered by a large crowd already gathered to see him off. The omens were good.

The most select from among James's well-wishers were already on the river in their own craft, pennants fluttering, eager to follow in his wake as he progressed through the city on the ebbing tide. A London newsletter described the scene:

About 8 yesterday morning his Royal Highness came in his coach to Putney where his barges and a shallop, double manned, attended him with the barges of all the persons of quality about town.[5]

The less affluent but equally enthusiastic followed in their wake in hundreds of small river craft, wherries, skiffs, shallops, gigs, smacks, hoys and pinks. Some were propelled by a single skuller, others by two oarsmen, or a four, or an eight, depending on their tonnage.

From the upper windows of the Shield Gallery, which towered giddily over the tumbling waters, the river looked like a great serpent lazily uncoiling itself, playfully flicking tongues of white fire at the many oars of the boatmen, who tried to beat down the flames with their twitching blades. It was a one-sided battle. The more the rowers slashed at the waves, the greater was the volume of white spume that rose up, appearing to make all their efforts at quelling the great river beast self-defeating. As well as oars, many of the boats carried sail. There were sails of every conceivable shape and size: jibs, lugs, luffs and lateens, spinnakers, spankers and gaffs. The royal barge carried no sail, but the flag of St George fluttered fore and aft, and the royal standard was hoisted aloft.

Those loyalists who could find no boat crowded the roof leads of the grand houses along the water's edge. There was much cheering, sounding of trumpets and letting off of firecrackers. Watermen continually shouted out at each other, with their usual vulgarity, to make room or risk being rammed. Black-winged gulls swooped and screeched, scavenging the tidal detritus. James stood in the forepart of the barge and acknowledged the cheering crowds by a slight movement of a raised hand. With his trained seaman's eye, he scanned the rooftops. It is most unlikely that Catherine Sedley was there to be seen. She was not an early riser and such sentimental gestures were not her style.

The royal entourage sailed past the steps of Westminster and Whitehall, past the gracious gardens of Northumberland House and Somerset House, past the Savoy Hospital, fallen into disrepair and offering sanctuary only to owls and beggars, and past the steps that led to the new Duke's Theatre, where Thomas Otway's *Venice Preserv'd* was still playing. The barge shot through the arches of London Bridge, where the waters raced and swirled. This most dangerous part of the river voyage was where many a small boat had come to grief. And then it was on past the Tower on the left and through the great hinterland of docks, crowding both sides of the river, and from where so many of the *Gloucester's* seamen had recently set out. They left the royal docks at Deptford behind on the starboard bow, followed by the gracious palace at Greenwich. Then came the impressive East India Docks at Blackwall, the great loop of the Isle of Dogs, the arsenal at Woolwich and finally they arrived at the low-lying gravel pits of Erith, situated just above Dartford Creek. They arrived at 11 a.m., a rate of progress not much slower than the equivalent modern journey by car. Waiting there was the royal yacht, *Mary*, freshly graved and ready to receive the duke and his entourage of favourites.

Captain Gunman, who was in command of the *Mary*, had left Deptford at six that morning and had anchored at Erith at eight. The uninitiated in the ways of the river could be forgiven for wondering why the *Mary* had not waited at Deptford rather than moving 10 or so miles further on towards the estuary, so making James's voyage in his barge that much the longer. The explanation is simple. By the time James had reached Deptford he had already missed the high tide, and so the *Mary* would have been stranded there until the evening. From Erith it was possible for the *Mary* to slip down river at any time of day. This constant attention to the state of the tides was second nature to Londoners of the seventeenth century, for whom the Thames was the main thoroughfare.

Another early riser, already waiting anxiously on the poop deck of the *Mary* and craning his eyes for a first sighting of the duke, was Samuel Pepys.

12

ERITH

Captain Christopher Gunman was a blustering, blunt-mouthed seventeenth-century sea dog; irascible, touchy, proud and pig-headed. But he knew the sandbanks and the estuaries of northern Europe like few others of his generation, and the black waters of the Kattegat ran in his veins. Pug-nosed and pugnacious, he wore his hair long and his leather boots tall in the outmoded Cavalier style. He was one of those strange amphibious creatures more at home between decks than on dry land. His language, his bearing, his beliefs all exuded the air of a man conceived upon the ballast of a flat-bottomed lugger and weaned on samphire and oysters.

He was of Danish extraction but had become a naturalised Englishman through a special Act of Parliament, and by 1682 he had been serving as a captain in the Royal Navy for nearly twenty years. He first made his name through the taking of the *La Vierge de Bon Port* in 1666, the first ship of the French East India Company to return to Europe with 'a great store of stones, emeralds, amethysts and topaz to a very great value'.[1] It was seized after a fierce five-hour battle off Guernsey, although it sank before the prize crew that Gunman sent on board could bring the valuable capture into St Peter Port.

The taking of a rich prize was the quickest way for a navy captain to make his fortune, so Gunman must have cursed his ill luck at having come so close, but he was not so unlucky as the sailors who drowned while trying to bring the damaged ship safely into port. Two months after this incident, Gunman lost his left hand in a skirmish with 'two Flushing men of warr' at the western entrance to the Channel: 'a little after the going down of the sunn I had my left hand shott away by a great shott from hee that had the 40 gunes'.[2] It is an odd coincidence that both Berry and Gunman, two key figures in the *Gloucester* sinking, had wooden stumps for left hands.

Three years later Gunman was appointed captain of James's personal yacht, the *Anne*, named after the duke's first wife. In 1677, he was transferred to James's new yacht, the *Mary*, named predictably enough after his second wife. The position of master of a royal yacht was not as potentially lucrative as being the captain of a rated ship as there was no chance of capturing a fat prize from the enemy. It was, however, something of a comfortable sinecure as it avoided the perils of a long posting to some pestilential foreign station such as the Caribbean, where yellow fever was rife. It also brought regular contact with the upper echelons of Stuart society. The yachts were largely used to ferry members of the royal family and foreign ambassadors around Europe and home waters. For Gunman it had the further advantage that the *Mary* was based at Deptford where he had a house, so he would also have seen more of his wife and children than most navy captains. Judging from his regular letters to his wife, he was a loving husband and attentive father. Nor did his maiming prevent him from becoming an accomplished pilot and surveyor. He produced a detailed draft of the Channel Islands, and Gunman Sand off Dover is named after him.

The numbers gathered at Erith were even greater than they had been at Putney. Gunman recorded in his journal that there were nearly 500 persons pressed together on the deck of the small yacht of which he had charge. Even allowing for some degree of exaggeration, it was clearly quite a throng. The *London Newsletter* recorded that 'the crowd that came to take leave of him was so great that the Captain spoke to the Duke to desire them to go off the yacht, for fear their weight should have forced the deck in'.[3] It was very much in Gunman's character to speak bluntly and forcefully whatever was on his mind; he did not stand on ceremony. But he was clearly a favourite of the duke's, despite his rough manners, for he had consistently used him as master of his personal transport for upwards of thirteen years. Gunman, like

Churchill, Legge, Berry and Mordaunt, had also been present at the infamous Battle of Solebay. He had been master of James's flagship, the *Prince*, during that particularly bloody encounter.

There were others present on the *Mary* that morning who took a less favourable view of Gunman's character. Thomas Bruce, 2nd Earl of Ailesbury, was a loyal supporter of James. He had been with the duke during the voyage down the Thames to Erith and was planning to accompany him to Scotland, but suddenly felt so unwell that he was forced to drop out at the last minute. In his memoirs, written some thirty years later, he thanked God for this merciful intervention and blamed the loss of the *Gloucester* unequivocally on Gunman. In Ailesbury's opinion, he 'merited death had there been law for it; he [Gunman] was brutal and positive, and certainly this melancholy wreck was owing to him. No one knew him better than myself, for he had transported my family several times, and myself, in particular twice.'[4] Ailesbury uses the word 'positive' here not in its modern sense but to imply stubbornness.

The earl goes on to relate how during one particular voyage on the *Mary* up the River Scheldt in 1679, en route to visit James in exile in Brussels, they took on a pilot for navigation who was discovered to be drunk. Gunman promptly lost his temper with the wretched Dutchman and would have thrown him overboard if Ailesbury had not intervened. From that point on, Gunman took on the navigation himself. Ailesbury, evidently a nervous traveller, appointed himself to the post of lookout and scanned the river for shoal water. The earl, who was only 24 years old at the time, claimed his eyesight was better than Gunman's, even if he wasn't a seaman. He signalled a difficult patch of water ahead but this assistance was not appreciated by Gunman, who exploded with rage and became abusive. 'He swore a bloody oath with some rude expressions,' is how Ailesbury delicately puts it in his memoirs.[5] 'On which I told him very fiercely that I would not be drowned through his obstinacy and folly, and that if he persisted, I would confine him in the bilboes.'[6] At this threat Gunman appears to have calmed down, and later in the voyage he requested Ailesbury not to report him to the duke. Ailesbury agreed to let the matter drop, something he afterwards regretted, for he felt that if he had reported the incident Gunman may have been dismissed from his command and the sinking of the *Gloucester* would, in that event, have been avoided. The anecdote is interesting not just for what it tells us about Gunman but also for what it reveals about Ailesbury. Gunman certainly comes across as hot-tempered, self-opinionated, intolerant of the views of others and jealous of his own authority. On the other hand, it is difficult not to feel some sympathy for a man who, having just discovered that his pilot is drunk, is now being told how to do his job by a young patrician with no direct knowledge of the sea.

Ailesbury was not the only one experiencing last-minute qualms about the Scottish voyage. Samuel Pepys was present among the many sycophants and dignitaries clamouring on board the small deck of the *Mary*. He had readily accepted an invitation from the duke to accompany him to Scotland and back but for some obscure reason he failed to inform his close female friends, such as the young widow Lady Betty Mordaunt, of his intentions. It was an omission that thoroughly annoyed her and later provoked her into taking a cruel revenge on him.

Pepys's secrecy with regards his intentions, not just with Lady Mordaunt, but also with others of his female admirers, such as the ladies of the Houblon family in Winchester Street, was probably in part due to the thoughtless independence of the unattached man. But it may also have reflected his general queasiness about what lay ahead. He was a timid traveller at the best of times, and the Scottish voyage could be notoriously rough. He probably wished to avoid tearful scenes of leave-taking in which the dangers of his proposed journey would have been pressed upon him. Less explicable was Pepys's obvious reluctance to take a berth on the *Gloucester*, despite James inviting him to do so. He had already written on 29 April to his friend Captain John Wyborne, commander of the *Happy Return*, asking for accommodation on his vessel instead. His letter suggests some apprehension about the forthcoming voyage: 'I mean to be very sick. Therefore pray let me have a little room with you if I come.'[7]

Captain Wyborne had in the past performed various favours for Pepys, including selling his 'black boy' for him, on a recent voyage into the Mediterranean, for 25 pistoles (gold coins), and reinvesting the proceeds in chocolate and sherry at Cadiz on the return. Little attention has been given to Pepys as a slave owner, which is surprising because the fact of it is far more shocking to any modern reader than his rather better-known sexual proclivities. Slave owning was not common in England at this period and it was not, strictly speaking, legal. However, it was becoming fashionable to have a black face among one's retinue of servants. In 1680, Charles II had requested of the East India Company that they procure for him 'three comely black dwarfs', two female and one male, and in 1682 the artist Pierre Mignard famously depicted his mistress the Duchess of Portsmouth in the company of a black child, or possibly one of the recently acquired 'dwarfs'. Pepys always liked to be at the forefront when it came to acquiring the latest fashionable accoutrements, but his dabbling with black servants obviously did not work out, for he sold him again very quickly.

James himself did rather more than dabble in slavery. He was both governor and major shareholder in the Royal African Company, which had a monopoly in the slave trade from West Africa to the Caribbean Islands. Slave owning in England may not have been very common but many Englishmen were becoming increasingly attracted to the lucrative profits to be made from the transatlantic slave trade. James, despite his reputation for being somewhat dimwitted compared with his elder brother, was possessed of a sharp nose for where the fast money was to be made. It was his involvement in the slave trade that most probably explains the presence of one of the more mysterious passengers on board the *Gloucester*, a certain William Freeman.

Freeman was a tough, no-nonsense, self-made merchant with extensive sugar plantations in the Leeward Islands. He had moved to London in 1674 to further develop his business empire. He was not exactly the kind of man one would have expected to be among James's special guests on board the *Gloucester* but he was possessed of an excellent knowledge in all aspects of the triangular trade between Britain, Africa and the West Indies, shipping as many as 5,000 slaves a year on his own account, a colossal number. He was also a fellow investor in the Royal African Company. With his profits from sugar and slaves he had recently bought a grand if somewhat dilapidated house at Henley called Fawley Court. Freeman was someone whom James was anxious to cultivate. For his part, Freeman was flattered by the attention and happy to act as James's agent in the same way that he acted for many other gentleman who wanted to get into the business of buying and selling slaves. He probably did not confide to James the details of his extensive French brandy smuggling activities, nor did James's patronage buy his enduring loyalty. When William of Orange invaded at Torbay in 1688 and made his way towards London, it was at Fawley Court that he was first wined and dined.

One of the attractions for Pepys in choosing to travel on the *Happy Return* with Captain Wyborne rather than on the *Gloucester* with James, was the potential company of Wyborne's 'pretty wife',[8] with whom Pepys was on good terms. 'Wherever your lady is (if she be with you) I kiss her hands and should laugh to see her in Scotland,' he wrote gallantly in his letter to Wyborne.[9] However, in the event his solicitations in this direction were to no avail. The *Happy Return* was apparently already full and could not accommodate him. Rebuffed by his old friend, Pepys still refused the offer of a berth on the *Gloucester*. Instead he opted for the *Katherine* yacht under the command of Captain William Davis, where the only other passenger of note was Lieutenant General of the Ordnance Sir Christopher Musgrave, a rather dour Cumbrian landowner of no particular note, and not, one would have imagined, a particularly entertaining travelling companion for someone of Pepys's disposition.

Once he had arrived safely in Scotland, Pepys was anxious to explain to his intimates that his travelling in the *Katherine* was his own choice, and that the duke had warmly requested his presence on the *Gloucester* but he had declined the invitation: 'though I had abundant invitation to have gone on board the Duke, I chose rather, for room sake and accommodation, to keep to my yacht, where I had nobody but Sir Christopher Musgrove and our servants with me'.[10] He was clearly concerned that his friends should not think he had been in any way slighted by the duke but this reclusiveness is not typical of the notoriously convivial Pepys and it seems likely that there were factors at work in his decision, other than the simple desire for private space. Perhaps, like some of the sailors who were prompted to write their wills, he had intimations of pending calamity. There had been a strange rumour, back in the previous January, circulating around the Royal Exchange, which was the main conduit in the City for maritime news, that Captain Gunman had been shipwrecked on the voyage to Scotland to visit James, Duke of York. The *Impartial Protestant Mercury* of 16 January 1682 had carried the following item:

> Twas discoursed upon The Royal Exchange that Capt. Wren, Capt. Gunman, Capt. Wilkes, and another, all four captains of his Majesty's Ships of War, who were on board the *Mary* yacht to Scotland to give his Royal Highness a visit were all cast away in the said yacht off of Tinmouth [Tynemouth].[11]

Gunman was indeed on his way to Scotland on the *Mary* on this date, but the rumour turned out to be false. Yet four months later, when James himself was en route to Scotland, there was indeed to be a disastrous shipwreck involving him, of far greater proportions than the one strangely anticipated the previous January.

After the *Gloucester* had wrecked, Pepys, like the Earl of Ailesbury, saw his decision not to go in that ship as a wonderful example of divine intervention from which he derived some self-satisfaction:

> Nor ought I to be less sensible of God's immediate mercy to myself, in directing me (contrary to my purpose at my first coming out, and the Duke's kind welcome to me when on board him in the river) to keep to the yacht. For many will, I doubt, be found lost as well or better qualified for saving themselves by swimming and otherwise than I might have been.[12]

Pepys is always endearingly frank about his own physical infirmities including, in this case, his inability to swim. But perhaps he was being less than frank about the true reasons behind his decision to avoid the *Gloucester* at all costs.

Meanwhile, at Erith, celebrations on board the *Mary* continued with much laughter and merriment. It was, however, a party of short duration. The tide waited for no man, not even the Duke of York. Near 1 p.m., according to the *Calendar of State Papers*, a little past noon according to Gunman (timekeeping was still something of an erratic art in the late seventeenth century, and Gunman's watch continually lagged that of his colleagues), the *Mary* yacht set sail for Margate Roads. The other yachts, the *Kitchin*, *Katherine* and *Charlotte*, followed. They sailed past Long Reach, Lidler's Reach, Gravesend, the Piles, the Oven, Blyth Sand, the Middle Ground, the Isle of Grain and the Buoy of the Nore, finally coming to an anchor in Margate Roads at 8.30 p.m., in 7 fathoms of water. Within half an hour the other yachts had caught up and anchored. Pepys hurriedly dashed off a letter to his friend William Hewer updating him on events. This would be his last chance to get a communication to land for some days. He was, as always, a compulsive scribbler.

13

THE NORTH FORELAND

The following morning at 6 a.m., the *Gloucester* frigate, in company with the *Happy Return*, the *Ruby*, the *Dartmouth* and the *Pearl*, weighed anchor from the Downs and headed northwards. There was a light wind from the south-south-west, and the weather was so hazy that they could not see the landmarks that would normally have enabled them to go through the Gulls. They went instead between the Break Sand and the Quorn Sand, taking as their guide point the Mill when it was in line with Broadstairs pier head. The *Happy Return* recorded having only 3 fathoms of water at one point, so it was fortunate to avoid grounding. But luck was with them and all the frigates came through safely.

At 8 a.m. they met with the Duke of York and the flotilla of yachts in Margate Roads off the North Foreland. Lieutenant Wetwang, writing up the logbook of the *Happy Return*, and Captain George St Loe, doing likewise in the *Dartmouth*, both record that there were five yachts in attendance. Only the four yachts already mentioned are ever identified by name, which would suggest that either both these officers were mistaken or that a fifth yacht was mysteriously in company but somehow overlooked in the accounts. The probable explanation is that these officers mistook the *Lark* frigate for a yacht. The *Lark* had sailed out of the Thames with the other four yachts and, being a sixth rate, with a burthen of 199 tons and a 74ft-long keel, it was not much bigger than the *Mary*, with 166 tons and a keel length of 66ft 6in. It would have been an easy mistake to make, particularly in the poor light.

At 9 a.m., James was rowed in his shallop from the *Mary* across to the *Gloucester*. Once he was aboard, the royal standard was hoisted on the main mast as evidence of his presence. In this period, even during hostilities, it was not considered to be a security risk to publicly advertise on which ship a key member of the royal household was travelling. The flag was red, blue and yellow, and divided into quarters, the first quarter containing the English prostrate lions and the French fleur-de-lis, the second quarter the Scottish rampant lion, the third quarter the Irish harp and the fourth quarter a repeat of the first.

The *Gloucester* fired a salute of twenty-seven guns to welcome James aboard. The *Happy Return* followed with a twenty-five-gun salute, and then all the other ships and yachts joined in. The cacophony must have been deafening and the smoke cannot have assisted with visibility, but such was the style of the times. Within about two hours the transfer of goods, persons and baggage had been completed, no mean feat in an open sea. It was probably at this point that James's personal strongbox, which was to be a subject of such controversy in later years, was loaded on board the *Gloucester*. Much of the bulkier goods had already been put on board in Portsmouth, and possibly also when anchored outside Deal.

The roll-call of those who had chosen to keep company with the duke was impressive. As well as Legge and Churchill, there was: Sir George Gordon, shortly to be appointed Lord Chancellor of Scotland; James Drummond, Earl of Perth, the future Lord Justice General; the Earl of Roxburghe; the Earl of Middleton; the Earl of Winton; the Marquis of Montrose; Lord Obrian; the laird of Hopetown; Sir Joseph Douglas of Pompherton; Sir James Dick; Sir David Falconer; Sir Charles Scarborough, personal physician to James; Lord Griffin; and numerous others, including a number of James's personal musicians, his huntsmen and key members of his household. Some of the lesser Scottish gentry went aboard the *Happy Return*, as did more of their personal possessions. Even so, the great cabin of the *Gloucester* must have been extremely crowded with so many notables and their servants aboard, for these ships were not designed for carrying large numbers of passengers. It was just as well that standards of personal space and privacy were less exacting than they are today.

At 11 a.m. the fleet made sail, the wind coming from the south. The course was set towards the north-north-east to avoid the sands of the Thames Estuary. At this point everything must have seemed set fair for a speedy and prosperous voyage. The wind was favourable and the haze had begun to lift a little. It might yet turn into one of those fine early summer days, full of promise for the future.

At noon it was standard practice for the navigators on all ships to calculate their position either through observation of the sun or by taking a bearing on a known landmark. If no landmarks could be seen and the sun was obscured, then the position had to be worked out by means of dead reckoning, which was based on distances and directions sailed since the previous known position, with some allowance being made for leeway and currents. The surviving logbooks, journals and narratives contain no mention of any direct observations, and so it is reasonable to presume that visibility was still too poor to make sightings on the sun. However, as all the fleet had only just departed from the vicinity of the North Foreland, the most north-easterly point of the Kent coast, even if this landmark was no longer visible with the naked eye, one might have expected some reasonable degree of consistency among the ships as to where exactly they were just one hour later. In fact, the evidence of the logs reveals some startling discrepancies. According to Lieutenant Wetwang, on the *Happy Return*, the North Foreland was bearing south-west 3 leagues at noon. Captain Allin, on the *Ruby*, made it south-west 5 leagues, a difference of 6 nautical miles. Captain Botham, on the *Pearl*, made their position the same distance off as Captain Allin, but in the direction south-west by south rather than south-west, a difference of 11¼ degrees. Such wide discrepancies of observation in a fleet that had only recently departed from a known point has three possible explanations: poor navigational skills among those responsible, a widely dispersed fleet implying weak central command, or wildly varying times between watches.

Early in the afternoon the weather changed abruptly. 'At two o'clock in the afternoon the wind shifted from the South to the West with much rain from the West to the North North West with thick foggy weather,'[1] is how Sir John Berry describes it in his

'Narrative'. Later that evening he refers to the wind shifting still further and starting to blow from the north-north-east. Christopher Gunman talks of 'dirty weather' and a wind veering about the compass before finally coming from the north-east by north.[2] The other captains were all agreed both with regards the deterioration in the weather and the change in wind direction.

At 8 p.m. the decision was made on the *Gloucester* to anchor up for the night. They had just made 'a short board to the North West' and come into 15 fathoms of water, at which they had tacked and stood into 20 fathoms.[3] The 15-fathom sounding was a useful warning sign that they were straying too near those dangerous sands on the north side of the Thames Estuary. Sir John Berry, in consultation with his pilot Captain Ayres, no doubt felt that it would be safer to anchor than try to continue to navigate past the Yarmouth Sands in the darkness. In this period ships did not always anchor up for the night, even in foggy conditions. The fact that they did so demonstrates the care that was being taken because of the importance of the passengers on board.

No doubt a number of toasts were drunk that evening. The first day of the voyage was over and there was no reason why all those involved should not have felt considerable satisfaction. The weather conditions were not ideal, but they were far from being severe. A number of the gentry would no doubt have been suffering from seasickness in the fresh winds but even so there was very probably plenty of alcohol going round. James himself was not a great indulger in wine, being altogether rather more puritanical in his drinking habits than his elder brother, but nor was he the most censorious. There were later to be suggestions that the reason so many of the gentry drowned was because many of them were dead drunk when the *Gloucester* foundered. Bevil Higgons, a near-contemporary historian and a supporter of James, made the following statement in his reply to Bishop Burnet of Salisbury on the subject of who was responsible for so many lost lives:

As to people of quality that were lost in this hurry and confusion, I am sorry to mention what was generally said and believ'd at the time, that some of them were in a condition that render'd it impracticable to wake them; so that in such a confusion, when every man is to save his own life, it is no great wonder that they were neglected, who could not shift for themselves.⁴

It is one of those insinuations that is easy to make and difficult to disprove, but if the number of bottles of good claret recently discovered on the seabed at the wreck site is anything to go by, sufficient stock had been laid in for quite a party.

As the *Gloucester* furled its sails and came to for the night, a cannon was fired from the quarter deck as a direction to the rest of the fleet to gather around their flag ship and follow its example. A trumpet would also have sounded from the poop deck to mark the beginning of the night watch. Sir John Berry calculated the *Gloucester*'s position to be 'the Naze Land bearing W by N nine leagues off'.⁵ They had covered approximately 25 to 30 miles since departing from the North Foreland some nine hours earlier, a fairly slow rate of progress that reflected the difficult conditions.

The *Pearl*, the *Happy Return* and the four yachts were all sailing in the immediate vicinity of the *Gloucester*. They let go their anchors, no doubt content to moor up for the night rather than continue to grope their way through the murky conditions. Captain George St Loe, on the *Dartmouth*, however, mistook the cannon shot for a signal to tack. The firing of a gun was indeed the usual method of warning for danger ahead and so the mistake was understandable. Captain St Loe made the following entry in his log:

> At 8 at night we heard a gun which we judged to be for tacking, we tacked and stood away NW by W til we spied two ships which stood to the Eastwards, we tacked and stood with them but a fog coming on very thick we lost the whole fleet this night.⁶

The identity of the two ships that the *Dartmouth* chose to follow is not clear but they may well have been the *Ruby* and the *Lark*, as they are the only two ships unaccounted for. According to the *Ruby*'s log, Captain Allin also chose to tack at 8 p.m., presumably for the same reason as St Loe on the *Dartmouth*. 'At 8 at night we tacked to the Northward and we had 26 fathoms water, and at 12 at night we tacked to the Eastward in 20 fathoms water.'[7]

Half an hour later, the *Ruby*'s captain, Thomas Allin, was alarmed to hear a great rushing of water, 'we had a great rush again' [against] the ship on the lee side and we heave the lead and found 15 fathoms water'. He was in the vicinity of the Galloper Sand, which was notorious for the sound it made of galloping horses and was the graveyard of many a fine ship, including most famously the *Royal Prince* during the Four Days' Battle of 1666. The impression Captain Allin gives in his logbook is that by assiduously lowering the lead at regular intervals he had sufficient warning of the danger of the Galloper and had taken the necessary avoidance action. However, a later examination of Captain Allin's logbook by the Navy Board reveals a different story. A nameless official tersely observes: 'runn upon the Galloper – but here only ownes a rush to leewards & that he heve the lead and found 15 fathom water.'[8] There is a further terse note in the margin of this manuscript, possibly added at a later date by Pepys himself, 'minces his running upon the Galloper'.[9]

It seems that Captain Allin had tried, unsuccessfully as it turned out, to cover up the grounding of his ship on the Galloper sandbank. It was a potentially fatal incident and one that he was lucky to escape from without more damage. All the same, it was a black mark against Allin. Meanwhile, the *Ruby* and the *Dartmouth* continued tacking back and forth through the night, trying unsuccessfully to make contact with the others.

All in all, the general impression one gets from these first hours of sailing northwards is that this royal entourage was pretty much a shambles. Navigation skills seem to have been of a poor standard, one ship had grounded on a sandbank, at least two ships had already got themselves lost from the main body of the fleet, the whereabouts of the *Lark* was completely unrecorded, and perhaps most seriously there was no agreed system of signals. It did not augur well.

14

LOWESTOFT LIGHTS

The following day, the small fleet, already somewhat diminished in its numbers, did not make a particularly early start by the usual naval standards. According to Sir John Berry, it was 8 a.m. before they weighed anchor and set sail. By this time on a May morning it would have been past dawn by three or four hours. Christopher Gunman mentions that it was 7.30 a.m. when they got under sail, but Gunman's watch invariably lagged behind the others and anyway 7.30 a.m. is still very much on the late side. The various logbooks offer no insights for the delayed start other than the fact that visibility was still poor. It was 'dark and hazy with a mistiness', according to Gunman.[1] But that was hardly an adequate explanation. The most probable reason is that crew and passengers were all sleeping in after a night of riotous celebrations. The wind was from the east-north-east and blowing hard. There was no sign of the *Ruby*, the *Dartmouth* or the *Lark*.

The fleet 'made a small trip to the South East'[2] and then at 9 a.m., they tacked and 'stood away North and North by East'.[3] At this stage of the voyage the courses followed by the fleet were most probably decided by Captain Ayres, the pilot on board the *Gloucester*. According to Sir John Berry, he was 'a person esteemed to be one of the best and ablest men to the Northward'.[4] By 'Northward' Berry was referring to the navigation of all those seas to the north of the Thames Estuary.

Pilots were selected for their intimate knowledge of the coasts and waterways and related hazards. Ayres was a pilot of many years' experience and had been employed on occasion by the Navy Board.

A Captain James Ayres was paid 10 guineas on 17 November 1680 for piloting the *Woolwich* warship from Gravesend into Leigh Road and 'from thence to Harwich', but he does not appear to have been used very regularly by them.[5] He did, however, have a long-standing relationship with the Duke of York, who had employed him as a pilot at least as far back as 1672.

Not everyone was impressed by the general level of competence of pilots, as was evident from Ailesbury's story of Christopher Gunman wanting to throw his pilot overboard when sailing up the River Scheldt. Samuel Pepys, when he was Secretary to the Navy Office, was very concerned about the need to raise the standards of the profession. He was an active supporter of Christ's College, a school that specialised in the teaching of those mathematical skills necessary for good navigation. Similarly, he was a member of the Trinity House Brethren, and was twice elected their Master. This august body acted like a guild for those involved in maritime affairs. They were responsible for all the lights, buoys, beacons, lighthouses and landmarks of the nation's waterways and coasts. Pepys was anxious to see Trinity House given the authority to regulate pilots through proper forms of examination and certification. He made a note in his *Naval Minutes*:

> We have often complained in the Navy of want of able pilots both in the River [Thames] and the Medway, and had under consideration how to supply the same, the able ones being worn out and men under-taking pilotage who be not approved by the Trinity House.[6]

There is strong evidence to suggest that Captain Ayres was one of those pilots 'not approved by the Trinity House'. After the shipwreck, Pepys makes one of his many notes to himself to check whether Ayres was 'ever duly entered upon the ships book … he being no regular pilot'.[7] According to Pepys, Ayres was only used on this occasion because he was 'a man that has heretofore served the Duke as pilot in the war, and in his voyage hither, and one greatly valued as such by him'.[8] In other words, Ayres was a personal favourite of the Duke of York's, his relationship having been forged, as so often where the duke was concerned, during his service in the Dutch Wars. It also implies that Ayres had been the pilot on the *Henrietta* yacht during James's recent voyage down from Edinburgh.

At noon, Gunman judged Orford Ness to be west by south 5 leagues off. Thomas Allin, on the *Ruby*, estimated the same landmark at around the same time to be north-west 8 leagues. The *Ruby* had met up with the *Dartmouth* in the early light of morning but neither ship had yet managed to make contact with the main fleet. The two lost frigates, sailing in company, were at that point some 10 miles or so adrift to the east, well beyond visibility in such poor conditions even with the aid of an 'optical tube'. Small refracting telescopes manufactured after one of Newton's designs and suitable for use on board ship were becoming popular at this time. Meanwhile, the *Lark*, commanded by the fretful William Gifford, still worrying about his inability to retrieve any men lost overboard, entered into the company of the fleet for the first time. Not for long, however. Before nightfall the *Lark* had again disappeared.

At 1 p.m. Captain Botham, on the *Pearl*, made the lighthouse of Orford Ness west 5 leagues. This was not hopelessly inconsistent with the Gunman position, but it already suggests that Gunman believed the fleet to be further north than his associates, an issue that was to become of critical importance before the day was out. At 1.30 p.m., Sir John Berry on the *Gloucester* made the steeples of Dunwich west by north 3 leagues off. This was before the cliff eroded and the churches fell into the sea. At 2 p.m. Lieutenant Wetwang, in the *Happy Return*, calculated that Orford Castle bore west-south-west 5 or 6 leagues. At 4 p.m. Captain Botham, on the *Pearl*, remarked that they were 'abreast of Sole Church'. Sole was an earlier name for Southwold. The trouble with all these entries is that they were likely to have been calculations by dead reckoning rather than observations on known landmarks. The fleet was groping its way slowly northwards, not knowing quite where it was in relation to the treacherous sands that surrounded the port of Yarmouth, the major navigational hazard between London and Edinburgh.

In the early evening, several of the lookouts must have made a simultaneous sighting of land. Sir John Berry, in the *Gloucester*, remarks that at 8 p.m. Lowestoft bore west-north-west 2 leagues. Wetwang, in the *Happy Return*, has Lowestoft west by north 7 miles off, also at 8 p.m. The two observations are impressively consistent. Captain Botham, on the *Pearl*, remarks that Lowestoft lighthouse bore north-west by west 5 leagues off at 8 that evening. The *Pearl* discrepancy is probably explained by the fact that it had just run into trouble. 'At eight at night had a short head sea: that our puttock shrouds broke and fore top mast came by the board,' is how the captain described it in his log.[9] In layman's language, they had hit a patch of rough water that had strained the ship to such a point that some of the cables that secured the top section of the foremast had given way, causing it to crash down. In attending to repairs, they had quickly lost company with the rest of the fleet. It was an excusable incident, but they were the fourth out of the six warships that had now become detached, leaving only the *Happy Return* and the four yachts still sailing in company with the *Gloucester*. Gunman also observed Lowestoft, which he spelt 'Laystow', around the same time as the others. He made his observation at 7 p.m., an hour earlier than the rest.

The fact that so many of the navigators independently made observations between 7 and 8 p.m. suggests that it had just become dark and the coastal lights were becoming visible for the first time. The establishment of lights on headlands at this period was largely left to the initiative of individual entrepreneurs, who erected a lighthouse and charged passing ships a fee for the benefit. There was some attempt by Trinity House to regulate this somewhat haphazard arrangement by issuing licences, but the combination of vested interests and muddled bureaucracy led to a generally confused situation, with lights appearing and disappearing according to the success or otherwise of the entrepreneur concerned. The lights themselves were relatively primitive affairs – baskets of coals burning on top of iron and wood constructions – and their reliability depended in part on the assiduity of those paid to tend them. It was not unheard of, in times of particularly wild and stormy weather, for the fires to be extinguished through neglect, just when they were most needed. But the evening of 5 May was not stormy and there were certainly some fires burning that night along the east coast of England.

Around the same time these sightings were made, a great argument broke out among the various navigators, and at the centre of the row was Gunman. The bones of the dispute are told in Gunman's journal. He was sailing in the *Mary* yacht ahead of the *Gloucester*, but when he saw the light burning on the coast he turned his ship and bore up under the *Gloucester*'s stern. The duke emerged from the great cabin on to the gallery, lent over the taffrail and a conference was held. 'The Duke asked me whether I thought we should weather the Newarpe without tacking. I informed him no for it was impossible.'[10] The Newarp was one of the most treacherous sandbanks off Yarmouth on the coast of Norfolk, and Gunman was clearly of the opinion that if the fleet did not change course immediately, they were in imminent danger of striking on it.

Gunman's advice on this occasion was clearly ignored but he was not the kind of man to take being overruled lightly. At about 8 p.m. (Gunman time) a second conference was held. 'I came up under the Admiral's stern being asked again whether we could weather the Newarpe. I said no and thought the pilot on board was mad if he did not tack off.'[11] Clearly the discussions were becoming increasingly heated and acrimonious. On this occasion Gunman's advice was taken and the fleet tacked off. What is not explained is why on the first occasion Gunman was ignored and yet on the second he was deferred to.

Sir John Berry's 'Narrative', on the surface at any rate, provides a more measured account of what happened:

The yachts being ahead and to windward bore up to us. His Royal Highness called Captain Gunman and Captain Sanders [in the *Charlotte* yacht] and asked their opinion, whether this course [north by east], without tacking to the southward, would carry us to windward of the New-wark and the sands without Yarmouth. Captain Gunman and Captain Sanders answered, we could not weather the sands, but must stand off; upon which the pilot, whose name was Captain Ayres, a person esteemed to be one of the best and ablest men to the northward, said we could weather the New-wark and all other sands, and was much dissatisfied that they should mistrust his judgement. His Royal

Highness said it would be a secure way to tack, and stand off till ten
or twelve o'clock at night, and then we should have room enough
to weather all the sands: upon which the pilot (though confident of
his skill) agreed, and we tacked and stood away S.E., a windward tide
under us.[12]

This appears to be a fair-minded account of what occurred that does
not unduly recriminate or try to allocate blame. But one of the most
noticeable aspects of Sir John Berry's 'Narrative' is that he manages to
avoid giving his own opinion about any of the crucial decisions that
were made, including the fatal decision to tack at 8 p.m. He was clearly
a man who knew how to keep his mouth shut. Indeed, one gets the
strong impression that he was very aware of the potentially explosive
nature of what he was writing about and was being extremely careful
to avoid saying anything that might possibly be construed as reflecting
badly on the duke, or have adverse repercussions for himself.

Even so, his 'Narrative' inadvertently provides some damning
evidence of the general lack of rigour regarding navigational standards.
He reports how, 'His Royal Highness said it would be a secure way to
tack, and stand off till ten or twelve o'clock at night', as if two hours
of extra sailing time would make very little difference one way or the
other. In reality, they would almost certainly have travelled another
6 to 8 miles in such an interval. This casualness merely underlines
how at this point there seems to have been an almost complete
loss of any precise control over the *Gloucester*'s movements. Pepys,
characteristically fulminating and censorious, certainly drew some
very unfavourable conclusions from his experience of this voyage
about the culpability of sea captains who abnegated all responsibility
for the navigation of their ships. Even the outspoken Pepys, however,
was careful not to mention Sir John Berry by name in this connection.
Berry was too powerful a figure.

Sir John quotes the duke as remarking that 'it would be a secure
way to tack', however it was a belt-and-braces approach. Take the
ship further out into deeper water and there would be very little
chance of running on the Newarp Sand, or any of the other sands

outside Yarmouth. That was true. But it ignored the increased danger of running on the Leman and Ower Sands. One of the underlying confusions behind so much of what was written at this time is that there was no clear understanding of whether the Leman and Ower Sands were to be regarded as part of the Yarmouth Sands or as a separate navigational hazard.

In retrospect, Captain Ayres was very probably right. There probably never was any need for the fleet to tack to the south-east at 8 p.m. The Newarp Sand is laid down at 3 leagues from the coast in late seventeenth-century charts, but modern Admiralty charts show it to be only 2 leagues from the coast. If the Lowestoft sighting was correct and the fleet was 2 leagues from the coast at that point, then they should have comfortably weathered the Newarp on a north-north-east course. It is true that by this time there was a strong wind blowing from the east, but against this they now had the benefit of a flood tide under them. Ayres was probably making his judgement based on his experience of the Norfolk coast rather than on what John Seller's chart said about the position of the sandbanks, and he would most probably have got away with it if Gunman and then the duke had not intervened.

Part of the problem for all those responsible for navigating James's small fleet from the Thames to Scotland was that there were three main alternative routes used at the time. There was what was called 'the colliers' route', which followed the coast even to the point of sailing within the Yarmouth Sands rather than outside them. Then there was the standard route for larger ships, including warships, which involved sailing on the outside of the Yarmouth Sands until the Newarp was safely past and then turning to the north-west, running through the Haisborough Gatt and passing on the inside of the Haisborough Sands, so keeping in sight the coastal landmarks. Finally there was the longer deep sea route, which passed on the outside of Yarmouth Sands, Haisborough Sands, and the Leman and Ower Sands.

Interestingly, Gunman had been on three voyages to Scotland during the previous year and on all of those voyages he had followed the coastal collier route. On all three occasions he was sailing in the

Mary yacht by himself, not as part of a fleet of warships, and so was better able to navigate through shoal water. It seems likely that Captain Ayres intended to follow the more usual route of sailing outside the Yarmouth Sands but within Haisborough Sands, which would also take him well to the landward side of the Leman and Ower Sands. In the event the *Gloucester* ended up following the deep-sea route out of sight of all landmarks.

Gunman, in a later paper on the subject of the *Gloucester* sinking, stated that the decision to take the deep-sea route was taken right at the start of the voyage by the Duke of York himself:

> … and in my hearing the Duke gave the pilot positive command the first hour he came on board that he should not go within the sands, but far enough without them all, upon which order I suppose Sir John Berry grounded his reason not to give anyone directions for going ahead'[13]

The difficulty with this instruction is we do not know for sure which sands exactly the duke was talking about. Was he referring to all the sands about Yarmouth or all the sands that might be encountered along the east coast, including the Leman and Ower Sands? If the latter, it is difficult to understand why the duke had been content for the fleet to sail more or less parallel with the coast at a distance of about 3 leagues the entire afternoon, since sighting Dunwich steeples at 1 p.m. That route was consistent with the standard course for warships, that is, passing the Newarp on the outside and then altering course to the north-west in order to come within Haisborough Sands.

There is also an issue about just who initiated this fateful mid-sea conference at 8 p.m. on Friday. John Berry, as so often, is rather evasive. He has the yachts bearing up to the flagship but it is unclear whether they did so in response to a signal or on their own initiative. Gunman's journal is similarly ambiguous. Both accounts have the duke speaking first but this may just have been the usual deference to a royal. Gunman's letter to his wife, however, dated 9 May and written from Edinburgh, is rather more revealing.

On Friday night, about seven o'clock, the wind at E., we were near Lisbon [*sic*] the yachts all a good way ahead. I bore up, and went back to speak with the Duke before night, to know what they intended to do. He asked me if on this tack we could weather the sands, and I told him we could not without standing off to the Southward.

But the pilot on board the Duke, by name Captain Eares, affirmed that he could do it very well, and that he knew better than anybody, either Gunman or Sanderson (of whom the Duke also asked the question). But, seeing they did not tack by eight o'clock, I ran up under them the second time, and asked what was the matter that they did not tack.

I was asked the second time if she could not weather the sand. I replied, 'No,' and stamped and flung my hat on the ground like a madman, saying I would not adventure the King's yacht to follow them.

This positiveness of mine the Duke beheld, and upon it commanded the pilot to tack, which – through much anger from the pilot – was done.[14]

From this account it is clear that Gunman's role was crucial both in starting the discussion and then returning to it a second time. The duke, typically, appears to prevaricate between the two highly polarised positions until he is finally persuaded by Gunman's rather more assertive style of argument. Sir John Berry appears to have entirely abnegated all responsibility. The final decision is made by the duke and the fleet tacks to the south-east.

This fascinating letter only seems to survive in E. Hallam Moorhouse's edition of *Letters of the English Seamen*, published in 1910. The reference to Lisbon is clearly a transcription error. Obviously, the spelling of Lowestoft has caused something of an editorial problem. One thing we can be fairly sure about in this complex and frequently confusing tale is that the fleet was nowhere near Lisbon.

By 9.30 p.m. Captain Ayres obviously felt that the fleet had gone quite far enough out to sea and it was vital they now tacked again to the north. Sir John Berry again provides the clearest account of this ongoing navigational dispute:

At half an hour past nine o'clock, the pilot being urgent, desired to tack again. His Royal Highness was still of the opinion to stand off longer, and asked his opinion: the pilot answered and said, he would engage his life, that if we tacked presently, we should, without hazard, weather all the sands.[15]

The word 'presently' in the above context implies 'immediately' and not 'in a little while', as it would today. Captain Ayres was overruled a second time, on this occasion by the duke himself. 'Notwithstanding all his arguments, (too long to enumerate), his Royal Highness commanded the pilot to stand a glass longer for more security.'[16] A glass means half an hour, that is, the time it took for the sand to run through the sand glass. It is a great shame that Sir John Berry felt that the 'arguments' were 'too long to enumerate', for Captain Ayres's thoughts at this point would have been of the greatest interest. It no doubt suited John Berry's purpose not to provide the detail of Ayres's testimony, however, for it would probably have placed him in the invidious position of having to question the wisdom of the decision taken by His Royal Highness.

Ayres is the silent actor in this drama, for none of his own writings have survived. He was court-martialled for his part in the wrecking of the *Gloucester*, but strangely the record of his trial is not to be found among the Admiralty records held in the Public Record Office. Their disappearance is particularly odd because the written transcript of a second court martial held on the same day on the same ship before the same officers, for the loss of the *Henry*, burnt by the carelessness of a watchman, has survived.

15

THE LEMAN AND
OWER

From 10 p.m. on Friday, 5 May, until 4 a.m. the next day, the small fleet of yachts and the two warships, the *Happy Return* and the *Gloucester*, sailed north-north-east and north by east. It was a rough night with a strong wind blowing from the east. Lieutenant Wetwang, on the *Happy Return*, refers to it as a 'stiff gale'. The ships made good progress in the darkness. According to Wetwang, they covered 12 leagues in the six hours, which is the equivalent of 36 miles or a speed of over 6 knots. This was a fast rate for a seventeenth-century sailing ship, particularly at night. According to Sir John Berry in the *Gloucester* and Christopher Gunman in the *Mary*, there was a slight shift off course at 2 a.m. from north by east to north. Wetwang does not mention it, which may explain why by 4 a.m. the *Happy Return* was 'to the windward' of the *Gloucester* – that is, further out to sea.[1] Both Wetwang and Berry mention a further shifting of the course at 4 a.m. towards the north-north-west (Berry) or north by west (Wetwang). This final change – the last before the fatal collision with the sandbank – was ordered by Ayres who, according to Captain John Berry's account, 'affirmed that this course would carry the ships out of all danger, and that we were past the Lemon and Oare [Leman and Ower]'.[2] The unfortunate Ayres could not have been more mistaken.

By 4 a.m., dawn had already broken. Gunman went below on the *Mary* yacht to get some rest. He had been on continuous duty for nearly twenty hours. He instructed his first mate, William Sturgeon, to come and call him should they come into shoal water. The *Mary* was out in front of the other ships. Ayres, on the *Gloucester*, also went off duty.

At 5 a.m., the linesman on the *Mary* cast his rope with a lead weight attached, marked with knots at regular intervals, and was shocked to discover a depth of only 7 fathoms. Gunman was sent for. He immediately realised the terrible danger they were in and ordered the helmsman to bear away to the west. The water depth quickly increased. Gunman then signalled to the *Gloucester* by waving the Union Jack seven times at the stern of the poop deck. Seven times indicated the depth of water of 7 fathoms. It had been daylight by then for nearly two hours and so the signal should have been clearly visible, but it was a little strange that Gunman did not also fire a warning cannon.

At first, the *Gloucester* appeared to follow the *Mary* towards the west, but in a very short space of time Gunman observed that the flagship was aground and beginning to fire guns, both as a signal of distress and as a warning to the rest of the fleet. All sources agree that at the moment the *Gloucester* struck, the *Mary* was sailing ahead on the larboard, that is the left hand or west side, of the *Gloucester*. The distance between the two ships was variously estimated as being somewhere between half a mile and one and a half miles.

In his 'Narrative', Sir John Berry makes no mention of observing the *Mary* either bearing off to the west or waving a flag of warning. But then he makes no mention of the *Gloucester* firing warning guns for the rest of the fleet, which it clearly did for they were heard both on board the *Mary* and on the *Happy Return*. Lieutenant Wetwang states that they heard 'a gun and then another', and observed that the *Gloucester* also 'put out a waft', a flag of distress.[3] If it had not been for these timely warnings the *Happy Return* would very probably have suffered a similar fate to the *Gloucester*, for it was following about half a mile astern. As it was, they were sailing at such a speed that it was no easy business to turn or 'wear' the ship. Wetwang provides a graphic description of the difficulties, 'Claped astays', that is tacked bringing the head of the ship into the wind, 'but would not stay, and had

7 fathom, so flatted in the head sails', to take some of the wind out of them, 'and hauled up the main sail and lowered the main top sail and in wearing had 9 fathoms and then 17 fathoms. So brought round to and came to anchor.'[4] It was a close thing.

Those on the *Gloucester* did not have the benefit of any advance warning. According to Sir John Berry, the linesman had 'just before sounded and had twenty fathom water' when the ship 'run ashore upon the west part of the Lemon [Leman]'.[5] He made the time 5.30 a.m., which is exactly what Wetwang made it. Gunman recorded the time as being 5 a.m. in his journal. He then changed it to 5.30 a.m. in his later report on the sinking, which was called 'An Abstract of Gunman's Cause'.

Sir John Berry provides the greatest detail as to what happened next. The *Gloucester* did not just strike the sandbank and come to a shuddering halt. Instead, it 'beat along the sand, not sitting fast. Whilst our rudder held, we bore away West, and upon every lift of the sea went off.'[6] In other words, it was bouncing along the top of the sand-bank, coming clear at every lift of the wave and crashing back down in the troughs. At this point there must still have been a strong hope that the *Gloucester* would pass over the ridge of sand and into deep water on the other side without serious mishap.

Hitting sandbanks was not unusual for a sailing ship; in most instances they survived without incurring fatal damage, as, for example, with the *Ruby* on the Galloper just two days previously. One of the problems for the *Gloucester* was that immediately before impact it had been running before a strong wind. It had probably been sailing at a speed of 6–8 knots. In addition, the Leman and Ower banks are very solid ridges of sand. The impact would have been considerable, for there had been no opportunity to slow the ship beforehand.

Sir James Dick, Lord Provost of Edinburgh, was a passenger aboard the *Gloucester*. His letter of 9 May to Mr Patrick Ellis, a merchant in London, graphically underlines the violence and shock of that initial collision, 'the helm of the said ship having broke, and the man being killed by the force thereof, at the said first stroke'.[7] In other words, the impact caused such a wrenching of the tiller that the man in charge of it had been crushed to death by the whiplash effect.

For some minutes the *Gloucester* continued to move in a westerly direction, still bumping along the surface of the ridge. The fact it was scraping along the top suggests that it must have hit the bank where there was approximately 3 fathoms of water over it at low tide. The *Gloucester* had a draught of 17ft 6in. 'At last,' continues Sir John, 'a terrible blow struck off the rudder, and, as I apprehended struck out a plank nigh the post, which made eight feet water in a moment'.[8] The word 'post' refers to the central structural timber at the stern of the ship, and 8ft is the depth of water that immediately flooded into the holds. The pumps were employed and materials for baling but it was already too late, 'the government of the ship being lost' now that the rudder had gone. The water rapidly increased 'as high as the gun deck' and the ship continued to beat along the sand, 'her head being cast about to the S.W. by W'.[9]

By this stage it would probably have been best to try and anchor on the bank in an attempt to stabilise the movements of the ship. 'However, the lifting of the sea forced her off the sand, and she went into fifteen fathom water, before we could let go one anchor, which proved the loss of many poor men's lives.'[10] Once in deep water they did succeed in letting go the anchors:

We anchored and brought her up almost head to windward, we still working with our pumps and baling, but to no purpose: the water increased so fast, that before the boats could take off the men, (though there was great diligence used) the ship sunk, and several of our men perished with her, myself hardly escaping by a rope over the poop, into Captain Wyborne's boat.[11]

It would doubtless have been better for all those concerned if the *Gloucester* had remained stuck on the sandbank. It would very probably still have wrecked, but it would have been a much slower process, allowing for a more orderly disembarkation. Sir James Dick remarked on this with his usual common sense:

Now if she had continued on the three fathom, and broke in pieces there, all would have had time to save themselves: but such was the misfortune, that she wholly overwhelmed and washed all into the sea that were upon her decks expecting relief by boats which certainly would have been if she had but staid half an hour more.[12]

Sir John Berry does not state how long it had taken from the moment that the *Gloucester* first struck until it sank, but Lieutenant Wetwang as usual supplies the missing detail: 'At a quarter past 6 oclocke sunke downe in 16 fathom the mizen top mast head just above water, being just upon high water.'[13]

It had been forty-five minutes from beginning to end. It was not much time for organising the sailors into doing what they could to try to save the ship, overseeing the evacuation of the duke and his entourage and finally saving their own lives, especially when one takes into account that when the *Gloucester* first struck most of those on board would have been asleep. Gunman, in his journal, agrees with Wetwang's estimate of forty-five minutes, 'And of all sorts there were above 150 men drowned, and all in less than three quarters of an hour.'[14] Samuel Pepys, in his letter to W. Hewer, also remarks on the brevity of the time between 'when she struck' and 'her final sinking', stating that 'there passed not, I believe, a full hour'.[15]

On impact the Duke of York had hurriedly thrown on his clothes and gone on to the deck to discover for himself what was happening. He appears to have been one of the first on the scene. Sir John Berry had immediately suggested that he should evacuate the ship, but at that stage the duke was unwilling to leave, not because he was frightened of getting into a small boat in such rough seas, although that posed a very real danger, but because he considered that there was still a chance that the ship might survive. 'I humbly desired his Royal Highness to have his barge hoisted out, to preserve his Royal person,' wrote Sir John, 'But, his highness was unwilling to have any boat hoisted out, considering the condition we were in, hoping as I did the ship might be saved.'[16] However, as the water level continued to rise, Sir John repeated his request for 'his Royal Highness to go away in his boat to the yacht' and this time 'his Royal Highness was pleased to condescend'.[17]

The duke was finally persuaded to leave through the large window of the great cabin, 'where his little boat was ordained quietly to attend him', in the poetic language of Sir James Dick, 'lest the passengers and seamen should have thronged so in upon him as to drown the boat'.[18] As it was, Sir George Legge had to hold off the pressing crowds at the point of a sword. Sir John Berry is careful to emphasise that 'his highness took as many persons of quality with him in the boat as she could carry'.[19] It is known that John Churchill was one of those favoured, and Sir George Gordon, soon afterwards appointed Lord Chancellor of Scotland, was called out for by James. The Marquis of Montrose was also fished out of the water, having tried to jump in the boat and missed.

Once the duke was safely away, another boat was lowered from the *Gloucester* and Sir James Dick threw himself into it, jumping from the shrouds. The Earl of Perth had already managed to get into this second boat, and shortly after Dick clambered in, the Earl of Middleton also jumped from the shrouds and crashed on to Dick's shoulders. The Earl of Winton, whom Dick refers to as the Laird of Touch, was also saved by this second boat.

Shortly afterwards it appears that discipline on the ship broke down and so many seamen threw themselves into this boat that a number of those left on the ship, such as the Earl of Roxburghe and Lord Hopeton, preferred to stay on the *Gloucester* than risk being overwhelmed. Sir James Dick also refers to a third boat, close by where the duke's boat was situated, that had turned over. 'We saw that at the Duke's boat there was another overwhelmed by reason of the greatness of the sea, which drowned the whole in her except two men whom we saw riding upon her keel, which they say were saved.'[20]

It is not clear whether this boat was another of the *Gloucester's* boats or was one of those sent off by the *Happy Return*. The latter is the most likely explanation. As soon as the *Happy Return* had anchored, they had 'sent away the pinnace, long boat and yaull' to help save the men on the *Gloucester*,[21] and the next day Wetwang makes the entry, 'we lost the long boat in saving the Gloucester'.[22] Some boats from the *Happy Return* certainly reached the *Gloucester* because Sir John Berry refers to 'escaping by a rope over the poop, into Captain Wyborne's boat'. Captain Wyborne took personal command of one of the small rescue boats, which says something for his bravery, for he could easily have sent one of his officers. The *Katherine* also had one of its boats overturn. Samuel Pepys mentions how they were 'prevented in our doing so much good as we would, by our own boat's being easily sunk by our side, and her men with much difficulty saved'.[23]

The weather conditions clearly made rescue in small boats an extremely hazardous business. Captain Gunman, in his letter to his wife, states that 'it blew hard and a great sea' while the rescue was taking place.[24] Sir James Dick mentions how 'the waves were so boisterous that we were like to be struck in pieces upon the wreck'.[25] Further on in the same letter he graphically describes the difficulty of disembarking with a gale blowing:

> We were like to be crushed in pieces by the yacht, which by reason of the great seas was like to run us down, till at length a rope was cast, which so managed that we came to the lee side, and there every man clam for his life, and so did I taking hold of a rope, and so made shift upon the sides until I came within men's reach, when at last I was hauled in.[26]

The danger of collision and upsetting when small boats were close to larger ones in rough seas was a very real one and Sir James Dick was in no doubt that the boatmen from the other ships had done their best: 'the four yachts came up as near as they durst, and sent off their boats to help; but all that could be done could not prevent this great loss of 200 men'.[27]

Sir John Berry, when describing the evacuation of the *Gloucester*, is anxious to give the impression that good order was maintained throughout, even as he admits that there was a great deal of distress and panic:

The government of the ship being lost, and everyone crying for help, yet amidst all this disorder and confusion, I could not but observe the great duty the poor seamen had for the preservation of his Royal Highness's person: when the barge was hoisting out, and lowered down into the water, not one man so much as proffered to run into her; but in the midst of all their affliction and dying condition, did rejoice and thank God his Royal Highness was preserved.[28]

Of course, as captain of the ship, Sir John was responsible for the maintenance of discipline to the bitter end and so he had something of a vested interest in claiming this. Certainly, it rather ignores the fact that George Legge was holding the crowds off at the point of a sword, as mentioned in a later account of the sinking written by his son. It also goes against Sir James Dick's observation that 'all the seamen and passengers were not at command, every man studying his own safety'. Dick also refers to two of the bedchamber men having drawn swords to hold the crowds off. Berry's remarks, however, give birth to one of the great British maritime legends, that of loyal sailors lining up to cheer the heir to the throne when they see that he is safe, even as they are going to their own death. As the immediate horror of the sinking faded, the duke proved himself very adept at exploiting this myth for his own advantage.

The sinking was, in reality, a desperate and gruesome business. Sir James Dick describes how many of those who were floundering in the water clutched at the sides of the boat he was in, only to have their grip loosened by those who were already aboard and who were anxious that their own safety might not be jeopardised by overloading:

… and being about mid way to the yachts, there were a great many swimming for their lives who catched all a dead gripe of our boat, holding up their heads above water crying Help; which hindrance was kept off and their hands loosed, telling them they would both lose themselves and us. This would not do to make them loose their grips; but they were forced by several in our boat, except one that took hold of me which I caused catch into the boat, lest I should have been pulled down.[29]

This is the struggle for survival at its most brutal and it is noticeable that Sir James Dick does not appropriate to himself any moral superiority for saving the one man who caught hold of him, admitting that he did it purely to preserve his own life.

A later anonymous report refers to how some of the drowning were mutilated to prevent them climbing into the duke's boat:

> But here I cannot pass in silence, that several Persons being Passengers, besides Common Seamen, committed themselves to the Sea, and those that could swim made up to the Boat where the Duke was, and grappled on the sides thereof, endeavouring to get into it, (but whether it was barbarous or justifiable, under such circumstances, I will leave the Reader to judge) their hands were ordered to be cut off as they strove to get into the Boat, grappling on the sides thereof; and thereby they were deprived not only of getting into the Boats that came to their assistance from the other Ships, but also of the ability of Swimming.[30]

If true, that would most probably have been carried out, on behalf of the duke, by John Churchill, who had gone into the boat armed with a sword. In the light of Sir James Dick's letter, the possibility does not seem at all unlikely. Samuel Pepys also makes a rather more oblique reference to the viciousness of the struggles that took place. In his *Naval Minutes*, written some years after the event, he is musing upon the building of the Ark and he asks of himself the question:

> … how they all agreed (contrary to all human practice in like cases of distresses, and particularly that of the *Gloucester* and the burning of London within my own observation) to see this means of safety enjoyed by so few persons, and oxen and asses, suffering the universality of mankind to perish without contention for a share in it.[31]

The *Gloucester* sinking had clearly impressed itself upon Pepys's memory as evidence of how at times of crisis the struggle to survive can become a brutally competitive business.

The boat that rescued Sir James Dick was rowed to the *Charlotte*, anchored at a distance of about quarter of a mile from the sinking *Gloucester*. The duke was taken to the *Mary*, where Christopher Gunman was captain, anchored at a short distance to the west of the *Gloucester* on the sandbank itself in 3 fathoms of water. Gunman received the duke 'on board just with a coat and breeches on, which was all he saved, – plate, linen, clothes, money, etc., all gone to the value of above £5,000'.[32]

Gunman was clearly flattered that the duke should choose to remain in his yacht to complete the remainder of the voyage rather than travel in the larger and roomier fourth-rate frigate the *Happy Return*. He obviously esteemed it a great honour that he was able to supply the duke with food, bed linen and silver plates for him to eat off. He wrote to his wife with evident pride:

> I would not, for all the sheets I am worth, have been without a pair of sheets this bout, for the Duke had neither linen nor victuals nor anything else, but of mine; and it did fall out that I was pretty well provided of all things, better than I used to be, both for liquor and for other provisions, for I gave him two or three dishes of meat each meal, with which he was well pleased. And I had two silver plates, enough for himself, always washing the one whilst the other was using.[33]

These were the days when each passenger or officer would have taken on board their own tableware, goblets and cutlery and all other necessaries for the voyage. Gunman sounds here like a man anxious to impress upon his wife that she need not worry he had disgraced himself, rather the opposite. He had acquitted himself most nobly in the domestic arena. It is a touching and rather revealing glimpse into the private life of this otherwise taciturn and irascible seaman.

Gunman was at this point no doubt immensely relieved that he had come out of this business as well as he had. His vessel was not the one that had been wrecked. And he had been instrumental in the rescue of the king's brother. He cannot have anticipated that, within one month, his entire world would be turned upside down and that he would find himself publicly disgraced and stripped of his office and livelihood.

At 7 a.m., just one and a half hours after the *Gloucester* first struck the bank, Gunman set off in the *Mary* for Edinburgh, in the company of the *Charlotte* and the *Katherine*. Captain Ayres, the unfortunate pilot, had been fished out of the water alive and was now under arrest on the *Charlotte*, where Captain Saunders was in command. 'Captain Sanders hath orders to secure him till he can be brought to trial for his misdemeanour,' wrote Sir John Berry, who clearly entertained no doubt as to Ayres's guilt.[34] The *Kitchin* and the *Happy Return* continued at the scene of the disaster until 8.30 a.m., when Captain Wyborne returned on board ship. They too then weighed anchor to continue their journey north.

At noon the weather was still too overcast for an observation, but Gunman calculated that he was off Spurn Head. At 7 p.m. he observed the light of Flamborough Head bearing west by south 5 leagues distant. The wind was east-north-east, 'a brave gale'.[35]

Meanwhile, Captain Botham, on the *Pearl*, had become separated from the fleet off Lowestoft when his foretop mast had come down, 'Plied to windward all last night that we might better weather Yarmouth Sand.'[36] At 5 a.m. the following day he saw the *Ruby* and *Dartmouth*, the two other ships that had become detached from the fleet during the first night of the voyage. These three frigates now continued in company until midday, when they too found themselves unable to weather the Leman and Ower Sands and were forced to tack. They were fortunate in that sight of a wreck upon the sands gave them ample warning that they were sailing into trouble.

Captain Botham made the following entry in his logbook: 'At 12 we tacked the wind at East by North because we could not weather the Lemmon and Ore Sand, whereon we see a wreck: at 8 at night it bore NW half West 2 leagues off but stood no nearer to it, being steep too.'[37] George St Loe, on the *Dartmouth*, apparently observed the wreck at 3 p.m. rather than at noon but otherwise provides no further detail. Thomas Allin, in the *Ruby*, also mentions seeing a wreck at noon upon the Leman and commented that it still had two masts standing. None of the three captains hazarded a guess as to the identity of the wreck, but the thought that it may have been either the *Gloucester* or the *Happy Return* must have crossed their minds.

The following lines, written by a seaman earlier in the seventeenth century, seem particularly appropriate for this dismal sighting of the *Gloucester's* masts:

> Aloofe, Aloofe, and come no neare
> The dangers doe appeare,
> Which if my ruin had not been
> You had not seen.
> I only lye upon this shelfe
> To be a mark to all
> Which on the same might fall,
> That none may perish but myself.[38]

16

HOLYROOD HOUSE

The three yachts, *Katherine*, *Charlotte* and *Mary*, pushed on ahead. The weather continued blustery and wet. They sailed past Flamborough Head and Coquet Island. They passed the gaunt crenellations of Tynemouth Castle standing proudly and gloomily upon the jutting prow of Tynemouth Cliffs. And finally, they came in sight of St Abb's Head. From there it was only a short haul around Inchkeith to the safety of Leith Harbour.

The newly graved *Mary* was the best sailer of the three and stayed out in front. Gunman noted proudly in his journal that although the other yachts crowded on 'top sail and sprit sail and what else they could make to come up with me which yet they could not doe'.[1] The wrecking of the *Gloucester* just a few hours beforehand and the loss of 200 lives had done nothing to diminish this sailor's love of speed. At 8 p.m. on a wet Sunday the *Mary* dropped anchor and the duke went straight ashore. 'In Leith Road where I safely landed his Royal Highness, God be praised,' noted Gunman with evident satisfaction.[2]

There was a great clamour within Holyrood House as the duke rushed straight there. He strode through the hallways and mounted the stairs to his wife's chamber with all his usual impatient vigour. According to the memoirs of Mary of Modena, which were preserved by the nuns of Chaillot, the convent to which she withdrew after the duke's death, the duke attended upon her straight away for he was anxious that she should not hear rumours of the wreck from anyone else, before being assured of his own safety in person. Apart from the understandable consideration that a husband may wish to show his wife, he was also no doubt mindful of her pregnant condition and the importance of avoiding any possibly calamitous shocks. The need for a male heir had never been more urgent.

Their reunion was an emotional one. Mary was so moved by James's dramatic story of the sinking and of the danger that he had run that she could not restrain her tears. She claimed that she still trembled several years afterwards when she thought about it.

James did not allow his recent traumatic experience to interfere with his busy schedule. The morning after his arrival, Monday, 8 May, he attended a session of the governing council in Scotland and made the appointments that had previously been agreed between himself and the king. Sir George Gordon was appointed Chancellor, the Marquis of Queensberry, Lord Treasurer, and the Earl of Perth, Lord Justice General. Before this he had already had a private audience with Lord Athol, who had entertained hopes of becoming Chancellor himself. James apparently managed to convince him that it was better that he should not pursue this ambition and took some self-satisfaction at this proof of his diplomatic skills. He also made arrangements for the establishment of a standing guard in Edinburgh to suppress the possibility of further riots of the kind that had taken place during his recent absence. He was anxious to complete his business in Scotland as quickly as possible and return with his duchess to England.

The following day he dealt with some personal correspondence, including a difficult letter to his former brother-in-law Laurence Hyde, the Lord Treasurer. Laurence's younger brother, Lieutenant James Hyde, had drowned in the *Gloucester* sinking. The result was not a masterpiece of compassionate prose, far from it. It was clumsy and halting in style:

I had not time yesterday to write to you by the flying packet myself, to have told you of the unfortunate loss of the *Gloucester*, but charged Churchill to do it; so that I shall say no more of it, but to assure you myself, that I am really troubled for the loss of your brother James. Really he would have made a very good man; for besides other good qualities, he was as unconcerned as any man I ever saw, and all they who got off after me say the same thing. I have now had an account of the loss of the ship's company, and find there were about 110 lost, besides those who belonged to me, and those who came with me; how many they were I do not yet know.[3]

He then turned with evident relief to relate various matters of everyday business that he had been attending to such as the issuing of warrants.

The editor of the Clarendon letters, a nineteenth-century historian named S.W. Singer, sees in this letter of James's 'something very like a want of feeling' and goes on to remark that the tone 'is not altogether in the best taste'.[4] What he is objecting to is James's apparent cynicism, in switching from reflections on mortality to petty private concerns. His criticism is to form a central part of that general trashing of James's character that took place during the nineteenth century, and which has continued ever since. Yet surely James is really doing no more than most human beings do in similar circumstances, that is distracting himself from the horror of death by immersing himself in the trivial and every day. He is perhaps doing it rather ineptly. He is evidently not a sophisticated penman like Pepys or Sir James Dick, but that does not necessarily mean he was not deeply affected by what had happened.

A wife may not be the most impartial of witnesses but according to Mary he was 'almost beside himself with grief, at the calamity which had been attended with the loss of so many lives'. She was also full of praise for his personal bravery at moments of crisis. 'He was the most intrepid of men and looked on danger with perfect coolness.'[5] It is also unlikely that Mr Singer would have considered it more admirable if James had reacted to the *Gloucester* disaster by having a complete nervous collapse and neglecting the business he had come on.

James's twentieth-century biographer, Professor F.C. Turner, similarly complains about another of James's letters written at this time, the one to his son-in-law William of Orange. Turner sees in it 'a very painful impression of callousness'.[6] He criticises James for turning too quickly from the considerable loss of life to his anger with the pilot.

It is true James blamed James Ayres for what had happened. 'It was the too great presumption of the pilot and his mistaking both his course and distance that was the cause of the loss of the ship.'[7] He goes on to regret that he did not have him 'hanged up immediately, according to the custom of the sea'.[8] But such anger is hardly the same as callousness. Anger is, after all, a common component of grief. James lived in an age when death was ever present. His father had been publicly executed. He himself had fought in the Dutch Wars, which were a grisly business. He may not have allowed himself to express fulsomely his more tender emotions, but that does not necessarily mean he did not have any.

Samuel Pepys's reaction to the shipwreck makes for an interesting comparison. Pepys wrote to his good friend Will Hewer on the very same evening that the *Katherine* reached Leith. Keen to be first with the news, he was obviously and understandably in a hyper-excited state. But what mainly comes across is his sense of personal satisfaction at the way things had turned out. As he saw it, his own life had been saved through an act of divine providence, namely his last-minute decision to travel in the *Katherine*:

> ... nor ought I to be less sensible of God's immediate mercy to myself, in directing me, contrary to my purpose at my first coming out, and the Duke's kind welcome to me when on board him in the River, to keep to the yacht; for many will, I doubt, be found lost, as well as or better qualified for saving themselves, by swimming and otherwise, than I might have been.[9]

This is all very Pepys and all very human. He is a little complacent that God should have singled him out for his mercy, but he is also anxious that Hewer and others should not think that his travelling in the *Katherine* meant that the duke had in any way slighted him. Quite the opposite. He had been particularly invited to go in the *Gloucester* but had decided for private reasons of his own to travel in the *Katherine*. There is a note of self-congratulation here that is not present in James's writing, and yet none of Pepys's biographers have taken him to task for callousness.

Also very Pepysian is the way he immediately goes on to respond to his experience in the manner of the trained bureaucrat and compulsive administrator. He wants to set up an enquiry 'into the care the Navy Office will be found to have used in providing for his safety and ship, with respect to the appointment of good and a sufficient number of pilots on this occasion'.[10] He remarks that it should not be left to the duke to select whomsoever he pleases. The Navy Office should 'interpose some immediate care of their own in it, as I am sure was heretofore done in my time'.[11] The touch of conceit is again typical. And as always with Pepys, at the same time that he is recommending actions for the national good, he is also thinking about how this situation can be turned to his own political advantage and the advantage of his coterie. He tells Hewer to give Lord Brouncker, a key figure in Charles's government, a 'hint' about this proposal of his, not just because he feels it would be of benefit in itself, but also because, 'I do privately think it will be very well received by His Highness, to hear of his Lordship's interesting himself of his own accord in this inquiry'.[12] Lord Brouncker was President of the Royal Society, and someone who Pepys was always keen to impress. What was good for Brouncker would also be good for Pepys.

Interestingly, it is Sir James Dick, whose letter on the *Gloucester* describes more graphically than anyone else the horrors of the sinking, who is perhaps guilty of the greatest lapse of taste. 'God make me thankful for this wonderful deliverance,' he writes of his own survival, and then in the next breath he adds:

> I believe I shall have trouble now that both my Lord Roxburgh and his man are lost, to recover payment of these bills – all my clothes and papers are lost, having nothing saved but the 20 guineas which were in my little pocket with my watch and the little box with my wife's ring and necklace, but for my papers I rolled them up in a handkerchief and put them off me, so that both the King's letter for the £1200 sterling and the account I filled with you are gone.[13]

Sir James Dick was a man of business and his mind naturally turned to the personal financial implications of the disaster. Nor was he the only one to suffer financially from Roxburghe's death. A list of Roxburghe's debts, drawn up on 15 May 1682, calculated that he owed £36,631 1s 11d ¼ (in pounds, shillings, pence and a farthing), a colossal sum at this time.[14]

Mr Singer, who also edited Sir James Dick's letters as well as James's, clearly considered that the subject of money should not have been mentioned in the context of the *Gloucester* tragedy. He cut the entire passage out of the printed version of the letters. It is necessary to read the original manuscript in the British Library in order to discover the details of what Sir James Dick lost, and what he managed to get off the ship with him. It is a strange kind of squeamishness.

17

SEETHING LANE

On the evening of 2 March 1669, some thirteen years before the sinking of the *Gloucester*, Pepys had held a small impromptu party at his house in Seething Lane. It was owned by the Navy Board but he had the occupation of it, so long as he was in their employ. It was a home he loved and had lavished much time and money on, continually changing the décor, the furnishings and the layout to keep up with the latest fashions in interior design. He had been there some years, having originally moved in when he first obtained his position with the Board back in 1660.

The guests that evening included Pepys's cousin, Roger Pepys, his wife and their two daughters. They brought with them a Mr Bellwood, 'a conceited silly fellow but one they make mightily of', remarked Pepys.[1] His Turner cousins, with their daughter Betty, and a sister called Dike, were also there. William Howe, a protégé of Pepys at the Navy Board, came with two 'strangers', Mr Ireton and Mr Starkey. Completing the guest list was William Batelier, who lived opposite. He came with his sister and two 'blackmore' servants. Batelier was a wine merchant who specialised in importing fine French clarets, and brought back presents for the Pepyses from his frequent trips across the Channel – not just wines but also the latest French fashions in books, songs and dresses. Mrs Pepys wore one of the dresses, 'My wife this day put on first her French gown, called a Sac, which becomes her very well, brought her over by W. Batelier,' Pepys noted proudly.[2]

The music was supplied by Thomas Greeting and two fellow musicians, a 'most excellent violin and theorbo, the best in town', the theorbo being a kind of lute.[3] Greeting probably played the flageolet, a woodwind instrument, although he was also highly skilled at the violin and the sackbut, a type of trombone. There was much dancing of jigs, which continued 'only with intermission for a good supper, till 2am in the morning'.[4] They danced by candlelight in Pepys's office.

Pepys was particularly taken with the dancing of the young Betty Turner, 'who did it mighty prettily' and who herself was 'mighty pretty'.[5] It seems that 'the Blackmore and blackmore maid' had been brought along specially to show off their proficiency at dancing, for they danced the final jig of the evening. The jigging was followed by more traditional country dancing. The party was a great success. Pepys recorded in his diary that the guests 'broke up with extraordinary pleasure'.[6] It was, he concluded, 'one of the days and nights of my life spent with the greatest content, and that which I can but hope to repeat again a few times in my whole life'.[7]

He then went on to describe in some detail the sleeping arrangements. The extended family guests stayed beneath his roof:

> … my cousin Pepys and his wife in our blue chamber – my cousin Turner, her sister and Theoph in our best chamber – Babb, Betty and Betty Turner in our own chamber, and myself and my wife in the maid's bed, which is very good – our maids in the coachman's bed – the coachman with the boy in his settle-bed, and Tom where he uses to lie. And so I did to my great content lodge at one in my house, with great ease, fifteen.[8]

It was Thomas Greeting, who usually arranged the music for these occasions, who had introduced Pepys to Drumbleby, a musical instrument maker. Pepys bought a flageolet from Drumbleby and greatly enjoyed playing it. It was like a cross between a recorder and a whistle, small enough to be carried in the pocket, so that it could be produced on any occasion for a little impromptu music making. In 1667, Pepys had engaged Greeting to visit the house in Seething Lane on a regular basis, and teach his wife the flageolet. He had it in mind that he and his wife should play duets together but Mrs Pepys was not very diligent about her homework. The lessons continued on and off for a couple of years, Pepys himself also deciding to take lessons, but the duets never quite happened, much to Pepys's disappointment. It was around this time that Greeting was appointed to the role of being one of twenty-four violinists at court.

By 1674, Greeting's musical standing had reached a level where he was appointed sackbut player and violinist to the Chapel Royal at St James's Palace in Westminster. Pepys sometimes attended the services at the chapel. He enjoyed listening to the music and equally he liked ogling Lady Castlemaine, the king's mistress; 'glutting' himself on her appearance was how he put it. It was an opportunity to indulge his two great passions simultaneously.

The following year, Greeting published *The Pleasant Companion*, or *New Lessons or Instructions for the Flageolet*. It contained popular songs as well as the instructions on how to play them, and was a great success, quickly going through many further editions. In the British Library there is a copy of the third, 'enlarged' edition. It came out in 1678, and was printed for J. Playford and sold in his shop near the Temple Church. Pepys must have been the original purchaser of this copy because it has his manuscript monogram on the last page. The lessons may have proved to be something of a failure, but Pepys was clearly still a great admirer of his tutor's musical accomplishments and still keen to improve his own performance.

Greeting was one of a surprisingly large number of musicians that James took with him on the *Gloucester* voyage. Were they there to provide party music on route? Was that what was taking place that first night when the *Gloucester* had lain moored up for the best part of twelve hours? Or was the intention to impress the Scots at the formal handing over of power to new representatives? On the other hand, perhaps James had been planning on a great musical fanfare to mark his re-entry up the Thames to Westminster. The exact purpose remains a matter of speculation, but that musicians were present in numbers is indisputable. Eleven can be identified by name. There was, for instance, a kettle drummer called Walter van Bright. He was one of those who was drowned, and his kettle drums were lost with him, for on his return to England James promptly ordered the purchase of a new set of drums and appointed a new drummer. There were also four trumpeters with silver trumpets. Two out of the four, Richard Deane and Simon Beale, were drowned, and it seems that all four of the trumpets went missing. On 5 July a royal warrant was placed for four new trumpets to replace those that had been 'lost at sea'.[9] Intriguingly, a trumpet engraved with the words 'Simon Beale, *Londini fecit* [made in London], 1667', turned up at Christie's exactly 300 years later for auction. It had been in the possession of the Legge family and was associated with the legend that it should always be blown at times of stress, or ill luck would follow. It seems possible that this trumpet had floated ashore in a wooden box, not far from a large atlas with Legge's name inside it, and that both items had been returned together to the Legge family.[10]

A warrant dated 25 August 1685 lists the following musicians as also having been on board: Thomas Farmer, Jeoffrey Ayleworth, Edward Flower, James Peasable, Joseph Fashion and Edward Greeting. They all must have survived the sinking. But it is noted against the last two names that their fathers were part of the same company of musicians and both of the older men drowned. Edward's father was Thomas Greeting. It is very strange that Samuel Pepys, a man who loved music, and was no mean musician himself, who had also been on the most familiar terms with Greeting, having had him visit his house on numerous different occasions, still chose to travel on a different ship. Indeed, nowhere in his copious writings does Pepys so much as mention Greeting as being among those who were lost in the *Gloucester* wreck. Another odd detail is that Thomas Greeting's pension to his widow was ordered to be paid by the Secret Service fund, a special Treasury cache of money of which the Stuart kings made use for a strange variety of purposes, few of which had much to do with spying.

There is a further curious coda to this whole business of the musicians on the *Gloucester*. In Mary of Modena's memoirs, she relates, as an example of James's compassion towards the ordinary people, how he had insisted on saving 'a poor fiddler' from the water against the wishes of his fellow survivors. Various subsequent myths have been elaborated down the centuries about this 'poor fiddler', including a persistent one that claimed the drowning man was so outraged at being labelled a 'fiddler' by James that he later left his service, plotted against him and was rewarded by William when he seized the throne. The version told by the early eighteenth-century historian John Oldmixon is probably nearer the truth. Oldmixon claimed to have got his information:

> … from a man of honour, who had it from one Flower, a musician, the only one of the Duke's band that could play on the lute. He was one of those whom the Duke left in the ship, and jumping into the sea he swam after the long boat; when he came near it the boat's crew were going to knock him on the head, but the Duke cried out, take him in, he's a fiddler. However, he afterwards turned him out of his band, because he would not turn papist. He was received into the family of the gentleman, from whom I received my information.[11]

Certainly, there was an Edward Flower who was one of the musicians on board the *Gloucester*, and it is also on record that he was the only one of the several musicians that survived the sinking to be continued in royal employment after James fled the country and William of Orange took over, all the rest being turned out.

18

FLOORS CASTLE

Not everyone was in high spirits during those early weeks of May. Lady Margaret Hay, Countess of Roxburghe, was far from sharing in Samuel Pepys's jolly humour. She paced the wild ramparts of Floors Castle with a growing sense of unease. One ship after another drew into Leith Harbour and dropped anchor and none of them could provide any definite news of what had become of her husband. Gradually her anguish turned to fury, and that fury was focused on James. She did not understand why James had not seen to it that the Earl of Roxburghe was saved alongside himself. He had called that upstart John Churchill into his boat but neglected to preserve the life of her dear Robert. She considered this lack of care a poor reward for the Roxburghe family's long years of devotion to the Stuart cause.

Margaret Hay was the daughter of the Earl of Tweeddale. She had married Roxburghe in 1675, when the two of them were both 17. Since then she had given birth to two sons, both of whom had survived infancy. Her portrait, painted by Gerard Soest around the time of her marriage, does not conform to the Lely stereotype of Jacobean beauty. She is depicted holding a lute, presumably symbolising harmony and feminine accomplishment, and she has a devoted spaniel at her feet. But both the lute and the spaniel are at odds with the rest of her appearance, which suggests a truculent, strong-minded, down-to-earth, blunt-mouthed woman. She is drawn as fat-faced and dumpy, with short podgy arms, and her fingers look as if they would be more at home in a washing tub than plucking lute strings. It is not the most flattering of portraits.

It is perhaps not surprising that Soest often had problems with his female sitters. Such was their frequent dissatisfaction with him that he refused to paint women altogether for a period of seven years. It seems, however, that Margaret Hay was quite happy with her portrait, for it was hung in the castle and has survived the test of time. Its directness certainly accords well with her outspoken criticism of James's behaviour.

In the absence of any official efforts initiated by James himself, Lady Margaret wasted no time in organising her own search party to recover her husband's body so that he could at least receive a proper burial. Her personal servant, Alexander Ramsay, was entrusted with the task. He arrived in Great Yarmouth at around 5 p.m. on Sunday, 14 May, which meant he had most probably left Edinburgh on the previous Wednesday. This was the same day that the final ship of the fleet had struggled into Leith Harbour, and any last hope that the earl might have been saved had finally to be abandoned.

Ramsay carried with him a letter addressed to Sir Thomas Medowe, which introduced him and explained the sad business he had come upon. This was the same Sir Thomas Medowe who just a couple of months beforehand had hosted that extravagant dinner to celebrate James's triumphant return to English politics. The change of mood could not have been starker. Medowe promptly sent for a local fisherman, John Grice, who owned a suitable vessel called the *Donald*. He gave Grice instructions to go with Ramsay out to the Leman and Ower sandbanks, to ascertain whether or not it was possible to discover the earl's body. Five other men were detailed to accompany them.

Ramsay must already have been exhausted after his gallop down from Edinburgh, but he left Yarmouth in Grice's small fishing smack at 2 a.m. the following morning. They had a fair wind and calm weather and by 8 a.m. they were out by the Leman and Ower sandbanks. Finding a wrecked ship in this period could be a very laborious business. It usually meant dragging a line or net across the bottom of the sea until it snagged on a submerged object. One of the problems with this method was that the vast majority of snags would prove to be nothing more than rocks or other obstructions on the seabed rather than the desired wreck. Ramsay and Grice, however, did not have that problem. When they arrived in the vicinity of the sandbanks, the top mast of the *Gloucester* was still showing clearly above the surface of the water. This suggested that the main body of the wreck was still holding together on the seabed very securely. They tied the smack up to the mast and sounded the depth of water, recording 17 fathoms. It seems probable that it was then high water. Ramsay then makes the following entry in his journal: 'They tried with divers engines to draw up or discover any that had perished.'[1]

It is most unlikely that Ramsay and Grice had a diving bell with them as such equipment was still extremely rare in 1682 and very expensive to hire and deploy. Also, usually two vessels would have been required for lowering the bell, while it is known that only the one fishing smack went out to the *Gloucester*. It is much more probable that the phrase 'divers engines' refers to nets, hooks, long pairs of tongs and specially designed optical tubes or glasses for aiding underwater vision.

The salvage team did not remain by the wreck for very long but rapidly concluded that there were no bodies to be recovered, or if there were they could not get at them. 'Their endeavours proved unsuccessful,' records the diligent Ramsay.[2] It seems likely that they never really expected to have any success and that the visit to the wreck was made to satisfy the concerns of Lady Margaret, rather than out of any real hope of recovering the earl's body. The *Gloucester* took around forty-five minutes to sink from the time of its first striking the sandbank. Most of those on board would by that time have come up on deck, leaving only the very drunk or the very ill remaining below. Even the incapacitated would probably have been roused and assisted by friends. The great majority of people at the point of final sinking would, as a result, have been washed clear of the wreckage.

During the time that Ramsay and Grice stood by the wreck, they removed three top sail yards, two caps and the flagstaff attached to the bowsprit. It was a bit of quick ad hoc salvage work, no doubt partly undertaken to prove that the wreck had been located. They were not on site for more than six hours in total – that is, for the duration of the flood tide – for Ramsay records that afterwards 'they stood to the Northward ... upon the coast of Norfolk ... the whole ebb (being 6 hours)'.[3] Their purpose in going north, rather than returning straight to Yarmouth, was to see whether they could find any bodies washed up on the shoreline. Bodies were certainly turning up. The *Domestick Intelligence* newspaper included a report from Yarmouth dated 16 May.

> This morning two sailors were cast upon this shore supposed to perish at the late dismal wracke upon the Lemon-Ore, about 20 leagues from this place, and we hear that the bodies of several others have been taken up at other places, being by the tides left upon the sands.[4]

Nor was it just the ordinary sailors whose corpses were being recovered. A report from London on 17 May stated, 'We hear the boats sent to careen off the Mouth of the Humber, have taken up the dead bodies of several persons in the late wreck of the *Gloucester* frigate, amongst whom are some persons of quality.'[5] It sounds as if these victims were discovered still floating in the water rather than washed up on the shore. Unfortunately, it does not give the identity of those who were recovered. The Earl of Roxburghe's body, however, was not among them, or if it was, the locals were not disclosing it.

Ramsay and Grice interviewed the masters of the colliers that plied up and down the coast, but no one had any information. They returned to Yarmouth on Tuesday 16 May at 2 p.m. Concerned that he should not be blamed in any way for not having carried out his orders to the full, the cautious Alexander Ramsay got Sir Thomas Medowe and John Grice to attest to the truth of his journal 'for the better satisfaction of those noble persons concerned'.[6] Grice was paid £9 for the hire of his smack, which presumably included the cost of the five other men involved.

Ramsay certainly seems to have been most conscientious in his efforts to carry out Her Ladyship's wishes. He now persuaded Sir Thomas Medowe to call in the assistance of the bailiff Thomas Gooch, an expert in local maritime matters. Gooch wrote to the Hon. William Carr Esq. in Edinburgh, presumably Lady Margaret's estate manager, assuring him of the very considerable efforts that were being made in this matter of recovering the missing body:

> Mr Alexander Ramsay employed for the search of the body of the Earl of Roxborough, came and applied himself to me and Sir Thomas Meadow, who with other persons of this corporation was not only willing but did give him the best advice we could, it being his great request to be advised by us in the business he came about.

He went on to detail the advice that he gave:

> He [Ramsay] have made tryall in a smack for two or three days without effect, but by our advise he is now wafting along the shore in the same smack to enquire at all places if any bodyes were taken up in any place on the coasts.[7]

In accordance with this advice, the indefatigable Ramsay left Yarmouth a second time on the evening of 17 May to coast between Yarmouth Roads and Happisburgh 'and to call at every sea port between this place and thither'.[8] A further £4 was charged by Grice for this extension of the hire of his smack but the results were similar to the previous efforts. There was still no information on the fate of Roxburghe.

The failure to recover the body only helped to increase Lady Margaret's lifelong bitterness towards James. Her attitude, though perhaps understandable, was not entirely reasonable. There were reports that suggested that James had called out for the Earl of Roxburghe, but that he had not answered. Sir James Dick was probably the last person to see Roxburghe alive. He had just succeeded in jumping from the shrouds of the quarter deck into a small and rapidly overcrowded boat. He had looked back at the *Gloucester* and glimpsed Roxburghe, together with his servant Mr Littledale and a few others, standing on the quarter deck. According to Dick, they 'would not follow' him, 'since it seems they concluded more safety to stay in the vessel, than to expose themselves to any other hazard, all which persons in an instant were washed off and all drowned'.[9] Whether Lady Margaret ever heard this account from Dick's own lips is not known. If she did, she was not consoled. She needed someone to blame. For the next seventy-one years she remained a widow, and haunted the elegant drawing rooms of the newly built Floors Castle in her black mourning gowns.

The Earl of Ailesbury was among those who thought the resentment displayed by Lady Margaret and her family unreasonable. 'I cannot commend that partiality,' he noted tersely in his memoirs.[10] He absolved the duke of having shown any particular prejudice towards Roxburghe. 'It might be done without thought, and not for want of goodwill towards noble persons that were drowned, and indeed very few escaped, unless those that could swim well.'[11]

It is true that Roxburghe was not the only notable on board who lost their life. Lord Obrian; the Laird of Hopetoun; Sir Joseph Douglas; Lieutenant Hyde; Hollis, the duke's equerry; a physician named Levington; and Captain Stuart were also numbered among the drowned. Nor was it just the rich and wellborn that suffered. The majority of those lost, of course, were seamen and servants.

There was a strange piece of flotsam that was handed in to the authorities and is known for certain to have come from the *Gloucester* wreck. It is an odd survivor of that grisly event. It is an atlas, a magnificent leather-bound volume of drafts and charts of the British coastline. Some of the pages are a little watermarked but otherwise they are unspoilt. Among them is a beautifully drawn view of the Channel Islands by Christopher Gunman. The volume was owned by George Legge and some years after its rescue from the waves it was gifted to the National Maritime Museum by Henry Legge, a descendant.

19

BARBER-SURGEONS' HALL

On 27 February 1663, Pepys had left his office at 11 a.m. and walked with commissioner Pett to the Barber-Surgeons' Hall, situated on Monkwell Street near the old Roman Wall. He had gone there to attend a 'very fine' lecture on the 'kidnys, ureters and yard'.[1] Pepys had taken a great personal interest in everything to do with kidneys and urethras ever since he had a gallstone removed by surgery in 1658. As for the 'yard', Pepys shared his era's surprisingly frank fascination with sex. The lecture took place in a grand room, at the end of which was positioned a large portrait of Henry VIII by Hans Holbein. The central feature of the lecture was the dissection of the corpse of a seaman who had recently been hanged for a robbery. The Company of Barbers and Surgeons had a royal licence to dissect four hanged criminals a year.

After a 'fine dinner' with 'good learned company', Pepys was invited to return to the hall, along with some other friends, and examine the corpse more closely. He records the occasion in his usual graphic style:

I did touch the dead body with my bare hand: it felt cold, but methought it was a very unpleasant sight. But all the Doctors at table conclude, that there is no pain at all in hanging, for that it do stop the circulation of the blood; and so stops all sense and motion in an instant. Thence we went into a private room, where I perceive they prepare the bodies, and there were the kidneys, ureters, yard, Stones, and seminary vessels upon which he read today. And Dr Scarborough, upon my desire and the Company's, did show very clearly the manner of the disease of the stone, and the cutting and all other Questions that I could think of.[2]

Pepys famously preserved his gallstone in a glass jar on his mantelpiece, celebrating the anniversary of its successful extraction every year thereafter.

Scarborough was an assistant and protégé of the great physician and anatomist William Harvey. He administered to Harvey on his deathbed and was reputed to have given him, upon his patient's request, the final dose of morphine that ended his life. Harvey bequeathed to Scarborough his medical instruments in his will. By the time of the Scottish voyage, Scarborough had risen through his profession to become the personal physician to the Stuart brothers. He was one of the passengers on board the *Gloucester*. He did not accompany James on all his travels but the fact that Mary of Modena was pregnant and was intent on returning to London with James as soon as possible was probably why the duke wanted Scarborough by his side on this occasion.

If the *Gloucester* passengers had consisted only of James's Scottish nobility friends such as the Earls of Winton, Perth and Roxburghe or the Marquis of Montrose, then Pepys's reluctance to be among them may be better understood. Pepys never felt himself entirely at home among blue bloods and certainly not among the Scottish aristocracy. Similarly, James's military colleagues such as Legge, Churchill and Jennings may not have been exactly to Pepys's taste. Pepys had not seen active service during the Dutch Wars and was not in a position to reminisce about the gruesome Battle of Solebay, even though his relation and great patron, Edward Montagu, 1st Earl of Sandwich, had lost his life on that occasion. Pepys would have had more in common with the royal musicians on board, especially as his former music teacher was among the selected players, but his evident reluctance to associate with them could possibly be attributed to the relatively low social standing that musicians held in Stuart society. They were, in some eyes, just a type of highly skilled servant, somewhat similar to cooks. Pepys's hypersensitivity to his social status may have made him want to keep his distance.

Still, there were passengers on board the *Gloucester* who fell into exactly the category of person that Pepys most enjoyed spending his time with, and pre-eminent among this last group was Sir Charles Scarborough. Pepys had known Scarborough for upwards of twenty years by the time of the Scottish voyage. He had sailed in his company before, most memorably on the occasion of King Charles's restoration in 1660. Both Pepys and Scarborough had accompanied Charles on the voyage over from Holland. They had all drunk and eaten together in Pepys's cabin, 'At supper three doctors of Physique at my cabin – where I put Dr Scarborough in mind of what I heard him say about the use of the eyes ...'[3] For Pepys and Scarborough to travel again together on the occasion of James's restoration to power and influence in England would have had a nice symmetry that would not have been lost on Pepys. It seems very strange then that he would have turned down an opportunity of spending time with such a learned and influential physician, a man he had always admired and been friendly with for decades, in favour of closeting himself on the *Katherine*, where he had only Sir Christopher Musgrave for company. There has to be another explanation for Pepys's out-of-character decision to rebuff James's invitation, apart from his excuse that the *Katherine* would afford him more room.

Scarborough was one of those who had to swim for his life when the *Gloucester* went down. He was already 67 years old, and so the fact that he survived at all was a testament to his fitness. As it happened, he was pulled from the water by the seamen of the *Katherine*, so he did spend the remainder of the voyage in Pepys's company, although he was hardly in a condition to be convivial. Pepys describes the moment of his rescue in his letter to Hewer of 8 May: 'we had also the good fortune to take up Sir Charles Scarborough, almost dead, and others spent with struggling in the water and cold'.[4]

Scarborough clearly made a good recovery because he was one of those, along with Pepys, honoured as a burgess of the town in Edinburgh, in a formal ceremony on 12 May. Scarborough had managed to survive by grabbing hold of a floating plank. He apparently had to struggle to get possession of it in competition with James's dog Mumper. Mumper was to become the centre of much historical controversy for the next 200 years, but the arguments that raged around the hapless dog only surfaced after James had lost the throne.

20

PORTUGAL ROW

News of the shipwreck spread quickly. The Earl of Conway wrote from Windsor to Secretary Jenkins in Whitehall on Tuesday, 9 May:

> I have worse news than this to tell you, which is by an express arrived just now from Hull we are informed that last friday night, the *Gloucester*, in which the Duke went, was cast away but the Duke is safe and went for Scotland in his yacht. In the night she ran on the Lemon and Ore Sands 16 leagues from the mouth of Humber. She was not under water til 6 next morning, so that I hope most of the passengers are safe, though tis said some are drowned but none named. The Duke did not sail thence till 10 on Saturday. 'Tis certain his Majesty has lost a very good frigate and I wish that may be the worst.[1]

Even the usually flippant Conway was not tempted to make a joke of it on this occasion.

At this point no one was quite sure what had happened or how many had drowned. Shipwreck was a daily occurrence and false information often circulated. Francis Gwyn also wrote from Windsor on the same day as Conway, but to the Earl of Arran. He provides more detail, but most of his additional material is mistaken. He does, however, give some useful information on just how the news had reached London so quickly, for it could not possibly have been posted down from Edinburgh in such a short space of time. Word had come from Hull via a Captain Coply. One of the yachts must have spoken to a fishing boat somewhere off Flamborough Head.

Samuel Pepys's correspondent Will Hewer summed up the mood of general confusion, as more and more contradictory reports began to filter through. He had received Pepys's letter in London on 12 May. It had been sent from Edinburgh on the 8th, a creditable speed of delivery considering it came by horse. Hewer replied from York Buildings the next day:

> We had some imperfect account on Wednesday morning, about 11 of the clock; it comeing from my Lord Conway, at Windsor, to Sir Leoline Jenkins's office, at White Hall, where I was then waiting at the Treasury Chambers, and was not a little surprized at the reporte, which in less than an houres time ran through the whole citty ... Some would have it that the Duke and all were lost – others, that all were saved, and the shipp only lost; but all generally concluded it to be a very unfortunate and unkinde disaster.[2]

Pepys's letter was probably the first detailed eyewitness account of the sinking to arrive in London. He had certainly despatched it at the very first opportunity and its contents were much in demand. Hewer provided an edited version to Sir John Banks, the financier, who was dining with the Lord Chancellor on the 13th. Banks was anxious to know all he could about the exact circumstances of the loss before that meeting. Pepys would have been flattered that it was his version of events that was being reported at influential occasions of this nature. He was, no doubt, equally flattered to learn from Hewer's reply to him of the anxiety that his friends had felt for his safety:

> You cann't imagine in what Consternation all your friends in generall were upon the Reporte of your being cast away, but more especially those at Crutched Fryars, Winchester Street, and Portugall Rowe, to whom I communicated your Letter, which was matter of noe small Joy and Satisfaction to them, they all joyne with me in returning God Almighty Thanks for his great mercy in directing you in your Passage as he did.[3]

James Houblon, one of five wealthy merchant brothers, was rather more humorous in describing the distress and relief his own household had experienced. He starts by describing the anxiety of the female members of his family (pointedly excluding himself from such weak sentiments):

> Mr Hewers Bringing with him last night your Letter of the 8th from Edinburgh was the most welcome alive to all your friends in my familey. For before that as you were numbred among the Dead by almost all the Cittie Except my selfe and some others, soe noe arguments could work upone my women and Girles to beleeve otherwise ...[4]

He then goes on to chide Pepys for his thoughtlessness in going on the voyage in the first place and in such a peremptory manner:

> You see and are like to be told soe when you Come home what your Iter Boreale hath Cost us and what it is to leave us on that sudain as you Did without either asking or for all that I knowe having our Prayers, Wee were all soe Angry at your Going.[5]

He concludes with some witty advice on the most sensible way to travel:

> You intend I hope to Continue your resolutions To Come home by Land, which is much desired; For I thinke by this time you are convinc't that a Scotch voyage with a ship Especialy of a greate Draught of water is more Dangerous then to goe to the Indies.[6]

Even while expressing his relief, Houblon is also not averse to a little sly teasing.

Sir John Evelyn was another who had been taken by surprise at Pepys's sudden and unannounced departure for Scotland, and he too confessed to the same feelings of anxiety followed by relief when he heard of what had happened:

I have been both very sorry and very much concerned for you since your northern voyage, as knowing nothing of it till you were embarked (though I saw you so few days before) and that the dismal and astonishing accident was over, which gave me apprehensions and a mixture of passions not really to be expressed till I was assured of your safety, and I gave God thanks for it with as much sincerity as any friend you have alive. Tis sadly true there were a great many poor creatures lost and some gallant persons with them; but there are others worth hundreds saved, and Mr Pepys was to me the second of those same.[7]

The first was, of course, James, Duke of York.

Pepys's friends who lived in Portugal Row and had been so afraid for his safety were Lady Betty Mordaunt and her sister Mrs Steward. Lady Mordaunt was twice widowed, rich, young and pretty. Pepys had known her since 1666 and often accompanied her to Vauxhall Gardens for a flirtatious stroll, or to the theatre, or even further afield to Wimbledon. When invited to her house for supper, he particularly enjoyed her lobster pie. The charms of the two sisters were obviously difficult for a man of Pepys's susceptibilities to resist. After all, as a friend, Thomas Hill, had once written to him, 'they are desperately in love with you and sigh out their Passions so prettily ... when you entertain them ... they acknowledge your humour the best in the whole world.'[8]

On hearing from Will Hewer that Pepys was safe, Lady Mordaunt immediately wrote Pepys her own letter. Its tone was both chiding and affectionate:

You can't imagine the trouble we have been in for you, and being you remember my dream, I must put you in mind of what you said to me that same day, that you had forgiven me a hundred faults and hoped I would forgive you seven, but I think this going into Scotland by sea is worse than a thousand.

Lady Mordaunt obviously felt that Pepys's behaviour in suddenly taking himself off, without any prior warning or discussion, was both reckless and thoughtless. She concluded her letter, 'I will assure you I had not my senses till I saw your hand. My prayers are heard. Adieu. God of his mercy preserve you.'[9] This mood of grateful piety did not last long. She was very soon plotting her own sweet revenge.

Pepys pointed out in his next letter to Hewer that no one need have experienced any concern on his behalf because he had told Hewer in a note sent on the evening of 4 May that he would be travelling in the *Katherine*. He was, however, doubtless secretly gratified at the extent of the dismay and worry he had caused. Pepys's male friends largely took his sudden disappearance to Scotland in good part.

Meanwhile, Pepys was thoroughly enjoying himself up in Scotland, his first trip north of the border. He spent two days with the duke, listening to government debates and even receiving the honour of being admitted to the Edinburgh Council and made a burgess and 'gild brother'.[10] This was just the sort of pomp that Pepys loved. He was most impressed by the combination of firmness and compassion that James showed in his administration of Scotland, 'being maintained with so much absoluteness and yet gentleness, to the rendering it morally impossible for any disquiet to arise in his Majesty's affairs'.[11]

When not attending on the duke he made a series of brief trips to nearby Scottish towns such as Stirling, Lithgow, Hamilton and Glasgow, describing the latter as 'a very extraordinary town for beauty and trade'. However, his overall verdict on the Scottish people was less than flattering. He declared that 'there is so universal a rooted nastiness hangs about the person of every Scot (man and woman), that renders the finest show they can make nauseous, even among those of the first quality'.[12] Houblon and Hewer both found this description of the Scots people very amusing.

Pepys decided against returning with the duke by sea in the *Happy Return*, nor did he take James Houblon's advice to return home by land. Instead he chose to go on a brief coasting tour of the towns of north-east England in the company of Colonel George Legge, in a yacht that was made available to them for the purpose. Sir George Fletcher and Sir Christopher Musgrave were also of the party.

Pepys's relationship with Legge had been far from harmonious in the past and so this teaming up with him as a travelling companion was somewhat surprising. Pepys was, however, always the pragmatist where his own career was concerned, and he no doubt realised that he might be jeopardising his future return to power if he continued to be on bad terms with the man who had become one of the duke's closest advisors. Past quarrels were carefully put aside. On the vexed issue of gentlemen captains, Legge had already been generous enough to agree with Pepys that some training would be beneficial, and as for the King's College position, there was now a far greater prize to be had, namely a return to the Secretaryship of the Admiralty. It seems probable that part of Pepys's purpose in going on this little jaunt with Legge was to reach an understanding with him as to how the future spoils of government would be divided when James returned to power, as was now looking increasingly likely.

After making their farewells to the royal party, Pepys and Legge travelled first to Berwick, arriving there on 17 May. By the 23rd they had reached Newcastle, where they were ceremoniously greeted by the mayor and aldermen and wined and dined in grand style. The following morning, they were made free burghers of the town and in the afternoon they rode to Durham, where they dined with the Archdeacon. 'Our business was so much to eat, drink and be merry,' wrote Sir George Fletcher, 'that we had not much time to talk of business'.[13] Pepys was equally impressed by the sumptuous quality of their reception, although being Pepys he could not resist a prim note of censoriousness, 'made a step to Durham, where the Bishop seems to live more like a prince of this than a preacher of the other world'.[14] From Durham they returned to Newcastle and from there they sailed for Scarborough and then for Hull.

As Pepys travelled south, he received regular letters from his friend Will Hewer in London. The news was most satisfying. First came word that the Attorney General was dead. Sir William Jones had been instrumental in the prosecution of Pepys for 'piracy, popery and treachery', an accusation that, though it was eventually proved to be totally false, had resulted in Pepys spending that unpleasant spell in the Tower. Pepys's response was characteristically robust: 'I thank you for the news about the death of that insolent and mutinous lawyer.'[15] No feigned tears or speaking well of the dead there.

Still more welcome was the latest gossip concerning the career of the infamous Colonel Scott, as detailed in Hewer's next letter:

> One Accident has happen'd here the last Week near in towne to be lamented, vizt Our friend Colonell Scott's being fledd for killing a Coachman, the Coroner having found it wilfull murther; meanes are using to buy off the Widdow who has three small children, but we are considering what to doe to prevent it.[16]

Hewer might have lamented the death of the coachman, being the good Christian that he was, but he knew very well that this news would delight his friend. It was Scott who had provided much of the false evidence against Pepys regarding his supposed supplying of France with coastal charts and secret details of England's defences. Scott had been shown to be both a fraudster and a fantasist on an international scale but to have him now publicly exposed as a murderer was a final vindication.

The circumstances of the coachman's murder reveal the seamier side of Restoration London. Scott had been drinking at the Horseshoe Tavern on Little Tower Hill. During the course of the evening he had ordered a hackney coach to take him to Temple Bar. When the coachman asked for his fare, Scott quibbled at the amount and ended up running his sword through him. Scott was described in the news sheets as 'a lusty tall man, squint eyed, thin faced, wears a perruque sometimes'. Mention was also made of how 'he hath been of Sheriff Bethel's club lately, and great with all the Popish evidences, plot drivers and discoverers'. Pepys was hopeful that Scott might be induced to confess the names of those who had put him up to making the original false allegations, in return for some deal that might save his life, 'nor do I doubt but, to save his own life, he will forget his trade, and tell truth,' wrote Pepys.[17] But in the event Scott's renowned facility with disguises enabled him to escape abroad again.

When Pepys arrived at Hull, on 27 May, there were two more letters waiting for him, both posted in London and bearing Hewer's signature. The first had been written on the 25th and was full of the usual gossip. Pepys's dear friend Lady Mordaunt had suffered from 'a shrewd fit of the stone'. The navy commissioners were still determined to continue with their plan for a wet dock at Chatham despite Pepys's objections. Finally, there was the troubling news that the ship *Henry* had been burnt to the water's edge 'by the carelessness of an old infirme man getting a Candle and leaving it burning in his Cabbin when he went to sleep', which incident was yet again being interpreted by some of the 'Fanaticks', the favoured term for the Puritan extremists, as yet further evidence of a Popish plot against the security of the nation.[18]

It was Hewer's second letter, however, that most alarmed Pepys. It was also dated 25 May, 'past midnight'. The content was brief and frustratingly elusive.

> Sir, There has something happened since my letter went to the Post-house of great consequence, and very ill both to you and myself and some other of our friends, which I dare not communicate to you with pen and paper, and therefore wish for your speedy return, which I hope in God you will defer no longer than bare necessity requires.[19]

Pepys was, understandably, extremely disconcerted. Had further plots against him been discovered? He wrote to Hewer the next day that it had caused him 'an inexpressible pain to aim at the ground of it, a thousand things running in my head'.[20] He cancelled his proposed trip to York and considered going back to London directly overland but could not obtain transport to get him there before 7 p.m. on Tuesday. It was then Sunday morning. He decided he would probably do better to return by yacht, 'I trust in God I shall be with you before that by sea'.[21]

Portugal Row was part of a fine street of new houses situated on the south side of Lincoln's Inn Fields, an area of London that was rapidly becoming very fashionable. Lady Mordaunt's house was virtually next door to Thomas Povey's, where Pepys was also a regular dinner guest. Povey was a wealthy merchant and another of Pepys's intimate friends. Povey had a portrait of the interior of his house painted by Samuel van Hoogstraten and hung it in the hallway as a piece of bewildering *trompe l'oeil*. It provides an interesting glimpse into a well-to-do domestic interior of the period.

Two black marble pillars frame an archway, through which can be seen a black-and-white-tiled floor, recently washed and polished, stretching away into the distance. From the apex of the arch is suspended a large iron volary. A green-winged songbird swings on its perch but makes no attempt to escape, although the cage door is open. An unseen servant has left a broom leaning against one of the black pillars. A pretty brown and white dog gazes affectionately upwards as if expecting to be petted. On the far side of the hall, a cat arches its back, apparently resenting the intrusion of the new entrant. Upon a hook on the right-hand pillar hangs a large iron key that speaks of housekeeping, of possessions and of secrets. A turkeywork-upholstered chair, richly coloured, stands upright against a wall. Above it is a map of the world encompassing both the East and West Indies. Ranged along the architrave are busts of ancient heroes. To the right is a solid wooden staircase with a polished balustrade and a stout newel post. On the lowest step, most appropriately, lies an opened letter.

Pepys was more impressed by Povey's well-stocked wine cellar than he was his hallway, but he was also entranced by another *trompe l'oeil*, this time by Robert Streeter, to be found in the small rear courtyard. It depicted 'a grotto and fountayne which in summer will be as pleasant as nothing in the world can be almost'.[22] Pepys had no sooner viewed this latest artistic wonder than he rushed out and commissioned some similar works for his own place.

Another near neighbour of Lady Mordaunt's was Charles Powlett. He was rather less entertaining than Povey:

For many weeks he would take a conceit not to speak one word; and at other times he would not open his mouth until such an hour of the day he thought the air was pure ... and took all sorts of liberties to himself many of which were very disagreeable to those about him.

It is hardly surprising to learn that he was 'much hated'.[23] Pepys had a particular reason for disliking him: he was another of those who had been behind the accusations of 'popery' that had landed him in the Tower.

When Pepys finally got back to London, he quickly discovered from Hewer the letter that had so disconcerted him had not been written by his old friend. The signature was forged. Pepys's suspicions quickly fell on the Ladies of Portugal Row. It very soon became clear that there was nothing for Pepys to be alarmed about other than the peevishness of a young woman who felt she had been slighted. Lady Mordaunt was evidently still cross with Pepys for having left London without so much as a goodbye, and even more cross when she heard that he was dilly dallying in the northern counties, so she and her sister decided to take their revenge by concocting this little piece of chicanery.

Pepys appears to have taken the outrageous trick played upon him in good part. He made the following note in his letter book:

This letter above written was founded upon one sent to me dated 25th May, ... who in a sportful revenge for my taking this journey without their knowledge designed to interrupt the pleasure of it and hasten me back before my time by a feigned letter from Mr Hewer, wherein his hand was so well counterfeited that I was easily imposed upon.[24]

This was a period when practical jokes were perhaps more acceptable than they are today. Even so, Pepys's frank admission of his own gullibility and his memorialising of it for posterity, copying the letter out word for word, reveals a surprisingly tolerant side to his nature when it came to the caprices of his young female friends.

21

TYNEMOUTH

On Wednesday, 10 May, James went on board the aptly named *Happy Return* to make arrangements for his forthcoming voyage to London and to check that the accommodation was adequate for his wife, daughter and somewhat depleted entourage. He was evidently satisfied with what he saw and he gave orders to Captain Wyborne to be ready to depart by the following Monday. James's immediate circle in Edinburgh expressed their amazement that he planned to leave again so soon and in particular that he designed to go once again by sea, especially given the duchess's pregnancy. They were equally amazed that the duchess was prepared to accompany him. She had written to Lady Bellasys on 20 April, 'I have really been so ill for these many months that I have hardly been able to writ at all.'[1] However, despite her poor health, and her propensity to be seasick even when she wasn't pregnant, she could still not be dissuaded from accompanying her husband. She declared that 'she should esteem herself happier in danger or trouble with him, than in ease and security without him'.[2]

Her lady in waiting, the Countess of Peterborough, was to travel with her. She was less sanguine, having lost her nephew, Lord O'Brien, in the *Gloucester* shipwreck. She asked that she might be allowed to go in a different ship from Mary for she was anxious not to agitate her with her own fears. Although she would have been most reluctant to voice it, perhaps she was also worried that the *Gloucester* wreck really had been the product of sabotage by the 'Fanaticks' and that the *Happy Return* would be similarly targeted.

James was coming to be thought of as an unlucky man where ships were concerned.

Early on the morning of 15 May, the duke and duchess's baggage was loaded. There was a considerable volume of it, for the duchess had been absent from her home in St James's for more than two years. While the luggage was being stowed, Sir John Berry came on board, a gun was fired, a pennant was raised upon the mizzen mast, and a 'Council of War' was held with all the various captains in attendance. The exact nature of the discussions that took place during that council is not known, but one can reasonably presume that the route to be followed was high on the agenda, together with some clarification of signals and a stress on the need for the fleet to stay together. Sir John would have been keen to avoid the shambles of the outward voyage. As it turned out, the return voyage was also something of a fiasco, albeit one with comical rather than tragic consequences.

Later in the day, the royal party came on board and the royal standard was hoisted on the main mast. Edinburgh Castle and all the ships anchored in Leith Roads saluted by firing their guns and the *Ruby* frigate answered all the salutes. Mary was hoisted on to the quarter deck by means of a specially designed chair and pulley system. She was still suffering from an injured knee incurred during her riding accident of the previous October which restricted her movements and this, combined with her heavily pregnant state, made the contrivance extremely useful. This is the first recorded example of a chair lift being used like this. Afterwards, it was to become common practice when ladies boarded ships. Mary was much taken with the device and many years later gave an exact description of it to the nuns of Chaillot. At 7 p.m. they weighed anchor, 'the wind at east a fine gale' and at midnight they anchored again 2 miles east of Inchkeith Island.[3]

Captain Ayres, under close arrest, had been transferred from a dungeon in Edinburgh Castle to the cockpit of the *Happy Return*, where he continued to languish in irons, with plenty of time to contemplate the ugly fate that awaited him. Captain Christopher Gunman, meanwhile, had been relieved of his command of the *Mary* and replaced by Captain Laurence Wright. Gunman also was on board the *Happy Return* but he was not confined in the cockpit. He saw nothing untoward in his altered situation, or if he did there is no inkling of it in his journal. On the contrary, he appeared to regard the move as a compliment to his navigational skills, for he assumed the duke had expressly requested the transfer so he could act as the ship's new pilot. 'He commanded me to attend on him into England this present voyage for the safe conducting him and the Duchess which accordingly I did.'[4]

The return voyage was slow with contrary winds and calms. At noon on the 17th they were off the Isle of May and at 8 p.m. the lights of Berwick were seen. The batteries of Bass, Berwick and Coquet Island all fired their guns as the fleet sailed past. At noon on the 18th, the Cheviot Hills were observed 6 leagues distant, so it must have been a clear day, and at 8 p.m., after dark, the lights of Witherington were glimpsed. At 4 a.m. the next day, the gaunt ruins of Tynemouth Castle on the prow of the great cliffs, with the sprawling walls of the priory next to it, could just be discerned glowering blackly in the pale light of dawn.

Tynemouth was the hometown of Thomas Browne and his wife Isabella. They had been married there in the parish church on 1 September 1680. He had been an able seaman on the *Gloucester* on its final and fatal voyage. He had been entered on board in Portsmouth on 22 April, however something must have happened in the days that immediately followed, because on 1 May, the day before the *Gloucester* left harbour, 'he made run'.[5] The cause of his running is not explained in the brief entry in Admiralty records entitled 'ordinary'. It may have been a woman or drink that took his fancy, it may have been a disagreement with a superior officer. It could even have been some doubt that crept into his head about the safety of the ship. Whatever prompted his sudden departure, later that same day he changed his mind and was 're-entered' on to the ship's books. It was an unfortunate change of mind. He was one of those who drowned off the Leman and Ower sandbanks.

Before travelling down to Portsmouth to enlist, Isabella and Thomas had been living in London and had one small daughter. The daughter's exact age is not given but her birth predated her parents' marriage. This was important. A legitimate child would have entitled Isabella to an additional £4 8s of bounty payment, but if the child was born out of wedlock she did not count. The Stuart brothers may have had endless illegitimate children themselves but they did not wish to be seen as encouraging profligacy and debauchery among the lower classes. A group of Isabella's old friends in Tynemouth were upset on her behalf at what they saw as the harshness of this decision and wrote to the Admiralty in protest. They claimed that Isabella and Thomas had actually been married 'two or three years before' the Tynemouth wedding, in Newcastle.[6] This earlier wedding would have made their daughter legitimate. The second wedding had been held, 'to give the greatest satisfaction to the world and upon some other considerations'.[7] The Navy Board clerks were not convinced. 'Of the truth of this we can not assure you,' they recorded soberly.[8] Enquiries were made of the minister of the parish church in Tynemouth but he was 'since dead' and so could not vouch as to whether the couple had been married previous to the Tynemouth wedding. The final decision of the Navy Board was characteristically bureaucratic: 'No allowance for the child. A bill ordered to be made to the widow.'[9]

It was somewhere in the vicinity of Tynemouth that there occurred another mishap. Its consequences were to be less disastrous than the sinking of the *Gloucester*, but it again suggests a lack of professionalism on the part of the Royal Navy. A vessel came by that failed to 'strike her topsails', which was the accustomed gesture of deference to a flagship flying the royal standard. Sir John Berry ordered a shot to be fired to draw this ignorant vessel's attention to their royal status and bring the impertinent stranger into line. Unfortunately, an overenthusiastic gunner on the *Happy Return* fired the shot straight through the other vessel's hull rather than across its bows as was apparently intended.

It immediately began to take on water and make signals of distress. The sinking of an innocent English merchant ship was not what James most needed right then to improve his standing in the country.

A boat was hurriedly lowered from the *Happy Return*, carpenters and men were entered into it and they rowed across to the damaged ship, which turned out to be the *Friend's Adventurer*, whose master was John Jefferson of Newcastle. Profuse apologies were made to the captain and the hole was successfully repaired with a section of lead sheathing. It was a lucky escape for all concerned. Whether the *Friend's Adventurer* ever got round to doffing her top sails is not recorded but it seems unlikely that those on the *Happy Return* were overly keen to press the point.

At dawn on 20 May, Whitby church was observed, and at dusk the lights of Flamborough Head. There was no question of sailing within the sands on this occasion. The fleet now stood deep into the North Sea. It was a lengthy detour and it wasn't until the afternoon of the 24th that Lowestoft finally came into view. The next day they were off Harwich and on the 26th they anchored at the Hope in the mouth of the Thames. There was the usual firing of cannon, and the royals transferred to the *Mary* for the final stage of the voyage.

As soon as Charles heard that the duke had arrived in the river, he set out from Windsor to Putney, entered into his barge there and met up with James and his party at Erith. The reunion was by all accounts an emotional one, not only because of his younger brother's recent escape from death but also because of the high esteem in which Charles was said to hold his sister-in-law. According to James's biographer, J.S. Clarke, Charles took Mary of Modena's side over the issue of James's mistress, Catherine Sedley. Charles apparently felt 'mighty love' for Mary, in part because he 'compassionated in some measure her sufferings more than the Duke'.[10]

The idea of Charles taking the side of the wronged wife in a situation of marital discord somewhat stretches one's sense of credulity. However, for the moment, the fraught issue of mistresses was put aside in order to concentrate on the crucially important public celebration for the returning duke and duchess.

The brothers and their consorts proceeded upriver, guns being fired all the way, until they reached Whitehall, where they landed. A large and joyous crowd welcomed them ashore. They progressed to Arlington Park, where they were entertained by the Earl and Countess of Arlington. The Lord Mayor of London and the city aldermen came and paid their respects. That evening there were fireworks, bonfires and the ringing of bells. When news of their safe arrival reached Edinburgh there were similar celebrations. A great bonfire was kindled in Abbey Close and another one on Arthur's Seat. There was much drinking and breaking of glasses, for which the Scottish Exchequer eventually footed the bill of 44 Scottish pounds.

On 31 May, Mary made her first public appearance to attend a special performance of *Venice Preserv'd* at the Duke's Theatre. The prologue John Dryden wrote for the occasion was not unrepresentative of the general feeling in the country:

> When factious rage to cruel exile drove
> The Queen of beauty and the Court of love,
> The Muses droop'd, with their forsaken arts,
> And the sad Cupids broke their useless darts …
>
> Distemper'd Zeal, Sedition, canker'd Hate
> No more shall vex the Church, and tear the State;
> No more shall Faction civil discords move,
> Or only discords of too tender love.[11]

The last line was perhaps a sly dig at the duke's now well-publicised marital problems but the general sentiment was clear. The country was being called upon to put an end to faction and unite behind the duke, and there was great hope that Mary would soon give birth to a male heir.

The duke's party did not have matters all their own way. According to Francesco Terriesi, ambassador in London from the court of Tuscany, there were certain members of the 'whig party' who went around the streets trying to put out the bonfires. They were busy, 'holding meetings, and writing, saying, printing with increasing malice all they can to render the person of the Duke odious to the populace'. Perhaps of rather more concern was the fact that intelligent and influential men such as James Houblon were also asking awkward questions about the duke's responsibility for the *Gloucester* shipwreck and the consequent large loss of life. In a letter to Pepys dated 13 May, he wrote:

> But now to come to the unfortunate wretches that have perished Certainly it makes a greate cry amongst the families in Scholtland [Scotland] that hath lost their relations as it Doth here, and the Circumstance of their losse is more aggravating then can be imagin'd, to be lost in Broad Daylight summer, and faire weather and with soe much helpe about them is intolerable. Some thinke the Duke's heate and Courage to save the ship, made him stay too long Abord and overlook the thoughts of saving the men ...[12]

Houblon was clearly picking up here on a remark made by John Berry that initially James had hoped the ship might be saved. Berry, however, is very careful not to imply any criticism of James, whereas Houblon's tone is very different. Houblon was a well-connected and successful merchant. He frequented the Royal Exchange and understood only too well the mood of the country. Lady Roxburghe was not the only one who wanted someone to blame.

22

ON BOARD THE
CHARLOTTE
YACHT AT GREENWICH

As far as the Stuart brothers were concerned, Greenwich was their particular playground. One of Charles's first priorities after taking the throne had been to commission the architect John Webb to build a new palace on the site of Henry VIII's Tudor ruin. By 1682 the work was finished. It was a great white slab in gleaming Portland stone, with four imposing columns on its east flank, and a grand entrance facing the river. The more elegant Queen's House, designed by Inigo Jones, which was situated further back from the river towards Greenwich Hill, fell into disuse. The fact that it had a road running through the middle of it was a drawback. Overladen carts driven too fast frequently collided with the cornice work, causing damage to the building's fabric.

Charles's new palace and the Queen's House were the only two buildings of the royal quarters that existed when the *Charlotte* was berthed in the river at Greenwich on its return from the disastrous Scottish voyage. The palace buildings had not yet acquired the grand symmetry that they possessed by the time Canaletto painted his famous view of Greenwich from the river in the 1750s, and which they retain to this day. All the same, it was still widely regarded as a very pleasant and healthy situation, convenient for Whitehall, but well away from the frequently sulphurous atmosphere of the crowded city. The brothers habitually kept their yachts moored on the river beneath the palace walls.

The better sort of Londoner would come to Greenwich on a pleasure trip. Pepys was one such frequent visitor. He once came with Lady Sandwich, and at another time with Lady Carteret, and on both occasions, they climbed the hill and admired the view. Pepys was impressed by the elms that had been planted recently, and the steps and terraces laid out in the French style that led to the old watch tower and the castle at the hill's summit. The castle was a ruin and in the last few years of the 1670s an observatory was constructed on its foundations. John Flamsteed was already working there as the first Astronomer Royal, but his grand new octagonal room proved not to be very useful for observing the skies and the telescope was housed instead in a small wooden shed nearby, a makeshift arrangement that was kept carefully secret from Charles.

In 1665, during the year of the Great Plague, the Navy Board was temporarily removed to Greenwich and Pepys came with it. He took lodgings with a Mrs Clerke. He also took advantage of her daughter, Mrs Daniel. This pretty woman's husband was a lieutenant in the Royal Navy, and it would have been more than his job was worth for either of them to complain of Pepys's unwanted attentions. In June the following year, Pepys was walking through Greenwich Park with both James and Charles when they heard cannon fire. It was the beginning of the Four Days' Battle against the Dutch. Two days later, Pepys met by chance with Lieutenant Daniel, who had been serving on the *Royal Charles* during the hostilities. He was 'all muffled up, and his face as black as the chimney and covered with dirt, pitch and tar, and powder, and muffled with dirty clouts and his right eye stopped with Okum'.[1] It was only a few hours beforehand that Pepys had spent some time with Mrs Daniel, 'alone a great while and I had the pleasure of her lips – she being a pretty woman'. He did not seem to see anything untoward in his behaviour towards her while her husband was off fighting.

Even when the plague time had passed, and Pepys was no longer lodging under the same roof as Mrs Daniel, he still liked visiting

Greenwich. He enjoyed listening to the nightingales when he walked from Greenwich to Woolwich, as he frequently did. He also enjoyed tucking into 'a dish of steaks' at the King's Head by the park gates. Such was his fondness for Greenwich that by the mid-1670s, when he was already a wealthy man, he commissioned the Dutch artist Henry Danckerts to paint the view from the top of the hill towards the river, with the marsh of the Isle of Dogs on the far side and in the distance the steeples and towers of London. It was to have pride of place upon the panels of his dining room.

On the morning of 6 June 1682, while the cherries were still ripening in the orchards that Greenwich was famous for, the *Charlotte* was being prepared, not for a royal jaunt down the river or to ferry some new mistress to a foreign port, but for an altogether different and more sombre purpose. It was to function as a chamber for the court martial of James Ayres, the hapless pilot on board the *Gloucester*. The main cabin of the *Charlotte* had wood-panelled walls that had been beautifully painted by the van de Veldes, father and son, with glorious views of recently constructed warships, such as the *Charles Galley* or the *Woolwich*, depicted in rich tones of gold and yellow. This cabin was to be the setting for these dismal proceedings.

Ayres, manacled and under guard, was brought on the back of a cart from the nearby Marshalsea Prison. The formal order for Ayres to be court-martialled had been given by the 'Honourable Commissioners for executing the office of Lord High Admiral of England' a week previous. It was necessary for the proceedings to be held on board a royal ship. The *Charlotte* was available and conveniently at hand.

It was a wet, clammy morning, with a westerly wind. Large numbers of people lined the narrow streets to stare at the spectacle of Captain Ayres being taken to his trial. The sinking of the *Gloucester* had caused a great stir both in Greenwich and in neighbouring Deptford, and it is likely that the families of the bereaved from both parishes were among the sightseers.

Rebecca Ford, for instance, lived in Deptford. Her husband, James, had been the carpenter on board the *Gloucester*, drafted in at the last minute because the Navy Board was not satisfied with the old carpenter, John Brookes, and regarded Ford as a more competent and altogether safer pair of hands. Ford had drowned. Brookes, who also went on the voyage, despite the low opinion of him held by his employers, lived to tell the tale. Ford was a highly esteemed and valued man and his widow received £33, as opposed to the standard £13 4*s* that the widows of able seamen received.

The Cranwells were another local family who would have taken a particular interest in Ayres's trial. Joan Cranwell was the widow of Francis, the *Gloucester*'s master cook. She lived in Church Street, East Greenwich. Thomas Plume, vicar of the old St Alfege Church, which was already crumbling and shortly to be demolished, wrote her a glowing testimonial, although he does not appear to have known her personally:

> We have enquired and are further satisfied in the truth of our former certificates in that Joan Cranwell is the sorrowful widow of Francis Cranwell, her husband, lately drowned in the *Gloucester*, a reputed, honest, poor man and she a very good woman.[2]

Francis had drowned along with his servant John Carter. Joan eventually received a payment of £13 15*s*, 11 shillings more than the standard payment. It does not appear that master cooks were rated anywhere near as highly as master carpenters.

Saddest of all the spectators, perhaps, was Elizabeth Bradford. She lived in East Greenwich and had been expecting to marry Thomas Phillips on his return from the Scottish voyage. On 1 April, a couple of weeks before he set out on the Portsmouth Road, he wrote his will. In it he mentioned being 'bound out to sea in his Majesty's ship called the *Gloucester*'.[3] The fact the *Gloucester* was to be used for this voyage had only just been decided and so this reveals the remarkable speed and accuracy of the maritime grapevine. The will itself states his motives for writing it, 'considering of the uncertainty of this transitory life', as it was phrased in that forlorn little document.[4] He described Elizabeth as 'his beloved friend and intended wife', and appoints her 'his true and lawful attorney'.[5] He could not write his own name and so he signed it with his 'mark', as did his three witnesses, Thomas Eames, James Johnson and Edward Symonds. One cannot help but wonder whether they were also sailors on the *Gloucester*. Certainly, there was a Thomas Symonds on board from neighbouring Bermondsey.

On the *Charlotte*, meanwhile, there was a great press of people assembled below deck, making it humid and fetid, but that did not deter the curious from piling on if they could obtain permission. Pepys was pre-eminent among the gawpers and the sightseers. This was the kind of occasion he would not have missed for the world. Chistopher Gunman was also present. He was one of the captains who had been assembled to provide evidence.

There had originally been a suggestion that Ayres should be tried in Edinburgh under the authority of Sir John Berry. Pepys mentioned it in his letter of 8 May sent from Edinburgh, 'The commission omitted to be given Sir John Berry, for holding a court martiall at his going out, is sent last night express, as I am inform'd.'[6] It seems he was wrongly informed. The trial was to be delayed for another four weeks. Anyway, it would hardly seem fair or reasonable that Sir John Berry, whom many thought should answer questions himself as to the cause of loss of the *Gloucester*, should be sitting in judgement on someone else in connection with the same loss. As it was, those who finally assembled on the *Charlotte*, ten men in total, could hardly be considered impartial. Gunman, Sanders, Wyborne, Allen, Gifford, Botham and St Loe had all captained other ships in the fleet that went on the Scottish voyage. Of these Gunman, and to a lesser extent Sanders, had been involved in a very public dispute with Ayres over the direction they should be sailing in, a dispute where Gunman's opinion had triumphed. Of the others, Allen, Gifford, Botham and St Loe had all captained ships that had become entirely lost and detached from the fleet right at the start of the voyage, which hardly put them in an authoritative position for providing evidence on the navigational skills of others.

The court's president for the day was Rear Admiral Sir Richard Haddock. He was an imposing man with a kindly, genial and intelligent face. He had a limp in his left foot resulting from a cannon ball injury during the infamous Battle of Solebay. There was hardly a senior serving officer in the navy who did not carry with him some scars of that recent battle.

The main item on the agenda was Ayres's trial, but prior to that it was necessary to deal with the loss of another ship, the *Henry*, a seventy-two gun second rate that was being used as a guard ship at Chatham. It was turning out to be a bad month for accidents to Royal Navy ships.

On 15 May, the *Henry* had caught fire. Fortunately, there was no loss of life, but the ship was now just a charred hulk. An 'ancient' sailor called Richard Wallis had recently been enlisted on the *Henry* and was expected to sleep, along with the other men, in a hammock on the middle deck. However, Wallis did not like his accommodation, 'finding it uneasy for him to get in and out [of the hammock] by reason of his age'.[7] So, he took himself off to bed down in what he rather grandly described as 'a cabin in the cockpit'.[8] It was little more than a small cupboard he was able to crawl into, and he made his bed there on some old, dried oakum that was lying around. Unfortunately, on the evening in question, while kneeling down to say his prayers, he dropped a lighted candle, a much-coveted luxury, but strictly forbidden. The oakum quickly blazed up and, despite trying to extinguish the fire with his bare hands, it spread rapidly. The boatswain, James Hawes, was called and buckets of water were thrown down the hatchway but it was not long before the entire ship had been consumed by fire.

It is interesting that the court were particularly concerned to find out whether 'anyone set him on work or persuaded him or enticed him to set fire on the ship'.[9] It seems they suspected arson. Obviously, the fear of deliberate sabotage by 'Fanaticks' was still very much a live concern. Wallis replied that it was entirely 'his own carelessness' that caused the conflagration and the court believed him.[10] His sentence was relatively lenient: he was dismissed from the navy and his wages forfeited. As further punishment he was made to stand for half an hour with his neck in a halter, the rope reeved to a gibbet.

Then it was Ayres's turn. Haddock, it seems, was disposed to think more positively about Ayres than many others present. According to Gunman, writing of the trial a few weeks later, 'the pilot' was Haddock's 'bosom creature' and he accused Haddock of opening his address with a 'harangue of praise' for Ayres.[11] Apparently, Haddock remarked to all present that 'he would pawn his salvation on the said pilot were he to go to sea again'.[12] It does not sound like the most judicial way of opening proceedings but it was really little more than echoing what Sir John Berry had already stated in the columns of the newspapers, namely that Ayres was 'esteemed to be one of the best and ablest men to the Northward'.[13] The last phrase implies that he was particularly expert in the waters of the North Sea rather than the English Channel.

If Haddock was inclined to be sympathetic to the prisoner there were plenty of others who thought differently. The duke himself had remarked (in a letter to his son-in-law the Prince of Orange, the man who was eventually to oust him from the throne) that the disaster had been caused entirely by 'the to[o] great presumtion of the pilot and his mistaking both his course and distance'. He went on to add, 'he was saved amongst the rest, by one of the yachts-boats, which had I then knowne, I had caused him to have been hanged up immediatly, according to the coustume of the sea, but now he must receve his doome by a court martial'.[14]

Pepys, in his first letter to his friend Hewer after the sinking, had similarly expressed his opinion that Ayres should be immediately hanged in Edinburgh, 'for the … satisfaction of those great families of this Kingdom, who, it is feared, would be found the greatest sufferers'.[15] His view on the importance of a death sentence had certainly not changed in the intervening weeks.

Strangely, while word-for-word testimony of the witnesses at Richard Wallis's trial can still be read in the National Archives, all traces of what was said later that same day during the examination of James Ayres have been expunged from the files. They may, of course, simply have become lost, a casualty of the passage of time, but with so much detail preserved for the other less important court martial that same morning, it seems unlikely. It is more probable that things were said during the course of the proceedings that it was perhaps felt best should be deleted immediately.

The verdict was a foregone conclusion. Ayres was found guilty. The question was the nature of the punishment he should suffer. He was condemned to prison in the Marshalsea 'in perpetuity'. There was uproar when the sentence was announced, many considering it far too lenient. It appears, however, that Haddock had stated in court that there was no precedent for hanging masters or pilots when a ship miscarried, no matter how negligent they may have been.

Pepys was one of those who was outraged. He considered such leniency set a very poor example. Being Pepys, he immediately made a note to search out the relevant precedents:

> Memorandum, to collect very particular accounts of the trials and sentences of court in the case of the pilot … reflecting well upon the consequence of those sentences, by which it is in consequence declared that no miscarriage of ship or fleet by any degree of ignorance in a master or pilot can be capital.[16]

Ayres was not the first ship's pilot to end up in the Marshalsea. He was not even the first to be sent there as a direct result of having wrecked a Royal Navy ship on the Leman and Ower sandbanks. A little less than ten years beforehand, a pilot called Thomas Wheeler was on board the *Kent*, a fourth rate. He had been commanded to take the ship from Woolwich to the Hope, where he was to be discharged. However, the ship's captain, John Wood, refused to anchor at the Hope and allow the pilot to disembark. England and Holland were at war at the time and there was much privateering being carried on by the Dutch against English merchant ships in the North Sea, and reprisal action by the Royal Navy. It seems the captain had decided that it was more urgent to seek out the Dutch privateers than bother with putting his pilot ashore. In the words of the pilot:

> Captain Wood by violence brought me to sea with him, and then slighted me and the master, and took away the charge from us both,

and, like a madman, ran the ship what way his fancy pleased him. If I but advised him to take in the top sails, or we should carry our mast by the board, he answered let the topmast and sail go to the devil.[17]

The captain certainly does not come out of this story in a very good light. He left the wrecked ship in the pinnace with only ten men and made for land. After reaching the coast somewhere near Boston in Lincolnshire, he abandoned the pinnace. A John Butler wrote to Secretary of State Joseph Williamson on 26 October: 'I informed you where Captain Wood left his pinnace … It being no harbour she will be spoiled, if she is not already.'[18] Butler took it upon himself to secure the pinnace at his own cost.

A boat was organised to go and seek out the wreck of the *Kent* and take off the 200 men who were still aboard with very little in the way of water or provisions. Captain Wood did not go on this vessel himself, leaving the master to take charge of it. It returned after three days of cruising having found nothing. John Butler, who seems to have been a respected citizen in the area of Boston, concluded that 'the vessel is gone to pieces and all the men lost'.[19] His knee-jerk reaction was to blame the pilot. He had only heard Captain Wood's version of events and so his remarks have to be seen in this context, 'Our seamen here wonder that, being daylight, they did not see the seabreak on the sands, but the pilot is doubtless most to blame and is punished for his folly.'[20] At that point nothing had been heard of the fate of the pilot and he was presumed drowned along with the rest of the crew. As it happened, the pilot and seven sailors had constructed a makeshift raft and left the wreck, still stranded on the sandbank, after a couple of days. Supplies of food and water were already running short. They were very lucky to be found drifting by Captain Richard White of the *Antelope*.

Even luckier were the men who were left on the ship as the boat that went to search for them was wrong in thinking they had all perished. After nearly a week of clinging to what little remained of the ship above water, a Dutch privateer sighted them and took pity on their plight:

This privateer, with much kindness, took them in, and was exceedingly kind and careful of them, laying beds in the cook room. And refreshing them with warm drinks, and resolved to have gone to Yarmouth, and with a white flag to have got off boats and so set them ashore.[21]

Before the privateer had had the opportunity of completing this act of mercy, however, it was intercepted by another Royal Navy ship, the *Portsmouth*, and taken captive. Captain Page of the *Portsmouth* was very impressed by the Dutch captain's generosity and was determined to present him to James, who was at this time the senior commander of the Royal Navy. This did not stop him, however, sending the crew of the privateer to Ipswich gaol.

Thomas Wheeler, the pilot of the wrecked *Kent*, also ended up in gaol but in his case it was the Marshalsea. On 19 November, he wrote to Samuel Pepys pleading his innocence:

> The Captain … took away the charge of the ship both from me and the lieutenant and the master, and took it wholly on himself, for when I sent to him to desire the ship might be put in stays and tack about, for I imagined we were near danger, he would not observe my directions, and soon after she was cast away, as the major part of the company (now through Providence saved) can testify.

He begged Pepys to help him, 'I therefore entreat you will stand my friend and assist me. That I may not perish in prison by want, having neither friends nor money to support me.'[22] There is no evidence that Pepys responded, and it would have been most out of character for him to have done so.

23

THE MARSHALSEA

James was quite clear in his own mind who was to blame for the *Gloucester* disaster: it was the pilot, Captain Ayres. After the trial this unfortunate man was taken under armed guard straight back to Marshalsea Prison. The Marshalsea was in Southwark and except for the Tower was the most important of the London prisons. It was directly under the control of the Crown and was particularly used for pirates, watermen and others who had committed maritime offences.

Prisons in the seventeenth century were run very much as a commercial enterprise. If you had sufficient resources you could buy in good-quality food and drink, walk in the prison garden, play bowls, inhabit spacious rooms and even purchase a day out, so long as an appropriate guard was included in the package. But for most, including Ayres, it was a squalid and miserable place. The Elizabethan and Jacobean writer Thomas Dekker, who had considerable experience of prison, provides a vivid account of what it was like:

> … nothing could be heard but keyes jyngling, doores rapping, bolts and lockes barring in, jaylors hoarsely and harshly bawling for prisoners to their bed, and prisoners reviling and cursing jaylors for making such a hellish din. Then to heare some in their chambers singing and dancing being halfe drunke; others breaking open dores to get more drinke to be whole drunke. Some roaring for Tobacco; others raging, and bidding hels plague on all Tobacco, because it has so dryed up their mouthes, with as many other franticke passions, as their be several men. [1]

The Marshalsea was not just for men, there were plenty of women incarcerated inside its walls, some of whom were permitted to mingle promiscuously with the male inmates. Most of the women were to be found in the poor quarters, where nine rooms were provided for some 300 inmates. The women's section was called the Oak.

One female prisoner, who had been incarcerated since the beginning of April, would have taken a particular interest in the arrival of James Ayres when word went round for what crime he was awaiting trial. Her name was Sarah Hunter, who was 56 years old and 'indigent', meaning she was without any means of supporting herself.[2] She would have been treated as one of the lowest of the low inside the Marshalsea, thrown in a cell with others in her wretched condition and given the poorest food and dirty straw to sleep on. A common bucket in the corner slopped out once a day was provided for the communal faeces in those overcrowded and stinking quarters.

She had two children still at home, the eldest of whom was said to be a boy aged 10. She was in prison for debt, as she owed Mark Lund, a brewer, more money than she could afford to pay. She most probably had a drink problem, like many in her sordid and impoverished condition, a vice that Mr Lund had, no doubt, been happy to exploit while she was in funds and when those funds were exhausted, equally happy to have her thrown in gaol.

This Sarah Hunter also had a grown-up son called John Hunter. He was a young seaman and he had set off to Portsmouth in order to sign on to the books of the *Gloucester* frigate around the same time that his mother had been put in gaol for debt. There was very probably a connection between the two events. It was only by enlisting that he had any chance of getting his mother out of prison. He was, however, one of the unlucky ones who had drowned off the Norfolk coast.

It is unlikely that Sarah would have known anything about the loss of the *Gloucester* while she lay incarcerated within the damp stone walls of the Marshalsea but the day Ayres arrived within those same walls, the reason for his imprisonment would have spread among the inmates like a contagion. When Sarah learnt the bitter news that the very man, whom so many were crying out against as being responsible for her son's death, as well as the deaths of so many others, was lying just a few feet away from her, she must have howled and raged against him.

It was a cruel irony that as a direct consequence of her son's drowning, she received sufficient bounty money – £13 4s – to pay off her debts and buy her freedom. She was released on 15 October 1682 after more than six months in gaol. Her credentials had been vouched for, in writing, by Robert Marriott, the rector, and Daniel Akines, the church warden, of the parish of St Paul's, Shadwell. She and her family must have lived in Shadwell along with the families of so many other seamen of the poorer sort. It is noticeable how vital the Church was in the administration of succour for the poor.

As a man of no great social standing, Captain James Ayres was an obvious choice for scapegoat. His navigational competence was soundly rubbished but it would be even more useful to James's cause if Ayres's calumnies went beyond simple human error. In short order, the rumour machine obliged. It was not very long before Ayres's loyalty to the crown was also being questioned. By this means, not just Ayres but the entire opposition party became tainted. In no time there was serious speculation that the shipwreck was all part of a plot to assassinate the legitimate heir to the throne, as hinted by a letter from a Mr Ridley to Sir Francis Radcliffe of Dilston: 'I must inform you that the pilot is a known Republican, but his Royal Highness, having a particular knowledge of his ability, and having done him many signal favours, trusted him.'[3]

24

DEPTFORD

If Greenwich was the playground for Charles and James when they wished to enjoy themselves aboard their private yachts, and Wapping was the home of the ordinary seamen, then Deptford was the beating heart of the Royal Navy, the place where the business of designing, building, fitting out, repairing, recaulking and victualling the great ships of war got done. It was also the place where the pay office was situated, the Clerk of the Cheque, as it was quaintly called. And, most crucially from Pepys's point of view, it was where the Brethren of Trinity House had their headquarters.

They were an immensely wealthy and powerful corporation, and Pepys made it his business right from the very start of his career to ingratiate himself with them. He was elected a younger brother in 1662, and rose through the ranks of their arcane bureaucracy to end up twice elected as master for separate terms of office. It is probable that some of the deep antipathy and vindictiveness that Pepys showed towards Ayres had its origins in the fact that he was not licensed to be a pilot by Trinity House. He was a freelancer, who owed his position directly to the patronage of James. Ayres had served James throughout the Dutch Wars and most crucially had been present at that great male bonding experience, the Battle of Solebay. Indeed, Ayres enjoyed such favourable status in the eyes of James that in 1675 the duke had ordered that, 'Mr James Ayres, pilot to the Duke of York and Prince Rupert is to have £30 as Royal Bounty.'[1] It would be very interesting to know exactly what Ayres had done to prompt such largesse but unfortunately the details are not provided. Ayres's favoured status must have annoyed Pepys the bureaucrat, who liked all lucrative appointments to be properly regulated, preferably by himself.

The geographical centre of naval Deptford was just to the west of the River Ravensbourne, better known as Deptford Creek. The poet Edward Walford described the Ravensbourne as a 'crystal rillet', but even in the seventeenth century it was little more than a stinking ditch at low tide. Westwards from the creek, Deptford could boast two wet docks, three great slipways, a basin for working on the ship's keel and lower strakes, and two mast ponds. A little way back from the river there were smiths' shops, forges for casting anchors, tar houses, mast lofts, cooper's sheds, rope yards and paint yards.

Deptford was where many of those closely connected to the navy lived, particularly the better-off sort. Sir George Carteret, the Navy's Treasurer, had a house there. John Evelyn, who was to become the Warden of Greenwich naval hospital, also made his home in Deptford. It was called Sayes Court. The property extended to 100 acres and its orchards stretched down to the banks of the Thames. It was here that Evelyn cultivated his famous garden. It included a 400ft-long holly hedge, 9ft high and 5ft in diameter, of which he was particularly proud. 'Is there under the heavens a more glorious and refreshing object,' he wrote.[2] It was also here that he constructed his innovative glass beehives, much admired by visitors. Pepys said that Evelyn 'must be allowed a little for a little conceitedness, by virtue of his great intelligence'.[3] All that remains of Evelyn's garden today is one rather sad mulberry tree held up on wooden crutches surrounded by a somewhat run down 1960s council estate.

Pepys was a frequent visitor to Deptford, both for pleasure and for business. He usually came by boat, which cost him 7s return, though he saw to it being paid for by the Navy Board. The pleasure partly consisted of visits to a Mrs Bagwell, who granted him sexual favours. It was a sordid arrangement entered into with the connivance of Mrs Bagwell's husband William, who was a ship's carpenter in Deptford. Mr Bagwell was hopeful that by making his wife available for Pepys's lustful desires, Pepys would do him the favour in return of procuring him a promotion. Mrs Bagwell seems to have gone along with the bargain reluctantly but diligently.

The business part of Pepys's frequent visits concerned such matters as seeing that the crews of the navy ships were properly paid off. Seamen's wages were often several years in arrears, a constant source of complaint for it meant the sailors had to borrow at high rates of interest just to meet their daily necessities. It was a situation that Pepys deplored and did his best to correct, but to little avail. The crew of the *Mary* were some five years in arrears, a situation that Captain Gunman was to blame for the problems that were very shortly to befall him.

Pepys never missed an opportunity for increasing his knowledge of navy business in all its many facets, it was what made him such a brilliant administrator. When in Deptford he would make a point of always following up some new aspect of the navy that had caught his attention, be it questioning the shipwrights about the design of the hulls that were being constructed, or examining the accounts of the victualling office, or familiarising himself with the latest innovative techniques that were being developed for the spinning of hemp. And, of course, even on business days he usually found the time for a visit to the Globe, now a betting shop, at the bottom of Deptford Church Street. He was rather partial to the 'burnt' wine to be had there. Nor was he averse to occasionally getting the skilled craftsmen of his acquaintance to deploy their skills to his own advantage. He asked Thomas Simpson, for instance, a highly accomplished naval joiner and cabinetmaker, to construct his bookcases. They can still be seen to this day in the Pepys Library in Magdalene College, Cambridge, and very finely constructed bookcases they are too.

There was an unexpected twist at the end of the Ayres trial that sent a particular shiver of anxiety through one of Deptford's best-regarded and longest-established residents, Christopher Gunman, who lived with his wife in the Treasurer's House. The details of what occurred are to be found in a fascinating document, written by Gunman himself and located among his papers. It is called 'An Abstract of Gunman's Cause'. It seems that the authorities were not satisfied simply with condemning Ayres to a lifetime in the Marshalsea; they wanted others to be punished, in particular those who might have failed to give the *Gloucester* an adequate warning of the dangers that lay ahead.

William Sturgeon – the mate on board the *Mary*, who was on watch when the *Gloucester* struck – had been one of those called as a witness during Ayres's trial. We do not have his testimony. As soon as the trial was over, however, the president, Sir Richard Haddock, wrote a note, which he gave to Mr Jones, the Marshal, authorising Sturgeon's immediate arrest and his committal to the Marshalsea. Gunman complained that neither he nor any of the other captains who had attended Ayres's court martial were consulted beforehand about this arrest, and he may have been correct in this. He must have learnt about it very soon, however. By Gunman's own testimony, set down in his 'Cause', during the next few days after the arrest, Sturgeon's wife was to be found 'running up and down' the streets of Deptford, trying to find witnesses who would swear 'that none of the fault lay with Sturgeon but all with Gunman'.[4] Gunman clearly wrote his Cause in a furious temper and as a direct riposte to those who had impugned him. He lashed out at everyone and the result was a great muddle. He contradicted himself repeatedly about just when he knew what, and much of what he wrote makes no logical sense. What does emerge between the lines, however, is fascinating.

A new trial was scheduled to take place on 13 June, again on board the *Charlotte*. Gunman claimed that he only attended the second trial 'in order to justify the mate',[5] which stretches credulity as he must have already heard something of all the furore that was going on in the streets and taverns of Deptford during the intervening week. According to Gunman, Sturgeon's wife's 'malicious solicitations' all failed, 'such as she brought to her husband in prison ... refused the said mate's desire, saying they would not forswear themselves for the world'.[6] He also claimed that prior to his appearance on the *Charlotte* the second time, on 13 April, he had had 'no charge given me, nor yet knew of anybody accusing me'. He went on to expostulate in a great explosion of anger, 'I do believe I am the first supposed criminal that ever was brought to trial without first having a copy of his indictment.'[7]

It is impossible now to get to the bottom of all the various accusations and counter-accusations that were flying around. According to Gunman's version of events, Sturgeon was owed sixty-two months in back pay. This is quite probable. In these circumstances Sturgeon, like most others in his situation, was forced to borrow at high rates of interest. The money lenders, hearing of Sturgeon's arrest, were desperate to get him freed, for fear that if he was condemned, they would never get their money back. It was these same money lenders, in connivance with Sturgeon, who supposedly came up with the plan for shifting the blame for the *Gloucester* tragedy on to Gunman. Gunman labelled the money lenders 'Fanaticks'. It was an easy smear to make but in the context of the rumours going round that Ayres had also been a republican and the *Gloucester* sinking was all part of a 'Fanatick' plot to make sure Monmouth got the throne and not the Catholic James, then it may well have been believed in certain influential quarters. Gunman's prose was a terrible muddle but even today it has a poetic power. 'I find this mate hath been tampered with in prison, all the Phanaticks in town, his creditors having been with him,' is how he describes what had occurred.[8]

Despite all his posturing and fury, when Gunman appeared on the *Charlotte* on 13 June, he found himself on trial alongside William Sturgeon, not simply present as a witness, which is what he claimed he had thought he was there for. The line-up of presiding captains was also different from what it had been the previous week. Not only was Gunman now in the dock instead of sitting in judgement, but Wyborne, the captain of the *Happy Return*, was this time appearing as a witness, and neither Sanders nor Gifford were present. The weather, on the other hand, remained very much the same. It was still pouring with rain, with strong blustering winds from the south-west. As June weather went, it was proving a terrible washout and the cherries were rotting before they ripened.

The case against Gunman was relatively straightforward. When the *Mary* first came into shoal water at 5.30 a.m. on 6 May, Sturgeon had called him on to deck, as previously instructed. Gunman had immediately given the order for the man at the helm to turn to leeward and also commanded that a flag be waved at the stern of the ship to indicate that there was shoal water ahead. According to the court, Gunman should have ordered for a gun to be fired as a warning and not just a flag to be waved. His failure to fire a gun was a contravention of clause 27 of the Articles of War Act, passed in 1661. Gunman argued that there was no time to fire a gun because no sooner than had the *Mary* sounded and discovered they were running into shallow water, the *Gloucester* had hit the sandbank. Several of the witnesses, however, who had served as officers on the *Mary*, testified that there was nearly fifteen minutes between the *Mary* first discovering shoal water and the *Gloucester* hitting the sandbank.

Gunman probably did not do his case much good by coming up with a plethora of excuses. Not only did he claim there was insufficient time, he also argued that he needed first to establish whether the sandbank was to windward or to leeward of him so as to be sure about which direction to turn in. Still more damning to his own cause, he remarked, 'for the sailing instructions alledged against him, he had not them, nor had them in ten years and doth not looke upon them for instructions to be always in force, but made for the present occasion and expedition and alterable'.[9] Gunman's comments about the Articles of War have an admirable bluntness, but he had just condemned himself out of his own mouth. It is not altogether surprising that the court found him guilty of 'neglect of duty', and 'adjudged that he be dismissed from the command of his Majesty's yacht the Mary and to be imprisoned during his Majesty's pleasure, and a year's pay to be forfeited for the benefit of the chest at Chatham'. As for William Sturgeon, 'the court do not find him negligent of his duty, and therefore do acquit him and clear him'.[10]

Gunman was incandescent with rage. He wrote in his 'Cause' that they 'might as well have sworn I did kill a man at the Barbadoes'.[11] He thought it was all part of a plot to lessen the guilt of Ayres. Pepys, who was there observing, felt the sentence was far too lenient. 'Very much to be bemoaned it is that the lives of those who miscarried had no more satisfaction exacted for them.'[12] He was particularly peeved that there was no independent witness allowed to be present while testimony was being taken, even 'though myself was known by the court to have come on board on purpose to hear the trial as being one that had hardly escaped bearing a share in the evil occasioned by Christopher Gunman and the pilot's misbehaviour'.[13] Pepys did not think that court martials should be composed entirely of naval commanders.

Gunman did not consider himself lucky to have escaped with his life. His mood, as he was escorted through the steadily falling rain to Marshalsea Prison, was black with anger and despair. As a man of some wealth and standing he would have been accommodated in relatively luxurious quarters, but this did little to mitigate the injustice and indignity he felt. It was as if he alone was being sacrificed from among the many ship's captains who took part in the Scottish voyage. Why should he be blamed, he argued, when four other ships had become altogether detached from the fleet?

Fortunately for Gunman, James was taking a keen interest in all the circumstances and details of these two courts martial. On the same evening that Gunman was committed to the Marshalsea, King Charles, at James's prompting, asked for a particular account of all the proceedings and proofs that had been placed before the court. By 19 June, just six days later, Gunman had been released and reinstated in his position of captain of the *Mary*. Gunman was suitably grateful. On 15 August 1682, on hearing that Mary of Modena, the Duchess of York, had given birth to a daughter, he gave each man on board the *Mary* 'a bottle of claret to drink prosperity to the Duchess and welcome to our new Princess'.[14] James, however, did not leave the matter there. On 1 October, Gunman wrote in his journal, 'His Royal Highness commanded Sir Richard Haddock and myself to become good friends as we had been formerly and would not let us part until it was so agreed on of all sides, and shook hands together in the Duke's closet.'[15] This small action shows a caring side to James's character that he is not always credited with. Finally, on 5 December, Gunman recorded in his journal, 'His Majesty was graciously pleased to remit my fine of a year's pay.'[16]

Pepys was far from happy at Gunman's exoneration, but he had to wait some years before he was in a position to exact his own special form of punishment. His chance did not come until after Gunman was dead and buried and Pepys was once more a Navy Board commissioner.

On 18 March 1684 Gunman had observed an extraordinary 'celestial phenomenon' from the deck of the *Mary* yacht moored at Calais Pier. 'This morning about 7 oclock saw in the firmament 3 suns with two demi rainbows; and all within one whole rainbow ... The sun towards the left hand bore East and that on the right hand bore South East of me.' He quickly made a sketch of it. 'I did sit and draw it as well as the time and place would permit me; for it was seen in its full form about the space of half an hour.'[17]

It was not long after this heavenly experience that Gunman fell from the same pier and injured his leg. The wound turned gangrenous and very soon proved fatal. He was 50 years old. John Evelyn attended his funeral on 26 March 1685 and later wrote of him in his diary as 'that excellent pilot and seaman who had behaved so gallantly in the Dutch War ... a sober frugal, cheerful, and temperate man, we have few such seamen left'.[18]

Pepys, on the other hand, saw in Gunman's death the opportunity he had been waiting for. He was not a man to forgive and forget. He promptly threw the sea captain's widow and children out of the Naval Treasurer's House in Deptford, where they had lived for many years. In their place he installed his own brother-in-law, Balty St Michel, who had previously helped Pepys out over the John Scott affair.

The Celestial Phenomenon, as it came to be known, was also not forgotten. Gunman's sketch was to form the basis for the spectacular backdrop used for the appearance of Iris in Dryden's opera *Albion and Albanius*. This was the first full-length opera to be put on in Britain and was staged at the Dorset Garden Theatre, where it opened on 6 June 1685, shortly after James's coronation. Like Otway's play of three years earlier, *Venice Preserv'd*, it was a thinly veiled panegyric, celebrating James and satirising his enemies. The opera made much use of elaborate visual scenery, winched into place by the enormous hidden machines for which the Dorset Theatre was famous. Iris's opening song once more made reference to James's near-miraculous rescue from the sinking *Gloucester.*

Albion by the nymph attended
Was to Neptune recommended;
Peace and plenty spread the sails
Venus in her shell before him
From the sands in safety bore him
And supplied the Etesian gales.[19]

25

HORSLEYDOWN

Word soon got around the port towns of Britain that there was money to be had if you were the widow of a seaman drowned on the Scottish voyage. Joan Smith was one such widow. Her late husband, Thomas, was the poor ship's swabber who had been let out of debtor's prison in the town of Sandwich, east Kent, so that he could sign on the *Gloucester*'s books when the ship was moored off Deal Harbour. He was already an old man when he was entered and he was one of those who, unsurprisingly, did not make it into a boat. His wife was described as 'a poor blind woman' aged 'about fifty years and very indigent'.[1] Blindness was a very common affliction in the seventeenth century, indeed Pepys was famously anxious about his eyesight. It was the explanation he gave for giving up writing his diary, although as it turned out his fears were groundless. He continued writing copious letters and memoranda for the next thirty years.

The lure of the bounty money prompted Joan to immediately set out for London. It is most unlikely she could have afforded a carriage, and walking was probably beyond her physical capabilities. She must have travelled up the old Dover road on the back of a cart during those wet days of early June. Joan had been married to Thomas for five or six years, so she had married him very late in life. It was stated that the two of them 'lived in this town and port [Sandwich, close by Deal on the Kent coast] and always behaved themselves very honestly'.[2] It seems that their debts were the result of the usual misfortunes that came along with age and illness.

When she reached London, Joan stopped in the house of Mr John Hopkins, a waterman. Perhaps he was a former friend of her dead husband. Mr Hopkins lived in Free School Street over against the Crown in Horsleydown, Southwark. A number of seamen on the *Gloucester* came from Southwark. Horsleydown was an area along the south bank of the river that stretched eastwards from Tower Bridge towards Bermondsey and is today very roughly the area of Shad Thames. In 1682, Tower Bridge was not yet built. There was only one crossing for those pedestrians, horsemen and carriage owners that did not wish to make use of a ferry and that was London Bridge, some distance further upriver.

The westernmost part of Horsleydown can still be identified because Horsleydown Stairs are still in existence. This would have been the point where watermen such as Mr Hopkins would have embarked their passengers for ferrying across the river to the Tower, situated almost exactly opposite. The school referred to in the name of the street was the free grammar school founded by Elizabeth I. It was demolished when Tower Bridge was finally built in 1886.

In 1682, Horsleydown was an area of decaying clapboard houses dating back to Tudor times. Pepys didn't think much of the place and avoided it if he possibly could. On 24 January 1666, however, he had found himself with no other option but to make his way through its narrow and sordid streets after visiting Deptford in the company of Lord Brouncker. They had gone together to Sir George Carteret's house, where they met William Howe, the same William Howe who a couple of years later Pepys was to invite to his own house for an impromptu dancing party where Thomas Greeting supplied the music. Howe showed them the chests with 'the poor sorry rubys which have caused all this ado to the undoing of W. How, though I am not much sorry for it because of his pride and ill nature'.[3] The rubies were part of the cargo of a fleet of East Indiamen captured by Pepys's great patron, Lord Sandwich. Sandwich had not handed the cargo over to the Admiralty commissioners as he was supposed to do by law. Instead he had distributed it widely among his followers and friends, which clearly included Howe. Howe had subsequently been examined before the Privy Council for embezzlement. Pepys clearly relished Howe's discomfiture, somewhat ignoring the fact that he had himself had been one of those favoured by Lord Sandwich's largesse. Pepys, with his usual subtlety, had managed to keep under wraps his own involvement in the widespread pilfering that went on.

While Pepys and Brouncker were examining the embezzled jewels, a huge storm blew up, which prevented them returning home by their usual method, which would have been to get a waterman to ferry them across the river:

> ... the wind being very furious, so as we durst not go by water, walked to London quite round the Bridge, no boat being able to stirre, and Lord, what a dirty walk we had, and so strong the wind, that in the fields we many times could not carry our bodies against it, but was driven backward. We went through Horseydowne, where I never was since a little boy, that I went to enquire after my father, whom we did give over for lost, coming from Holland. It was dangerous to walk the streets, the bricks and tiles falling from the houses, that the whole streets were covered in them – and whole chimneys, nay, whole houses in two or three places, blowed down. But above all, the pales on London Bridge were blown away, so that we were fain to stoop very low, for fear of blowing off of the bridge. We could see no boats in the Thames afloat, but what were broke loose and carried through the bridge, it being ebbing water. And the greatest sight of all was, among other parcels of ships driven here and there in clusters together, one was quite overset, and lay with her masts all along in the water and keel above water. So walked home, my Lord away to his house, and I to dinner.[4]

The state of the buildings in Horsleydown had not improved much by Charles Dickens's time. In *Oliver Twist* he describes the houses as having:

> ... crazy wooden galleries, common to the backs of half-a-dozen houses, with holes from whence to look on the slime beneath; windows, broken and patched, with poles thrust out on which to dry the linen that is never there; rooms so small, so filthy, so confined, that the

air would seem too tainted even for the dirt and squalor which they shelter; wooden chambers thrusting themselves out above the mud, and threatening to fall into it, as some of them have done; dirt-besmeared walls and decaying foundations.

It was in this area that Joan lodged. As she was blind, she could not see the rags of washing hung out to dry on the crank galleries or the rats running in the gutters, but she could still probably smell the stink from Jacob's Ditch and hear the cries of the watermen as they touted for custom. She had most likely never been to London before. It must all have seemed very strange and confusing. What was most bewildering were the requirements made of her by the Navy Board officials. It turned out she had made the long journey down the Dover Road without the appropriate paperwork from her parish priest. Without it she could not claim the bounty money that she had come all this way for.

Joan was distraught. She did not have sufficient funds to get back home to the Kent coast, acquire the required documentation, and try a second time. She had almost certainly needed to borrow money for the long journey she had just made. It was then that someone, either Joan herself or one of her acquaintance, hit on the idea of forging the certificate. Joan could not have accomplished this unaided for it is most unlikely she was able to read and write, even before she went blind. Someone must have helped her. Possibly it was John Hopkins, the waterman she was stopping with, who came to her aid. Watermen had a reputation for being lawless.

Whoever conceived of it, the plan did not work. The certificate that was produced cannot have been very convincing. Enquiries were made of John Pigot, vicar of St Mary's church Sandwich, where Joan and her husband had lived. He wrote back:

We do acknowledge that about 6 months since the churchwardens of this parish gave the said poor woman with their hands a certificate to recommend her to the charity of some adjacent parishes for the release of her husband then in prison, but other certificate we doe disown.[5]

From this it is apparent that Joan, right from the start of 1682, had been trying to get her husband out of prison, where he languished until he could pay off his debts, but Sandwich parish were not willing to bear the whole expense of relieving his debts alone and so were helping Joan canvass other parishes to make a contribution. This looks pretty much like buck passing from one parish to another without much in the way of results.

Thomas Smith was still in jail when, on 3 May, the *Gloucester* arrived and anchored in the roads off Deal. It had then been hastily arranged between his creditors and the parish authorities that Smith was to be released from prison on condition he enlisted on the ship. It seems the *Gloucester* must have had a shortage of swabbers. The creditors, no doubt, would have required a lien on his future wages in return for facilitating his freedom.

By the end of June of that year, things were looking very bad for Joan. She was facing prison herself, not just for debt but also for forgery. It was then that her sister intervened to try and help. She pleaded with the church wardens 'to testify that the said Jone Smyth was the wife of Thomas Smyth a seaman said to be drowned in the Gloucester'.[6] Her desperate appeal was successful and the church wardens of Sandwich issued a genuine certificate dated 19 July. The clerks in the Navy Board, however, were still not satisfied. They wanted further and better particulars. The church wardens replied once more in a state of some perplexity:

> Whereas you are pleased to require us to declare what we further know or can learn for the satisfaction in this affair we do answer, that we know, nor can learn, nothing more of it unless that the said Jone Smith, upon the news of her husband's death unadvisedly went up to London without a certificate from the Parish and then finding a certificate to be necessary did (as it is evident) forge one when she might easily have obtained a true certificate from the Parish had she at first required it.[7]

This account is almost certainly correct and one detects a slight note of exasperation on the part of the wardens that the Navy Board cannot put this together for themselves. After all, Joan Smith was a blind old woman, unlikely to be well versed in the bureaucratic niceties of the Navy Board. To do justice to the latter, however, in this instance they did show some compassion. Joan eventually received her £13 4s.

26

WAPPING STEPS

It was no great surprise that Ayres had been found guilty of negligence. The judgement discreetly overlooked the Friday evening before the sinking, when the duke had summoned Gunman and Sanders in their respective yachts to bear up to the *Gloucester*, and had asked their captains to give him their opinion as to what courses they should be following. Gunman had responded very volubly with a great pantomime of ill temper, shouting that the course the pilot was following was 'mad'. Sanders had been more tactful but had clearly sided with Gunman. The upshot was that Ayres was overruled, just as he was overruled a second time at 9.30 that same evening when he wanted to turn to the north and James had requested that he should continue to tack off for another half an hour. But none of that absolved Ayres from the charge that he was the one who had responsibility for the *Gloucester*'s navigation. It was also inarguable that it was Ayres by himself who, at 4 a.m. on the Saturday, made the fateful decision to turn to the north-west, in the belief that all the dangerous sands were by that point well behind them. Clearly, he could not have been more wrong. In just over another hour they crashed on to the Leman and Ower sandbanks. As James put it succinctly, he was 'out in both his course and his distance'.[1]

It was reported in the newspapers from Scotland that the only defence Ayres had offered while in prison in Edinburgh was, 'The late great storms had moved the Sands far distant from the place they were before.'[2] The excuse has a rather desperate and plaintive ring to it, as if he hardly expected to be believed. A careful examination of the relevant charts that have been laid down over the last 200 years reveals that there has indeed been a gradual movement of the main ridges of the Leman and Ower. They have travelled towards the north-east, but only in the order of about a quarter of a mile over the entire period, which is equivalent to about 6ft a year. Movement from a previously known position definitely does not explain why the *Gloucester* hit one of them. Equally important for the purposes of navigation, the soundings taken over the sandbanks, which give the depth of water at low tide, have hardly changed at all. Ayres may have been better advised to point an accusing finger across the river in the direction of Wapping than at the recent stormy weather.

At the beginning of the seventeenth century, the East End of London had largely been open fields and orchards. By 1682, it was covered with small tenement buildings crowded along a maze of dead-end alleys and narrow lanes. The houses were generally two storied with a garret, wooden framed and infilled with 'Flemish Wall'. They were the product of speculative builders such as George Care or Mr Fox, who gave his name to Foxes Lane. After the Great Fire of 1666, the authorities wanted all new building to be of brick construction, but the old style was cheaper and was in some ways better suited to the marshy land close to the river, and so it persisted.

London was the fastest-expanding urban area in Europe, already twenty times bigger than its nearest English rival and soon to become the largest city in the world. It was sucking in people and money and commodities not just from the English hinterland, but from every corner of the globe. Trade was the great moving force behind this remarkable growth. Silks, spices and chinaware came in from the Far East; gold and ivory from Africa; sugar, rum and hard woods from the Caribbean; hemp, fir and iron from the Baltic; fish and furs from the Americas; sea coal from the north; wines from France. And it all came in through the docks of East London.

Along with this growth in trade went a boom in shipbuilding. The great wooden skeletons of the newly built hulls with their gaunt arching ribs and giant knees, trusses and stanchions, dominated the river shoreline. The *Gloucester* had been built at Limehouse dockyard, just a little further down the river from Shadwell. But shipbuilding was not the only boom industry. Everywhere you looked there were rope yards and sail yards, timber yards and tanning yards. Clustered near the Tower there were gun makers and iron founders, providing the ordnance that the larger vessels carried for protection against privateers and pirates. The demand for beer was also on the up, as water contaminated quickly on a long-distance voyage. The Red Lion Brewery at St Katherine's was one of the biggest in London. Glass was becoming increasingly popular, both in houses and ship's cabins, and Michael Rackett had his glass factory in Lamb Alley on the south side of Goodman's Yard.

The most crucial part of this rapidly expanding economy was the workforce of sailors. Wapping has always been seen as the very centre of London's sailor town, a noisy, brawling, drunken and frequently mutinous district, famously depicted in Thomas Rowlandson's watercolour painting of Wapping Stairs. In 1682 it was not a distinct parish, being lumped together with Whitechapel, but Wapping already had a reputation for its great concentration of mariners.

Right at the beginning of the seventeenth century, John Stow famously described it as 'a continual street or filthy strait passage with alleys of small tenements or cottages ... inhabited by sailors'.[3] Two hundred years later, things had not changed much. A German tourist, Johann Archenholz, remarked that 'the east end, especially along the shores of the Thames, consists of old houses, the streets there are narrow, dark, ill paved; inhabited by sailors and other workmen who are employed in the construction of ships'.[4] It was in these crowded and bustling streets that many of the *Gloucester*'s sailors lodged.

They were men like Magnus Alison, who left a widow called Katherine. James Benning was another local sailor, and his widow was called Susan. She had a child to maintain but she received no payment because the father was a former husband and therefore did not count. Robert Browne of Wapping had also drowned. He had wed his wife Joan in the Chapel of Trinity in the nearby Minories two years earlier. They had no children. Thomas Champain was another local victim and his wife Frances was pregnant. She received £4 8s for the child in her womb. Mary, widow of Francis Davis, was also pregnant. She already had two children, Francis, 10, and Philip, 4. She received £32 1s 8d in total, which even counting the money for the children suggests that Francis must have been a sailor of some importance; a boatswain perhaps or a quartermaster's mate.

The list goes on. Judith, widow of William Rutter; Elizabeth, widow of John Seymour; Sarah, widow of John Shand; Joan, widow of Robert Stowe; Katherine, widow of Walter Young, 'the late cooke's mate' and 'one of those persons that was unfortunately drowned'; Anne, widow of Richard Soloman.[5] Mr Soloman had been a midshipman, a position of some standing. His wife was 'in a distressed condition having contracted several debts which are unpaid we therefore recommend her to your charitable consideration', wrote her priest.[6]

It is also common to find in the list that there were big differences between the children's ages. Anne Thorne of Wapping, widow of Allen Thorne, the quartermaster on the *Gloucester*, had one child, 10-year-old Dorothy, and was expecting another. The frequent gaps in childbearing were no doubt partly because of the husband's extended absence on board ship, but probably also a result of infant mortality rates. There is no doubt that the people of Wapping were badly hit by the *Gloucester*'s sinking.

Not all the housing in the area was of poor quality and mean proportions, nor were all the inhabitants sailors, although they did make up about 50 per cent of the local population. There were also men and women of modest wealth who lived in the more substantial houses along streets such as the Lower Shadwell Road, fronting the river. These were for the most part merchants, ship owners, large inn keepers, builders, chandlers and coopers. They were people like Widow Craven, who owned a thirteen-room house close to Cod Piece Row. Her husband, John, had been a shipwright. Or there was the enterprising blacksmith, Philip Wright, who owned a crane on Bell Wharf and hired it out to those merchants who wished to make use of it for unloading their ships. The ship owner and East India merchant Thomas Bowery had a shop on Mansell Street that sold the much coveted Chinese blue and white porcelain. His wares were aimed at the new rich living in London's fashionable West End, rather than sailor's wives, who could only ogle the fabulous tureens through his shop window. The poorer classes purchased their more humble pots from William Knight, owner of the Hermitage Pot House on Hermitage Dock.

Another well-heeled Wapping merchant was Sir William Warren. He was a great importer of timber from Scandinavia and also a great friend of Samuel Pepys. Pepys often visited him in his 'pretty and neat and well furnished house', always going the smart way, which was by water from Custom House Stairs to Wapping Stairs.[7] This avoided the sordid road route described by John Stow.

Pepys arranged many of the contracts by which Warren sold his timber to the Navy Board. It was widely rumoured that it was through his friendship with Warren that his own considerable wealth was accumulated. There was undeniably in this part of London a complex set of personal and mercantile interconnections that was like a giant web, mirroring the entangled streets. Pepys was not averse to accepting backhanders; he knew how the system worked. It was what made him such a proficient rooter out of corruption when it came to examining the accounts of others who had dealings with the Admiralty commissioners.

News of the *Gloucester's* loss caused a great stir. There was doubtless much gossip in the numerous Wapping taverns, such as the Black Eagle by Wapping Stairs, or the Town of Ramsgate down by the wharves, about the court martial of the pilot and where the blame lay for so many deaths. But no one, it seems, not even the inquisitive and combative Samuel Pepys, thought of looking into a very particular shop that lay at the very heart of this maritime community, a shop that Pepys, for one, was very familiar with.

One of the darkest and narrowest streets, in this parish of narrow and dark streets, was Little Hermitage Street. It led past the roaring furnaces of the Hermitage Pot House towards the black waters of the river by Hermitage Stairs. Hanging over the alley at the top of the stairs was a sign with a mariner's compass painted on it and, perhaps more ominously, an hourglass. Inside the shop was an extraordinary store of ingenious mathematical instruments. The aspiring navigator could purchase here a back staff or a cross staff, a quadrant or a telescope, an hour glass or a running glass, pocket sun dials and horizontal sun dials and universal equinoctial ring dials. The owner of the shop was John Seller, aged 50 in 1682, and at the height of his success as a supplier of the latest navigational inventions to the seagoing trade.

Seller was not just a purveyor of mechanical instruments. Some ten years or so earlier he had the bright idea of branching out into the lucrative business of supplying charts. Up till then, the production of sea atlases had been entirely dominated by the Dutch. At some point in the 1660s, Seller came up with a plan for diverting that rich source of revenue into English hands, or more particularly his own hands. He took a ship to Holland and acquired a set of worn-out copper plates that had been used to produce Dutch charts some fifty years before. Back in England, he employed an engraver to sharpen up the lines and then he set about producing what he called his own 'sea waggoner' under the new title *The English Pilot*. The enterprise was an enormous success and Seller's atlas rapidly became the standard work of navigation in the English language for the English seas, even though almost all the charts in it were of Dutch origin, except one by Christopher Gunman of the Channel Isles, and another by Jonas Moore of the Thames Estuary. The latter was acquired without Moore's permission and before he had properly finished it, but that was a mere nicety.

Seller dedicated his new atlas to James, Duke of York – always a good move. In return, and somewhat ironically considering the manner in which he had acquired the charts in the first place, Seller was granted a royal monopoly on his *English Pilot* for the next thirty years, to prevent it being 'counterfeited' by others. He was also issued with a royal warrant that appointed him Hydrographer to the King, an honour that he proudly printed at the front of the next edition.

This was all very fine and patriotic but when it came to laying down the position of the Leman and Ower sandbanks there was a problem: no one had a clue where they were, neither the Dutch, nor the English. The chart of the River Thames in Seller's *English Pilot* of 1671 shows an 'Orri Sand' 4.5 leagues off the coast and an unnamed bank 6 miles

Johan Danckerts's painting shows James in the stern of a small boat being rowed away from the sinking *Gloucester*, while red-coated soldiers take an axe and a sword to those still in the water, desperately trying to climb aboard.

Probably painted in 1672 or 1673 towards the close of the Third Dutch War, James is shown in characteristic martial pose, drawing on classical imagery.

ne of a series of sumptuous portraits of Mary of Modena commissioned for James's Coronation in
85. Her richly embroidered dress, ornamented with pearls and gold, complements the jewels of the
own placed to her right, and is balanced by the white cockatoo to her left, suggestive of purity of soul.

A superb portrait that reveals both the truculence and intelligence of Samuel Pepys. His lifelong frien
William Hewer, also had his portrait done by Sir Godfrey Kneller around the same time.

epys was impressed by Danckerts's view of Greenwich and commissioned an almost identical painting or his own house.

Left: Painted a few years after the sinking of the *Gloucester*, by which time Sir John Berry had been made vice admiral of the red squadron. The ship in the background flying the red ensign his flagship, probably the *Henrietta*

Opposite left: Portrait of Sir Charle Scarborough. The anatomical drawing in the open book is from Vesalius and establishes the sitter a a physician, just as the watch and the prisms on the table symbolise his interest in mathematics and science. The view in the background is of Rome.

Opposite right: Painted in the mid-1680s when John Churchill was aged about 35, he still has the boyish good looks that Barbara Villiers, among others, found so alluring. The armour establishes h military credentials.

Opposite: This portrait of Lady Margaret Hay was commissioned for her wedding to Lord Roxburghe when she was just 18. The arch lute signifies harmony.

Left: Christopher Gunman's right hand rests on the muzzle of a cannon, establishing him as the captain of a man-of-war. The loss of his left hand is discreetly hidder by his sleeve, unlike in the Berry portrait, where the sitter proudly displays his stump.

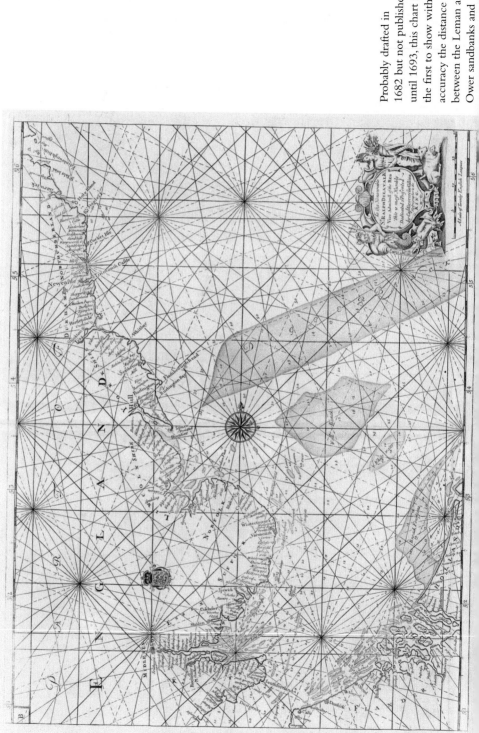

Probably drafted in 1682 but not published until 1693, this chart is the first to show with accuracy the distance between the Leman and Ower sandbanks and further out, or 6.5 leagues off the coast. A second and more detailed chart places an 'Orrey Sand' 6 leagues from the coast, and the 'Lemmon Bank' 7 leagues from the coast. The name Ower is a corruption of Orre, which comes from the Anglo-Saxon *ore*, meaning a strip of land between two waters. In Seller's charts the Orrey or Orri is the inner bank and not the outer one as it is in most subsequent charts.

But the confusion over nomenclature is not really the problem. What matters is where they are positioned and at what distance from the mainland. Both sandbanks are seriously misplaced. In Seller's chart of the Thames, the inner bank is laid down approximately 12 miles nearer the coast, and the outer bank 9 miles nearer, than accurate modern Admiralty charts place them. The second chart is not much better, the error being more in the order of 8 miles for the inner bank, and 9 miles for the outer bank.

In a later edition of the atlas the accuracy of the information being supplied about these two sandbanks had not improved, and if anything it had got worse. Seller writes that:

The Owery is a sand which beareth from Winterton Ness North East almost 7 leagues distant; it lyeth in the sea NW and SE, being in length about 4 miles ... the Limber is a sand which beareth from Winterton Ness, N by E, half Easterly, and from Hasborough ENE distant from either of them about 4 leagues.[8]

It is noticeable that here the order of the sandbanks has become reversed. The Leman, or Limber, as Seller now has it, has become the inner one and the Owery, or Ower, is the outer. The nomenclature is now consistent with most subsequent charts. But the positions given have become even more wildly inaccurate. The Leman is now stated as being just 12 miles distant from shore, 14 miles adrift from where it really is, and the Ower is still laid down 9 miles adrift from its true position. The accompanying chart carries the grand dedication:

A draught of the sands, channels, bumpes, beacons and sea marks upon the Coast of England from the South Foreland to Orford Ness, discovered by Captain Gilbert Crane and Captain Tho Browne, Elder Brethren of Trinity House. The sea coast surveyed by Jonas Moor Esquire and published by the special licence and approbation of his Royal Highness the Duke of York.[9]

It is difficult to believe that either Crane or Browne had actually spent much time plotting the position of the Leman and Ower sandbanks.

After the furious row on the evening of 5 May between Gunman and Ayres over the direction they should be sailing in, it is not difficult to imagine that Ayres would have gone to his cabin and consulted his sea charts. It is highly likely that the charts would have been those printed and sold by John Seller. Working on the basis of these charts, the courses he followed should have taken the *Gloucester* well beyond the Leman and Ower sandbanks with a very comfortable safety margin. Even if he had consulted contemporary Dutch charts by the likes of Pieter Goos or Arnold Colom of Amsterdam, they would have been of no better assistance. They also laid down the sandbanks in completely the wrong positions. Hardly surprising then, that the only explanation James Ayres could think of was that 'the late great storms had moved the Sands far distant from the place they were before'.[10]

Pepys was something of an expert when it came to the history and development of English cartography and the way in which it had relied heavily on Dutch charts. Some years before the *Gloucester* voyage, Pepys had 'decided to collect from Mr Seller a list of sea charts and books on navigation printed in English, showing how the books of charts under several titles borrow all from Waggoner'.[11] As a result of this study Pepys was well aware of the deficiencies of Seller's charts. He had even had a conversation with Captains Gunman and Sanders about the problems. 'They [Gunman and Sanders] say that even Seller's new maps are many of them little less than transcripts of the Dutch maps, some of them even with paper pasted over and names scratched.'[12] One might have thought that with his expert understanding, Pepys would have felt some sympathy for the plight of a man who had come to grief, at least in part, because of the shortcomings of English cartography. But no such sympathy was forthcoming. He still wanted Ayres hanged.

It was largely as a result of Pepys's criticisms about the state of English map making that, in 1681, the naval authorities took it upon themselves to do something about it. Pepys noted in his *Naval Minutes*:

> Trinity House tells me that they have made their application to the King that the coasts of England may be generally surveyed anew, they appearing universally to be laid down false, and particularly Scilly 10 minutes more North than it ought to be; by which our ships have been always to this day exposed to ruin, and infinitely more have miscarried than were ever heard of to have done so. And that this has arisen upon our having still depended and governed ourselves by the Dutch draughts.[13]

The discrepancy regarding Scilly that Pepys noted was no greater than the error regarding the Leman sandbank.

Later in that same year, Captain Grenville Collins was appointed by the Admiralty to produce a set of new charts for the coastal waters of Britain. This was to be a very different project to John Seller's. He was to 'make a survey of the sea coast of the Kingdom by measuring all the sea coast with a chain and taking all the bearings of the headlands with their exact latitude'.[14] Collins was a practising seaman and hydrographer with much first-hand experience of the business of charting unknown waters, having spent time as a ship's master both in the Southern Seas and the Mediterranean. Unlike Seller, he knew what he was doing.

By the summer of 1682, shortly after the wrecking of the *Gloucester*, Collins in the navy yacht *Merlin* was diligently sounding around the Leman and Ower sandbanks and calculating their distance from the Norfolk coast. He got the distance right to within 1 mile. His entire mapping of the English coastline took another six years as it was often delayed by a lack of funds from the Crown. The engraving of the charts took a further five years and the complete atlas of sea charts was only finally printed and published in 1693, under the title *Great Britain's Coasting Pilot*. It was the first major survey of Britain's seas carried out by an Englishman and it was to remain constantly in print for the next 100 years, going through numerous editions.

In the *Coasting Pilot*, Grenville remarks:

The Leman and Ower are two very dangerous Sands, the innermost is the longest and is called the Leman, the body of which lieth from Haseborough North East by East about 8 or 9 leagues: This sand hath in length North West by North about six Miles, and at Low-water hath not above six, seven and eight foot water. This sand is steep too having twenty two Fathom close to it. The Ower lieth 2 or 3 Miles without the Leman, and lieth in length NW by W about 3 miles, on which is 9 foot at low water, and is steep too, having 22 fathom on each side of it and 22 fathom between the two sands.[15]

The consistency of this information with that revealed by the modern charts, produced with all the benefits of satellite navigation and echo sounders, is remarkably impressive.

Interestingly, and also somewhat puzzlingly, Pepys never appreciated Collins's great survey, as this characteristically critical remark reveals:

September 21, 1693. This day Mr. Lee the globe-maker came to show me some draughts, which led us to discourse about Collins's late Book of Sea-Charts, that let me into a large field of enquiries into the faults even of this work of his, and those many and great, and many things only copied therein.[16]

Pepys does not provide the supporting evidence for what these 'many and great' defects were. It is an off-the-cuff swipe and probably had more to do with Pepys's poor opinion of Collins than the quality and accuracy of his charts. The truth is that Pepys had been carrying on a campaign against Collins ever since he had first obtained the commission for his great survey. The origins of the dispute are difficult to unravel, but it appears that Pepys did not consider that Collins should have been allowed to produce his *Coasting Pilot* under his own name. In Pepys's opinion the survey should have been under the direct control of Trinity House. One suspects, as so often with Pepys, that an element of turf war was clouding his judgement.

27

THE QUEEN'S HOUSE

It wasn't just the likes of Lady Roxburghe and James Houblon that were critical of James's actions during the sinking of the *Gloucester*. Some of the reports that soon came out in the newspapers had the potential to be far more damaging. The inaccurately titled *Impartial Protestant Mercury* of 12 May 1682, for instance, contained the following damning remarks:

> We have a painted relation of the misfortune which says that none were suffered to go into the first boat but which his Royal Highness called for, which were about 40, of which one or two in mean habit and unknown.[1]

Reading such lines, Lady Margaret must have wondered why her husband had not been chosen when so many others had been, including some of low birth. In reality, forty people would never have been able to fit into the small shallop that James went off in, and if some of low rank were included, it was probably those who were fished out of the water at James's insistence, against the wishes of his bedchamber man, John Churchill. But it was a story that went through many elaborations and which was to dog James for the rest of his life, and even for several centuries after his death.

The wave of sympathy and popularity that James experienced at his homecoming was a not an entirely spontaneous demonstration of the nation's goodwill. It was, to a very large degree, cleverly orchestrated by his news managers and image makers. Manipulation of the media is not a recent invention. Seventeenth-century monarchs were greatly preoccupied with how they were portrayed and went to some extraordinary lengths to control the public's perception of their every deed. Such control was vital to the creation of that sense of mystique and invulnerability that underlay the doctrine of divine right and the exercise of absolute power. It is not coincidence, nor simple vanity, that there is a plethora of portraits of James II in various martial and triumphalist poses. In the light of the hostile versions of the *Gloucester* disaster that were already slipping into the press, it is not surprising that as soon as James landed he should set about putting his own particular gloss on what had happened. It was with this in mind that James's agents, at the earliest opportunity, paid a visit to the largely derelict and abandoned Queen's House in Greenwich Park.

Some years back Charles had agreed to the conversion of part of the downstairs of the Queen's House into an artist's studio. It was let to Willem van de Velde the Elder and Willem van de Velde the Younger, the pre-eminent marine painters of the seventeenth century. It seems their Dutch nationality did not get in the way of their popularity with the Stuart brothers. They specialised in views of naval battles such as the Four Days' Battle of 1666, or even more crucially the Battle of Solebay in 1672. The elder van de Velde would sail with the fleet and in the midst of scenes of mayhem and devastation was to be seen on deck busy with his sketch book, drawing both from the life and the death. As a result, the paintings have the dramatic power of first-hand reportage. However, the father and son's work was not limited to naval engagements. They also depicted ordinary maritime life, royal yachts in harbour, East Indiamen being loaded from lighters, merchantmen under full sail with a following wind, and ships in storms with sails close reefed.

There can have been few more appropriate locations for their studio than Greenwich, where they could observe the myriad of hoys, ketches, pinks and wherries that crowded the Thames waters on a daily basis. They occupied the downstairs rooms on the north side, where the light was more suited to their work. The house accounts record their presence. 'March 1675 charge was made for three pairs of deale shutters for three windows in a lower room at the Queens Building nexte the parke (where the Dutch painters worke).'[2]

On James's return to London, the van de Veldes were approached about a somewhat unusual and delicate commission. They were requested to produce a dramatic representation of the *Gloucester* sinking. As was usual with the van de Veldes, the painting that resulted was impressive for the accuracy of its detail. On this occasion neither of them were on the ship, but they must have listened carefully to first-hand accounts. The wind direction, the time of day and the boisterousness of the waves are all consistent with the known facts. The original is apparently lost, but a possible copy survives in the National Maritime Museum. It shows a dramatically stormy sky and choppy sea with the *Gloucester* sinking by the stern, fore and main top sails still set, but the sails on the mizzen brailed up. The duke is already in a crowded barge, which is being rowed towards the *Mary*, shown close hauled in the background, a short distance to the west.

The painting manages to communicate a powerful sense of both danger and urgency. The focus is on James being safely ferried away from the sinking ship as a brilliant ray of dawn sunlight pierces through the heavy banks of grey cloud. The symbolic message would not have been missed by a seventeenth-century audience. God was shining his merciful light on the true heir to the throne, preserving both his life and the future well-being of the kingdom. The horrors of the Civil War were still fresh in the collective memory.

The van de Veldes's studio was, like most artist studios of the period, something of a factory. The original artwork was no doubt conceived and drawn by the van de Veldes themselves, but it would have been finished off by others, and then copied by their numerous different assistants. The idea was to have this heroic image of James disseminated as widely as possible. After the paintings had been produced and the market for them saturated, there would also have been successive editions of etchings of the same dramatic scene. Etchings were keenly sought after by the less affluent who still wished to advertise their loyalty.

This propaganda war was not limited simply to the production of paintings. Across the river at the Royal Mint, a medal was struck to commemorate James's miraculous escape, just as similar medals had been struck after his victories in the Dutch Wars. On the face of it was a bust of His Royal Highness with the inscription round it, *'Jacobus Dux Eboracensis et Albanensis G.B.F'*. The reverse depicted a ship sinking in the ocean with a rock surmounted by a fort in the background, symbolising the permanency and strength of the crown. The medal was inscribed with the words *'Impavidum Feriunt'* to emphasise James's fearlessness in the face of all danger. Other examples, with the same words but slightly altered images, suggest that it was a highly popular item and went through several editions. Such medals were a common feature of the period and were eagerly collected throughout Europe.

The message that James's iconographers wished to convey was emphatic and unambiguous: his survival was clear evidence of God's design that he should be the next king of England. His triumph over danger was similar to previous triumphs during battle and therefore reminded the nation of his physical bravery and his martial prowess. Perhaps even more important, however, was the way in which the story could be used to convey the selfless loyalty of the sailors. Their patriotism and love for James was a lesson and example to the rest of the nation.

It was the written word that reached the largest audience and that was most suitable for conveying this version of events, and numerous scribblers and poetasters hurriedly went into print with a variety of panegyrics and Pindaric odes on the wondrous devotion of the English tar. It was probably Sir John Berry who had first given birth to this legend when in his 'Narrative', he referred to:

> ... the great duty the poor seamen had for the Preservation of his Royal Highness's person: when the barge was hoisting out, and lowered down into the water, not one man so much as proferred to run into her; but in the midst of all their affliction and dying condition did rejoice and thank God his Royal Highness was preserved.[3]

James Macpherson's *Extracts from the Life of James II* continued the same theme, 'Those left, as they were ready to sink gave a great Huzza! when they saw the Duke of York safe.'[4] Clarke, in *The Life of James the Second, King of England*, expanded the story further, drawing out the political implications:

> … those therefore who were thus abdandon'd (tho ready to be swallowed up) gave a great huzza as soon as they saw his Royal Highness in safety, to the no less honour to the English Seamen for their intrepiditee and zeal, than the Duke's for having so great an esteem amongst them, when such endeavours were used to render him the object of all men's hatred.[5]

It was left, however, to the poet Nathaniel Wanley to describe the moment in the most high-flown and ludicrous manner:

> As soon as they perceived the boat clear of the ship and the Duke out of danger, they all of 'em threw off their caps and made loud acclamations and huzzahs of joy as if they had attained some signal victory over their enemies and in this rapture sunk to the bottom of the sea immediately, at the same instant concluding their lives and jubilations.[6]

James reciprocated this fabled show of loyalty by ordering the Treasury to make the special payments of bounty money to the dependants of those seamen who had drowned, their widows and their children, as well as mothers who had lost sons on which they were reliant, and daughters, who had lost fathers and had no other means of subsistence. The payment was equivalent to eleven months' salary and was traditionally only paid for dependants of seamen who had been lost in battle not shipwreck (the latter being much more common). The payments were made on this occasion with the bureaucratic caution that 'it was not to be esteemed a precedent', and was only made 'in respect of the preservation of his Royal Highness' Person'.[7]

James's generosity was not entirely confined to the dependants of sailors who had drowned. He also gave the Treasury orders to pay up until 2 June those seamen who had survived. This was four weeks of extra salary beyond the norm. The usual procedure was that when a ship wrecked, the contract of employment was terminated automatically, a harsh prescription, particularly as many ships sank far from home and the survivors were faced with the cost of making their own laborious way back. It was presumably intended as an extra incentive for the men to take care of the vessel in their charge and not abandon it negligently.

There were other reports of James's largesse that were not confirmed in the official records but which may, nonetheless, have been true. *The Loyal Protestant*, for instance, in its edition of 18 May, states that 'the two trumpeters who went with his royal highness were saved by swimming and when they came to Edinburgh his Royal Highness according to his wanted generosity gave them 40 l [pounds] a piece to buy them clothes'.[8]

The bounty payments were all part of the campaign to convert what could have been a public relations disaster into a triumph. The duke's survival was to be broadcast to the world as definitive proof of both God's special care and also the love the seamen held for him. The impression given, at least so far as the bounty payments are concerned, is that James was anxious that he should be seen to be doing the right thing. He had enjoyed strong support from the seafaring community in the past and he could not afford to alienate them now. The bounty payments were well received and as the Treasury footed the bill it did no harm to the Stuart pockets.

The net effect of James's effort to win over the hearts and minds of the English people was brilliantly successful. The story of his escape from the *Gloucester* shipwreck, far from damaging his reputation, helped to augment it. This triumph was followed on 15 August by Mary Modena giving birth. The fact that the baby was yet another female was disappointing both to the parents and to Charles. Somewhat sadder was her death at just three weeks old. However, Mary was still young, and there was still the strong possibility of a male heir being produced. The goodwill of the country continued. Three years later James was to succeed to the throne with minimal opposition.

28

GRESHAM COLLEGE

The second half of the seventeenth century was a period of huge curiosity about the natural world, leading to an explosion of interest in experimental science. Much of this interest was centred around and stimulated by the Royal Society. It was founded in 1661 and was soon to be based in the old Tudor buildings known as Gresham College on Bishopsgate. Pepys became a member in 1665, proposed by his Navy Board friend Sir William Brouncker, the society's first president. In December 1684 he was to be elected president. Pepys was fascinated by all the new inventions that were being devised, particularly those that had relevance to the navy such as more accurate time pieces or improved methods of caulking a ship's seams, and he regularly attended meetings, but never aspired to being an experimental scientist himself. Rather, he was elected president for his organisational and administrative abilities.

The dominant creative force in the Royal Society during the 1660s and '70s was Robert Hooke. Other members, Isaac Newton pre-eminent among them, may have ultimately contributed more to scientific progress, but no one was more prolific and diverse in their interests than Hooke. He was allotted rooms in Gresham College itself, and promptly had a hole made in the roof of his living quarters and installed a large telescope through it. He was perhaps not the ideal tenant. But it wasn't just the sky that fascinated Hooke. He was equally interested in what lay beneath the surface of the water and, with his usual imaginative fecundity, devised a whole range of instruments for exploring beneath the seas.

Pepys, Hooke and others, such as his good friend Lord Brouncker, often went to the King's Head near Chancery Lane after Royal Society meetings and continued to discuss the scientific issues of the day over a hearty meal accompanied by claret. On one such occasion Pepys quizzed Hooke as to what it was that caused 'discords in music'. He was not entirely satisfied by the answer he got and noted in his diary, 'will at my leisure think of it more and see how far that doth go to explain it'.[1] Hooke could be equally unimpressed by Pepys. He wrote in his own diary for 19 Dec 1676, 'Mr Pepys, Master of the Trinity House, made a long speech to no great purpose.'[2]

Hooke was far from being the only scientist of his time interested in devising new engines and instruments for exploring beneath the sea. Sir Robert Moray reported to the Royal Society on how diving bells could be used to recover lost cannons. The bronze guns of the Swedish warship *Vasa*, lost in Stockholm Harbour in 1628, had recently been salvaged using a diving bell and as a result there was much interest in their potential for working other lost shipwrecks with valuables on board.

Human diving without the aid of bells was similarly a subject of interest, particularly the diving of the black slaves used for pearl hunting and the feats of endurance shown by the Caribe divers employed on Spanish shipwrecks lost in the New World. There was much contemporary speculation in the intellectual salons of London as to just how deep a man could dive, without the aid of engines and other contrivances, and for how long he could stay beneath water. Nathaniel Wanley, who had written so enthusiastically about the miracle of James surviving the wreck of the *Gloucester*, published a book called *Wonders of the Little World* in which he described divers being able to stay beneath the surface for up to forty-five minutes without the aid of any breathing apparatus. He was somewhat prone to exaggeration.

Both the Stuart brothers were fascinated by all the talk of exploration beneath the seas, not so much from the scientific perspective as from the possibilities it opened up for obtaining treasure. It was very appropriate to the times that in Pierre Mignard's portrait of Charles's mistress, Louise Kerouaille, Duchess of Portsmouth, painted in 1682, she is depicted being offered by a young black person a cornucopia shell full of pearls and coral, exotica from beneath the sea.

The Eldorado for seventeenth-century treasure hunters in British waters was the *Florencia*, a Spanish Armada galleon lost in Tobermory Bay off the Isle of Mull in Scotland. It was widely believed to have been carrying 30 million silver pesos when it sank. The salvage rights belonged to the Argyll family, but Charles had the 8th Earl put to death early in his reign for his supposed part in the execution of Charles's father, and so appropriated the salvage rights to himself. The courts, however, saw it differently, and awarded future salvage rights to the 9th Earl.

One of James's first acts while he was running affairs in Scotland, during his virtual exile, had been to arrest the new earl on the grounds of his refusal to sign the Test Act, which involved swearing loyalty to the Church of England, an act that James himself did not sign, but James was given a special dispensation. So, once again the rights to this great hoard of wealth reverted to the Stuart brothers.

James commissioned a professor at Glasgow University called George Sinclair to salvage the treasure from the Tobermory galleon. Sinclair was the author of the ground-breaking *Ars Nova et Magna Gravitatis et Levitatis*, published in 1669. In it he writes:

> The farther the bell is lowered into the water the higher the level of the water rises in the interior of the bell, and, conversely, when the bell is raised towards the surface of the water so the level of the water in it is forced lower because at only slight depths the pressure of the particles of water becomes less and the internal air expands … the greatest possible equilibrium is established between the water, which strives to force itself to the top of the bell, and the air, which strives with the same force, to hold down the water. The diver is under uniform pressure over the whole of his body, in the one case from the water, in the other from the air. He does not feel the weight of the water in any way.[3]

Up until Sinclair, most famously Leonardo da Vinci, but many others also, had assumed that all that was necessary for a diver to penetrate beneath the waves was a breathing tube from the surface, ignoring the fact that the weight of water as a diver went lower would very rapidly make breathing impossible unless the air that was being breathed was also compressed, so that it was equivalent to the weight of the water forcing the chest inwards.

Sinclair was licensed by James to salvage the *Florencia* and he diligently worked away at it for years, but recovered almost nothing. All that has survived of his efforts is one silver peso encrusted with marine growth that somehow ended up in the Hans Sloane collection, now in the British Museum. However, the fault did not lie with Sinclair or his diving bell; the legendary hoard of wealth had never existed. Charles was much luckier with his investment in the *Concepción* project in 1683, which first put the Caribbean on the treasure-hunting map. He made a huge return on his money, as also did Richard Haddock, the astute naval captain who had presided over the trials of Ayres and Gunman.

Almost from the moment that the *Gloucester* had slipped beneath the waves, it had acquired the reputation of being a ship in which great fortunes had been lost. Gunman was one of the first to suggest it. On 9 May he wrote to his wife from Edinburgh, 'The Duke came on board just with a coat and breeches on, which was all he saved, – plate, linen, clothes, money, etc. all gone to the value of above £5000.'[4] The duke was, of course, just one of many wealthy men on board, all of whom would have travelled with their own silver plate, money and jewels. 'Two Letters from Scotland', published by John Morice shortly after the loss, stated:

> Tis judged that in money and other valuable things, which all perished in the sea, will amount to above £30,000 besides the ship herself, with her guns and furniture, being a third rate ship, new fitted and mounted with 58 pieces of ordnance.[5]

The parliamentary chronicler Narcissus Luttrell repeated the same figure of £30,000 in an entry of his *Brief Historical Relation of State*

Affairs dated 13 Mary 1682. It was a colossal sum at that time. The Modenese envoy in Paris, Gaspare Rizzini, tells the same story of all the silverware and all the money of many persons, together with other items of great value, perishing in the vessel. Intriguingly, shortly before the *Gloucester* departed, James had asked the French Ambassador in London, Monsieur de Barillon, where he should invest his private money. It seems he had an embarrassment of personal cash on his hands.

It is quite possible that there was far more of value lost in the *Gloucester* wreck than was reported. During the months of March and April 1682, the royal yachts *Mary* and *Katherine* were making voyages to Holland and bringing back gold coin. On 3 April 1682, for instance, Captain Davis of the *Katherine* was directed to sail to Rotterdam and 'receive on board such money as shall be sent to you by order of Mr Cooke, goldsmith, within that time [6 days] and then you are to return with it to Greenwich'.[6] This item comes shortly before a specific instruction sent to Sir John Berry on 25 April 1682 in which he is told that no 'goods or merchandise upon any pretentions whatsoever' were to be shipped on the *Gloucester* frigate or any other of his Majesty's ships in the Scottish fleet, 'gold and silver only excepted'.[7]

George Seton, 4th Earl of Winton, was one of the wealthiest men in Scotland by virtue of his extensive salt and coal interests. His agent in Rotterdam wrote to Seton at the address of a Mr James Foules, a gold merchant in London, where presumably Seton was picking up his post while travelling as part of James's entourage. Foules's letters refer to four separate shipments of gold being made on Seton's behalf throughout March and April. There has to be a possibility that some of this gold was subsequently shipped on the *Gloucester*, and there is certainly evidence that some of it was destined for Scotland. One thing for certain is that soon after the *Gloucester* sinking, Seton felt the need to spend £505 12s with Alexander Reid, a goldsmith, for replacement silver plate.

The Admiralty never moved very fast, but by the beginning of July they had taken the decision to attempt a relocation of the *Gloucester* wreck. A Navy Board minute stated, 'The Mary and Charlotte [yachts] be ordered to go and find out the *Gloucester* wreck and see what can be saved of her.'[8] What happened to this expedition is unclear. It is evident from Gunman's journal that he never sailed. On 17 July Gunman was ordered instead to carry the Ambassador of the Emperor of Fez of Morocco into the Downs and then return to Greenwich.

But thoughts of salvage had not been abandoned entirely. On 25 July 'at my Lord Brounker's', it was 'resolved that the *Kitchin* yacht upon her return from Diepe be ordered to take on board the diver and seek the Duke's plate which was lost with the *Gloucester* when she was cast away'.[9] It seems that the Navy Board's thinking had become rather more focused since its previous order on this subject. Firstly, it was recognised that the services of a professional diver would be required if they were to make any progress at all with recovering valuables from the *Gloucester*. Secondly, the salvage expedition now had a specific objective, namely the recovery of James's silver plate.

The diver was William Harrington of London, who described himself as a mariner, and he was backed financially by two London merchants, Cornelius de Gildir and Samuel Sowton. The three of them together had recently been granted an exclusive patent for fourteen years on:

> ... a new invention being several tools, engines and instruments ... for the weighing or recovering from under water, ships guns and goods by any accident or shipwreck, lost in the harbour or at sea ... your petitioners having already expended above £450 for the making and working their engines ...[10]

There followed much lengthy debate on what share the king or lord high admiral should rightly reserve to themselves, with precedent ranging from anything between 10 and 50 per cent. After prolonged negotiations the projectors or salvors stated that 'they will rather choose to suffer their said invention to sinck, and be lost than to proceed therewith to no advantage'.[11]

It appears that the financial terms were eventually agreed upon, but even then there were further problems. A yacht was proposed for the voyage to the Leman and Ower sandbanks to attempt relocation of the *Gloucester*. However, this yacht or more probably the captain of it, was not agreeable to the salvors. Harrington wrote to Sir Richard Haddock, comptroller of His Majesty's Navy, in the following terms:

> The *Kitchin* yacht was that which his royal highness proposed and designed for me to go in upon the business I have undertaken and therefore I am willing to stay for her rather than have any other. I went to Greenwich purposely to discourse with Captain Crow, before he set sail for Diep and he tells me he can not undertake to find the *Gloucester* wreck among sands where he is not well acquainted and therefore does desire that John Grice of Yarmouth (the man that your honour paid for salvage of some rigging belonging to the *Gloucester*) may be directed with his boat to go along with him. He having taken his departure exactly from Yarmouth and being a good mathematician knows more directly how to find the boat than anybody else.
>
> He desires likewise that a spare anchor and cable may be prepared for him (by that time he come back from Diep) to ride the yacht by near the wreck in a gale if need bee that no time may be lost but that I may be ready at hand to make use of all opportunities of fair weather.
>
> And I for my part do only request of your Honourables to lend me three coile of rope which I will be answerable for at the end of the voyage, viz 1 of I inch, 1 of 2 inch, and 1 of 3 inch, and four wooden buoys for me to clip upon the wreck as soon as I come at her that I may not be in danger of losing her, although her masts should happen by storm to be carried away.
>
> If I find the wreck and it please God to send good weather I do not question but I shall answer his Royal Highness' expectation, and the good opinion you have been pleased to have of me.
>
> Your Hon. And most humble servant, Will Harrington, July 28th 1682.
>
> I will wait on your honour tomorrow morning before I go to Derby House.[12]

Some agreement was eventually reached because on 5 August Captain Crow of the *Kitchin* received the following orders:

You are hereby directed and required to receive on board his Majesty's yacht under your command Mr Herrington and with the first opportunity of winde and weather transport him unto the Lemon and Oare there to assist him in finding out his Majesty's ship the *Gloucester* lately cast away there and to endeavour finding some of the Duke's plate and then to return to Greenwich.[13]

On 9 August, John Grice of Yarmouth, captain of the *Donald*, was instructed 'to goe off with Captain Crow with his boat to search for the *Gloucester* and to give what assistance he can in finding of her and of anything belonging to her'.[14] But after that date there is nothing. It is possible that Mr Harrington's engines failed to work as predicted. It is more probable that they were never even put to the test. Continuous gales had swept through the North Sea throughout the latter half of May and June and it is very likely that the *Gloucester*'s masts had been washed out, making relocation virtually impossible. On 9 September, Captain Crow was directed to return to Erith. The whole expedition had ended far too quickly and nothing further was heard from Mr Harrington, mariner of London.

29

STEPNEY

St Dunstan's church in Stepney has always been associated with marsh folk, mariners and the sea. Even today, glimpsed from the distance through its fine wrought-iron gates, it is not unlike a stout ship, a Hanseatic cog, that has somehow become beached on dry land. It is best approached from the south along a fine avenue of lime trees. It is here that Sir John Berry, captain of the *Gloucester* when it sank, is buried. The Latin inscription on his memorial stone gives little away about him. It seems he was as discreet in his death as he was throughout most of his life.

Berry was a man who early on had learned the virtue of keeping his mouth shut, and it was a facility he displayed to great advantage in the aftermath of the *Gloucester* sinking. He had been the captain of the ship and yet in his detailed account of what had occurred, written just a few days after the event, he reported the opinions of others and the decisions that were taken, as if he was no more responsible than a disinterested onlooker. It was a talent for discretion that served him well, and yet within just a few years of the *Gloucester* sinking, he was to be a crucial player in a plot against James that was as bizarre and outrageous as any of the many intrigues that bedevilled this era. A close, hard look at Sir John Berry is key to understanding James's downfall.

In the later part of his life Berry lived in a substantial house in Stepney with his wife and numerous servants. They had no children. Close by lived several relatives including his younger brother Thomas Berry, who had served as lieutenant on the *Gloucester*. In the immediate area there also existed a small retinue of skilled sailors who followed Berry faithfully from ship to ship as his commands changed, men such as Cornelius Balling, midshipman, Richard Chenney, gunner, John Jones, surgeon, John Spurrier, gunner's mate, or Allen Thorne, quartermaster. Stepney was very much part of maritime London along with Wapping and Shadwell but it was a definite rung up the ladder from its more notorious and noisy neighbours. Berry was the central figure in this all-important and well-established maritime community.

It had not always been so. In his early years Berry had lived a life of such swashbuckling adventure that Robert Louis Stevenson might well have scripted it. He was born in 1635, which made him more of an age with James and Pepys than the younger generation of Legge and Churchill. His father had been a vicar near Exeter who had had his property, living and a large library of books confiscated during the Civil War. He died when John was only 17, the second eldest boy of nine children.

Having few other opportunities in the world, John Berry signed on as an apprentice to a ship owner called Robert Mering in Plymouth. He was captured by the Spanish on his first voyage and ended up spending a considerable stretch of time in a Spanish gaol, which did him no great hurt, according to his biographer. By the time he was released, his master had fallen upon hard times and was unable to keep him on as an apprentice, a setback that Berry, with characteristic resourcefulness, managed to turn to his advantage. He went to London, and on the credit of his recommendation from his previous master, obtained the position of boatswain on a Royal Navy ketch called the *Swallow* under the command of Captain Insam.

The *Swallow*, together with two frigates, was directed to the West Indies, but ran into a hurricane in the Gulf of Florida. Both frigates sank and the *Swallow* only survived by cutting down its masts and jettisoning all its guns and provisions, including food. Berry and his shipmates spent the next sixteen weeks eating fish and drinking rainwater, until they washed up on the coast of Campichea (Mexico) where they were able to reprovision the ship and sail to Jamaica. Once there, the *Swallow* was refitted, Berry was appointed lieutenant, and they were ordered to hunt down a notorious local pirate, whom they finally managed to corner in a bay off the Isle of Hispaniola.

When the Second Dutch War broke out in 1665, Berry was appointed as the captain of a sloop called the *Maria*, in which he took thirty-two prizes and for this exceptional service he was promoted to the captaincy of the fifty-six-gun, third-rate man-of-war *Coronation*. He was again sent to the West Indies, this time as the commodore of a fleet of nine ships. There he was involved in a fierce battle with the French fleet off St Christopher's in which he burnt the French flagship. Later he served in the Mediterranean. When the Third Dutch War broke out, he was given the command of a seventy-gun ship called the *Resolution* and he was one of many among James's intimate circle who was present at the Battle of Solebay. During this battle he so distinguished himself he was immediately afterwards knighted by James, who is reported as having said to him on the occasion, 'as our thoughts have been now upon honour, we will hereafter think of profit, for I would not have so brave a man a poor knight'.[1]

Sir John Berry's history is illuminating because it demonstrates the way in which the Commonwealth, for some, was a period of great social mobility, particularly for an enterprising officer in the navy. Berry was very different from both Legge and Churchill in that he did not come from the aristocracy but from relatively poor, if literate, origins. He was every inch the professional seaman, a thoroughgoing tarpaulin. But by the time of the *Gloucester* sinking he had accumulated considerable earthly possessions and an enviable standing in the world. He was indeed, as James had promised, no longer a poor man, and he was obviously anxious not to jeopardise his hard-won gains with a rash word at an ill-chosen moment.

His memorial in Stepney church might be tight-lipped but the magnificent portrait of him by Michael Dahl is somewhat more revealing. He sat for it near the end of his life and it shows a man overweight and heavily jowled, fond of the good things in life, shrewd, humane, quietly acquisitive. Like many self-made men in this precarious age, an age that saw the first great surge towards mass materialism, Berry liked money and what money could buy: coffee, wines, clothes, carriages, houses, furniture and self-portraits. The fingers of his right hand, protruding from a lace cuff, are long and slender and suggest a delicacy and refinement of manners quite at odds with the swarthiness and coarseness of his seaman's features. He was a talented player of the violin, commended by Samuel Pepys, no mean musical aficionado himself. Berry's left hand, by contrast, is a visual shock. It is a wooden stump, a blunt reminder of his thirty years at sea fighting the Dutch, and the brutal personal cost of those wars to so many sailors.

But Berry was not quite all he seemed, not even in this portrait. Like so many of his contemporaries, who were also self-made, he was a man with a secret, a secret that very probably played a large share in ultimately undermining his loyalty to James. He had, before the Restoration, acquired considerable lands in Kent, on the cheap from dispossessed Catholics. Once James became king and started to adopt militantly pro-Catholic policies, Berry began to worry that he would soon come under pressure to restore his newly acquired lands to their original owners. It was perhaps for this private reason, as well as the larger considerations of national politics, that Berry was later to be a principal player in an extraordinary plot to kidnap George Legge, who by then was Admiral of the Fleet, if Legge should show any resistance to William of Orange's planned invasion of England. This was hardly the kind of loyalty that James may have expected from a sea captain whose career he had gone out of his way to promote.

30

FAVERSHAM

On 2 February 1685, Charles was in his rooms in Whitehall when he emitted a strangulated scream, which was shortly followed by an apoplectic fit. For the next few days, six physicians were constantly in attendance. Sir Charles Scarborough, personal doctor to both Charles and James, and one of the survivors of the *Gloucester* sinking, was the most senior among them. A series of remedial measures were hastily applied: blistering, bloodletting, purging, cantharides and scarifying. More than fifty different medicines were administered in total, including spirit of human skull, white hellebore, powdered pearls, goa stone and opium. Nothing that could possibly be tried was left undone. On the morning of 6 February, Charles remarked that no one would ever know how much he had suffered. A few hours later he was dead.

Scarborough performed an autopsy the next day. It was noted that the vessels of the brain were fuller of blood than was ordinarily found and the ventricles were engorged with a serous liquor. The lungs were sound but full of blood. The heart was in good shape and the lower body sound, only the liver, kidneys and spleen too full of blood. A plaster of Paris death mask was taken, which object, like so many such curiosities, ended up in the vast and miscellaneous collection of Sir Hans Sloane.

After a long and troubled wait, James finally ascended to the throne with a minimum of protest; the image makers had done their work well. Charles was dead and the nation collectively decided to give James their trust and unite behind him.

However, the mood of goodwill did not last long as James's open Catholicism and increasingly pro-French policies soon alienated large swathes of the political classes. Ironically, when Mary of Modena at last produced the much longed-for healthy male heir in June 1688, it did not play to James's advantage. By then there was a majority in the country who profoundly mistrusted him. A male heir brought up a Catholic was the last thing they now wanted. Within another six months James and his wife found themselves once again in exile, this time in France.

George Legge was in charge of the fleet that was assembled at the mouth of the Thames to intercept any invasion attempted by the Protestant William of Orange of Holland, who was James's son-in-law. William was married to James's eldest daughter, Mary. Legge was in an unenviable position. The fleet itself was in good shape, partly as a result of Pepys's recent return to power within the Admiralty, but many of its commanders were very unhappy with James's blatant favouring of Catholics and Catholic commanders, and some of the seamen had become openly rebellious. The difficulties of Legge's situation were compounded by the false information, innocently handed on by Pepys, that William was intending to land his invading force in Yorkshire. In the event, favourable winds and a helpful covering of fog enabled the Dutch fleet to slip past the English undetected, pass down the Channel and land William's hotchpot army safely at Torbay on 5 November.

There is nothing to suggest that Legge deliberately conspired to facilitate William's invasion but it is equally clear that he, like so many, was very unhappy with James's recent handling of his affairs, and he had no enthusiasm for a potentially disastrous sea battle. William, whose fleet was outclassed and outnumbered by the English, was equally keen to avoid a naval confrontation. So, as a result of contrary winds, Sir John Berry, the second in command of the fleet, was not required to kidnap his senior officer and stage a mutiny. The final betrayal was to take place on land and was to be carried out by another of James's long-standing favourites.

When James heard about William's invasion in the west, he set off for Salisbury to take control of the army. It was there that he held a crucial meeting with his senior military officer, John Churchill. Churchill was the man that James had summoned first to share his boat when the *Gloucester* was sinking. That trust proved to have been devastatingly misplaced. Churchill had, in fact, been in close contact with a number of well-placed supporters of William for at least six months before James set out from Windsor.

Churchill had clearly been sounding out the waters and weighing up his options for some considerable time. On 7 November, a still-unsuspecting James appointed Churchill as lieutenant general of the army. By the time James arrived in Salisbury, large numbers of troops had already started going over to the other side and Churchill had done very little to stop them. By 24 November, Churchill decided that the desertion rate was so great he could risk joining them. He left James a long self-justificatory letter in which he claimed his decision had been 'actuated by a higher principle', and that it was not in 'his inclination or interest to desert'.[1] In truth, his decision was very much in his interest, as subsequent events proved. James was devastated. He was described by one onlooker as riding 'backwards and forward continually with a languishing look, his hat hanging over his eyes and a handkerchief continually in one hand to dry the blood of his nose for he continually bled'.[2] Out of that original band of brothers whose bonds had been forged during the great Battle of Solebay twenty years back, only George Legge had remained steadfast in his loyalty, and even his goodwill had been tested to the limit.

In this distressed state, James hurried back to London, only to discover that his second daughter, Anne, had defected in the company of Churchill's wife, Sarah. The coup was complete. At this point James suffered what was almost a complete nervous collapse. He tried to flee the country disguised as the footman to Sir Edward Hales, a loyal and long-standing servant to the Crown and known Catholic. They went aboard a small 30-ton boat and attempted to escape down the Thames early on the morning of 12 December. But it seems that someone must have betrayed them, because their boat was intercepted off Sheerness by about forty local fishermen in three smacks. James was not recognised at first, perhaps because by this time he was looking so ill and distraught as well as unshaven, but Sir Edward Hales was identified, and both men were apprehended and taken to Faversham. More than 300 guineas in ready cash was found in the men's luggage, which money was promptly seized. James was later to complain about how the fishermen 'carried themselves very brutish and indecently to him'. His complaints fell on deaf ears.

Captain Marsh, the owner of the local brewery, now in the possession of Shepherd Neame, came to view the prisoners and recognised James. Both men were placed under close arrest and lodged in the Queen's Arms. The Earl of Winchilsea was sent for. He was Lord Lieutenant of Kent, and a stout Anglican. He lived in nearby Canterbury, so it did not take him long to arrive. James pleaded that he might be allowed to flee the country under cover of darkness in the customs house's boat but Winchilsea was not to be persuaded. James was returned to Whitehall under armed escort, where he was delivered into the hands of William, while Sir Edward Hales was taken to Maidstone gaol.

One of the ironies of this somewhat desperate and farcical episode is that the last thing William wanted right then was to deal with the problem of what should happen to James. Therefore he contrived to allow him to escape a second time, on this occasion via Rochester and with greater success. William had very wisely decided that it was preferable to have James abroad than to make a martyr of him by cutting off his head. And so James crossed the Channel yet again, towards his third and final exile. He landed at Ambleteuse and made his way via Abbeville to Paris, where Louis XIV of France graciously received him and offered him the Château de Saint-Germain-en-Laye as a temporary residence. James was to remain there for the last twelve years of his life.

Pepys had seen which way the wind was blowing even before the final days of James's frenetic dithering. He had accompanied James as far as Windsor, when James had first set off to meet up with Churchill. It was there that he left him to continue the journey by himself. But before the two men had separated Pepys presented his king with a bill for £28,007 2s 1¼d for past services rendered. It was a colossal sum of money and it was very like Pepys to calculate it down to the last farthing. James signed it. Pepys took it back to Buckingham Street with him, but the bill was never honoured.

Pepys was out of office and was to spend the rest of his days fulminating against the inadequacies of the current administration, rearranging his much-loved collection of books, and failing to write his complete history of the English navy, an endeavour in which he was encouraged by his friend John Evelyn.

John Churchill was to rise to become the Duke of Buckingham and owner of Blenheim Palace. John Berry continued to enjoy his lands in Kent. And the luckless George Legge was put in the Tower of London, where he soon fell ill and died.

31

CHARTWELL

Winston Churchill moves restlessly from study to library and back again. He is in his beloved Chartwell House, out of office and out of funds. To help pay the bills, he is writing another of his weighty histories. This time it is a four-volume biography of his lineal ancestor, John Churchill, Duke of Marlborough. He has come to that interesting episode early in John Churchill's career when the *Gloucester* sank. Winston is aware of the many historians down the centuries who have written about that catastrophe, more celebrated names than perhaps have written on any other shipwreck. He is familiar with the accounts by Burnet, Ailesbury, Oldmixon, Lediard, Macaulay and Chesterton – to name just a few. He sits at his large mahogany desk, which is positioned by the window and overlooks the garden. He starts to write his own version. He scribbles hastily, perhaps too hastily.

He begins by making a point of correcting 'previous histories' for placing the Leman and Ower sandbanks 'off the Humber', stating in a footnote that 'they are actually thirty miles to the south of it'.[1] In reality, the distance is more like 80 miles. He then compounds the error by placing the Leman, bizarrely, 'three miles off Cromer', when it is in fact nearer 30. Unfortunately, it is not just his map reading that is at fault. He states 'the sea was calm' when the logbooks and journals of the ships involved make it quite clear that conditions were extremely choppy. He also makes the mistake of thinking George Legge was saved in the same boat as James when it is evident from Pepys's account that he went off in a different boat and was taken into the *Katherine*. His remarks on the number of lives lost is similarly cavalier. He states that 'forty were saved out of the three hundred souls on board'. A considered analysis of contemporary accounts would suggest that around 150 people drowned out of approximately 330 on board.[2]

None of the above errors are of particular importance but when it comes to making a judgement on James's behaviour during the sinking, and consequent upon that, on his entire character, then accuracy is vital. Churchill's main source is the private papers of John Churchill's wife, Sarah. He quotes her version in full and declares at the end, 'There can be no doubt that this is the real story.'[3]

Actually, there can be every doubt. Sarah wrote her account in her eighties, more than fifty years after the event, and long after she and her husband had abandoned the Stuart cause in favour of the House of Orange. It is worth examining her criticisms of James's actions.

She blames the large loss of life on James 'obstinacy and cruelty' in not abandoning the ship earlier:

> If he would have been persuaded to go off himself at first, when it was certain the ship could not be saved, the Duke of Marlborough was of the opinion that there would not have been a man lost.[4]

This is clearly an absurd exaggeration, but the accusations against James of indecisiveness and delay had predated his loss of the throne.

Just a few days after the sinking, James Houblon had voiced similar rumours about James procrastinating unnecessarily:

> Some thinke the Dukes heate and Courage to save the ship, made him stay too long Abord and over look the thoughts of saving the men who knew their Desperate Condition but would not (in Good manners to him) provide for their safety while he staid with them.[5]

Sir John Berry had also delicately intimated in his 'Narrative' that perhaps James lingered longer than was wise. The most damning evidence for delay, however, comes from the son of James's most stalwart supporter. William Legge, writing in 1723, in order to defend his father's reputation concerning the *Gloucester* wreck, provides some new and damaging information:

> After the ship had struck, he [Sir George Legge] several times pressed the Duke to get into the boat, who refused to do it, telling him that if he were gone, nobody would take care of the ship, which he had hopes might be saved, if she were not abandoned. But my father, finding she was ready to sink, told him if he staid any longer they should be obliged to force him out: upon which the Duke ordered a strong box to be lifted into the boat; which, besides being extremely weighty, took up a good deal of time, as well as room. My father, with some warmth, asked him whether there was anything in it worth a man's life. The Duke answered that there were things of so great consequence, both to the King and himself, that he would hazard his own life rather than it should be lost.[6]

This strongbox and what it may have contained has been the subject of much subsequent speculation. The most common presumption is not that it contained his gold or his jewels, but his memoirs. James was known to take very seriously the business of recording the details of every passage of his life for posterity. He was a compulsive memorialist, covering thousands of pages with his own version of history. If it is true that the strongbox contained his own writings then his efforts were ultimately in vain. These diaries, that he was to take lovingly to France with him when he fled the country in 1688, did not survive the French Revolution.

But the immediate point is not whether James's journals were preserved, but how credible is this story of the strongbox in the first place. It is told in some detail and it is difficult to believe that George Legge, or his son, would have entirely made up the story. On the other hand, Gunman, who received the Duke of York onto the *Mary*, makes no mention of any strongbox, 'The Duke came on board just with a coat and breeches on, which was all he saved, – plate, linen, clothes, money, etc., all gone to the value of above £5,000.'[7] This might suggest that the story was a fabrication, but James himself, in his letter to Sir Lawrence Hyde of 9 May 1682, provides some interesting corroborating evidence not only to the strongbox's existence, but also to its contents:

> I was yesterday at Council, where I acquainted them with the choice his Majesty had made of his great officers, and gave those that were present their warrants, which I took out of my strong box when the ship struck, and put them in my pocket, and so they escaped being wet.[8]

There is no mention here of trying to save the strongbox itself, merely the most important of its contents. The implication is that the strongbox went down with the ship.

Even presuming that James did waste valuable minutes attempting to remove his strongbox full of state papers, how culpable does this make him? He was clearly not guilty of trying to save his own personal effects or money at the expense of sailors' lives, a common enough occurrence in maritime disasters. And it can reasonably be argued that his concern that the proper processes of government should be continued uninterrupted when he finally reached Edinburgh was a respectable one. It is also quite possible that there were confidential papers in the box that James did not wish to risk falling into the wrong hands. How could he be sure if he left it behind him that others might not rifle it or take possession of it? The looting of sinking ships was not uncommon. James may well, and not unreasonably, have considered it to be a dereliction of his royal duty to leave the most important contents of the box behind.

This certainly seems to be his attitude in his affronted response, as described by William Legge. No doubt James's behaviour was exasperating to the likes of George Legge, Churchill and Berry, who could see discipline beginning to break down, but it hardly amounts to Sarah Churchill's accusation of 'a false courage to make it appear, as he thought he had what he had not'.[9] James was in the unenviable situation of being damned if he did and damned if he didn't.

There is also the question of just how long a delay was incurred by this removal of despatches. The various journals, letters and logbooks written by eyewitnesses show a remarkable degree of consistency on how long the *Gloucester* remained above water. From the point of striking to the point of sinking was no more than forty-five minutes to an hour at the most. The *Gloucester* beat along the sand for some minutes while those aboard were woken from their sleep, got dressed hurriedly and came up on deck. By the time that it had been established that there was 8ft of water in the hold, at least a quarter of an hour had already elapsed. After the duke's shallop had gone it was probably another fifteen minutes before the *Gloucester* came off the bank.

According to John Berry's account, and it is Berry who provides the best chronology for these events, the duke was already on board Captain Gunman's yacht before the *Gloucester* came off the sand. It must have taken the best part of fifteen minutes to transit the quarter of a mile between the *Mary* and the *Gloucester* in those rough seas. After the *Gloucester* came off, it righted itself, and those aboard spent some time still trying to save it, for it was anchored and the head turned into the wind. It was only then that it sank, albeit very suddenly. This sequence only leaves fifteen minutes at the outside for the entire process of disembarking the duke. Any delay cannot have been more than five or ten minutes at most. It no doubt seemed like an age for those who were anxious for him to be gone so that they could set about saving their own lives, but it would hardly have enabled more boats to go back and forth between the yachts and the stricken *Gloucester*.

James was clearly sensitive on the question of the number of lives lost and whether or not more might have been done to save them. In his memoirs he makes several counteraccusations of his own. In James Macpherson's *Extracts from the Life of James II*, he remarks, 'many more might have been saved, had it not been for the timorousness of the boatmen, hindering them from coming near the ship, when they thought her about to sink, for fear of sinking with her'.[10] But again, this looks like another example of needing to find someone to blame rather than a careful analysis of events.

Sir James Dick mentions that 'four yachts came up as near as they durst and sent off their boats to help'.[11] We know that John Berry escaped in Captain Wyborne's boat sent from the *Happy Return* shortly before the *Gloucester* went down, a boat of which Wyborne himself took command. We know that Sir James Dick got off in a boat that went to Captain Sanderson's yacht, the *Charlotte*, but we cannot be sure whether this boat was one of *Gloucester*'s own or came from the *Charlotte*. We know from Pepys that George Legge got off in a boat that went to the *Katherine* and that the *Katherine*'s own boat was 'sunk by our side, and her men with much difficulty saved', which would suggest that the boat that saved Legge most probably belonged to the *Gloucester*.[12] This is also supported by Lieutenant Wetwang's log, which records taking in 'the Duke's shallop, the *Gloucester* barge, and ours, and tooke the *Gloucester* long boat in a tow'.[13] We also know from Gunman that he sent a boat from the *Mary* and that this picked up twenty-six men. Finally, we know that Dick saw one boat overturned with considerable loss of life. Everything considered, it does not really seem as if the boatmen did not do their best to effect a rescue in very difficult conditions.

The second defence that James offers in his memoirs is that if the *Gloucester* had been anchored when it was on the sandbank there would have been no loss of life. 'Had not too much haste been made to clear her all the passengers and seamen might have been saved.'[14]

The advantages of early anchoring are obvious. It would have allowed the carpenters and officers to gauge accurately how dangerous a condition the *Gloucester* was in, and if the damage looked as if it was fatal, then at least it would only have sunk in 3 fathoms of water and the decks would have remained above sea level. This might sound like a sensible manoeuvre in theory, but in reality it was not quite so simple. John Berry has provided the answer in his 'Narrative': 'The lifting of the sea forced her off the sand, and she went into fifteen fathom water, before we could let go one anchor, which proved the loss of many poor men's lives.'[15] The failure to successfully anchor in such adverse circumstances is hardly a surprise.

Of course, if it was not the timorousness of the boatmen that caused such high loss of life or the failure to anchor on the sandbank itself, then James's fallback position was always that the wreck would never have happened in the first place if not for the error of the pilot, James Ayres.

Sarah Churchill's most stinging remark is reserved for James's supposed regard for saving the lives of his dogs and his priests at the expense of everyone else. She endorses what the historian Thomas Lediard has to say on this subject. Lediard in turn has got his 'facts' from Bishop Burnet's *History of His Own Time*.

Burnet was short, plump, witty, malicious, extremely clever and a devoted gossip. In his history he wrote:

> The Duke got into a boat and took care of his dogs, and some unknown persons, who were taken, from that earnest care of his, to be his priests. The long boat went off with very few in her, though she might have carried off eighty more than she did. One hundred and fifty persons perished: some of them men of great quality. But the Duke took no notice of this cruel neglect, which was laid chiefly to Leg's charge.[16]

Burnet started his history in 1683, the year after the *Gloucester* sinking, but it was not published until well after James had fled the country. It was Burnet more than anyone who was responsible for the new version of the *Gloucester* sinking, the version that was to become standard for the next 300 years. But again, it is worth looking closely at the substance of his claims.

Sir John Berry is quite explicit on the question of whether or not the duke's boat went off only half full. 'The barge was hoisted out, and his Highness took as many persons of quality with him in the boat as she could carry.'[17] Pepys provides some revealing further detail:

> The Duke himself, by the single care of Colonel Legg, was first sent off in a boat, with none but Mr Churchill in her, to prevent his being oppressed with men labouring their escapes: some two or three, however, did fling themselves after him into her, and my Lord President of Scotland, by the Duke's advice, endeavoured it, but, falling short, was taken up out of the water by him.[18]

There was clearly a pressing need to get the duke away from the sinking ship before a crowd of people rushed his boat, endangering everyone. Pepys alludes to an increasing loss of discipline, but the duke, far from being selfishly preoccupied with his own safety, is presented as actively giving encouragement to others to join him in his barge, in particular the Earl of Winton, Lord President of Scotland and the Marquis of Montrose. It is Sir James Dick's account of the evacuation that is, as usual, the most graphic:

> When the Duke had got his clothes on, he enquired how things stood, she being sunk nine feet of water in her hold, and the sea fast coming in at the gun ports, and all the seamen and passengers were not at command, every man studying his own safety, forced the Duke to go out at the large window of the cabin, where his little boat was ordained quietly to attend him, lest the passengers and seamen should have thronged so in upon him, as to drown the boat; which was accordingly so conveyed , as that none but Earl Winton, the President of the Session, with two of his bed chamber men went with him, but were forced to draw their swords to hold people off.[19]

Clearly there was a considerable degree of chaos on board, and in this situation, James's safety was prioritised, but this is a far cry from making him guilty of the cowardly selfishness suggested by Burnet, Lediard and Sarah Churchill. Burnet suggests that eighty more men could have been saved in the duke's boat had he not abandoned the ship so peremptorily. This is nonsense. The duke escaped in a small barge or shallop that was suspended beneath the great cabin of the ship and which even at full capacity would not have held more than a dozen people. It is significant that the observant Sir Dick refers to it as a 'little' boat, not a long boat. Mary of Modena states in her memoirs that 'the Duke's boat held but six persons, besides the rowers'.[20]

Ten or twelve people is indeed about as many as a boat of this kind could be expected to carry. It is known that the Earl of Winton and the Marquis of Montrose together with two bedchamber men, one of whom was John Churchill, were all in the boat with James, which, with the rowers, would have made it already almost full to capacity. Contrary to James neglecting the welfare of others, it appears he spent some time summoning key members of his household and future administration to his side. William Legge, not himself an eyewitness but defending his father's reputation some years after the event, states how, 'before he [James] went off, he enquired for Lord Roxburgh, and Lord Obrian, but the confusion and hurry was so great, that they could not be found'.[21] He also called out for the Earl of Aberdeen to be saved, referring to him as 'my Lord Chancellor', an appointment that was planned, but which he had not yet taken up.[22]

As for the damaging smear that James cared only for saving his dogs and his priests, this was as ill-founded as the argument that the boat he went off in could have held eighty more, but it was eagerly repeated by Sarah Churchill, and it has been often requoted since. It was obviously intended as an attack on James's Catholicism but there is no evidence that any priests went in the boat with him. The only priest that is known to have been travelling on the *Gloucester* was Pere Ronche, Mary Modena's almoner. None of the eyewitness accounts make any mention of him, but Mary's memoirs refer to him as having been saved on a plank. As she was herself a fervent Catholic, if James had taken him into his boat with him it seems very probable that she would not have been too embarrassed to mention it. There was also a ship's chaplain, Nathaniel Adams, who had only been appointed to the *Gloucester* on 19 April 1682. Whether he survived the sinking is not known, but he would not have been a Catholic.

It is possible that the rumour about priests had its roots in the story of Thomas Jory, or Jewry. The Earl of Ailesbury, in his memoirs, relates the following anecdote:

There were about four in the shallop besides the Duke next the stern. A bold, saucy fellow, Tho. Jewry, a foot huntsman, had the address to get into the shallop and lay under where the Duke sat, and it was imagined that some baggage had been thrust in, but they perceiving him at last, the mariners would have thrown him into the sea, but the Duke forbad them, saying he was a Christian, a very pious and Christian thought but ill interpreted.[23]

This suggests that it might have been James's remark about the man being a Christian that led to the ill-founded rumour of priests being given special favour. Thomas Jewry was certainly not a priest and appears quite independently of the *Gloucester* tragedy in a list of members of James's household dated Christmas 1677. Here his surname is spelt 'Jory' and he is described as one of the huntsmen to the foxhounds, as Ailesbury had indicated.

As for the dogs, William Legge disposes of this malicious rumour in short order:

> And I believe his reflection upon the duke for his care of the dogs to be as ill-grounded, for I remember a story (that was in everybody's mouth at that time) of a struggle that happened for a plank between Sir Charles Scarborough, and the duke's dog Mumper, which convinces me that the dogs were left to take care of themselves (as he did), if there were any more on board; which I never heard until the bishop's [Burnet's] story book was published.[24]

But the truth no longer mattered. It is clear that, as soon as James lost his throne, the loss of the *Gloucester* was widely reinterpreted in a way that suited the Whig faction, who were, after all, the victors. The sinking from then on was to be seen as emblematic of the near sinking of the 'Ship of State'.

This rewriting of history is nowhere more evident than in the new paintings that were produced. One of the most striking hangs in the National Maritime Museum. It is attributed to the Dutch artist Johan Danckerts, although it cannot have been painted by him. It shows James in the stern of his boat cuddling his spaniel. A man who may well have been a priest is seated beside him, and various members of his entourage are wielding axes and swords at those hapless survivors struggling to get out of the water and haul themselves to safety. It is a damning indictment of James's behaviour. It is also completely historically inaccurate in numerous respects. It shows, for instance, the sandbank sticking in a mound out of the sea with numerous figures walking upon it, when in fact the sandbanks even at their shallowest were always covered by 10 to 12ft of water. It also shows two ships with double tiers of portholes in the background, when in fact only the *Happy Return*, fitting this description, was in the vicinity.

This piece of propaganda cannot conceivably have been painted by Danckerts because he died while James was still on the throne. It would have been very rash for anyone to have commissioned such a painting at such a time, and equally foolhardy of Danckerts to execute it. It is, however, a very dramatic and revealing political statement.

The wise words of David Hume in his *History of England*, published in 1754, are well worth remembering in the context of James, and the question of his responsibility for those who died in the *Gloucester* sinking: 'Every action of every eminent person, during this period, is so liable to be misinterpreted by faction, that we ought to be very cautious in passing judgement on too slight evidence.'

32

PORTSMOUTH REVISITED

In all the swirling fog of blame and counter-blame that surrounds the sinking of the *Gloucester*, there is one obvious question that no one ever seems to have asked. What condition was it in when it left Portsmouth dockyard in early May 1682? Furthermore, and rather less obviously, could there be a connection between its condition and Samuel Pepys's decision not to sail on it? The answer, if it is to be found anywhere, lies in the murky waters of Portsmouth dockyard.

The *Gloucester* had been built at Limehouse on the River Thames by the shipwright William Graves in 1654. It had been part of a huge naval building programme undertaken by Cromwell's Commonwealth in the early 1650s that outstripped the capacity of the Royal Dockyards and which explains the use of a private contractor. Mr Graves charged £5,473 15*s* for the completed hull, which was a rather more competitive price than the cost of similar ships being built simultaneously in the Royal Dockyards at Chatham and Portsmouth. The debate about the respective merits of private enterprise versus state monopoly was just as hot a topic in the late seventeenth century as in the early twenty-first. Graves was part of a family dynasty of shipbuilders and had inherited the business from his father, John.

The *Gloucester* was 26 years old when it set out on its final voyage and it might be considered strange that the safety of the heir to the throne was to be entrusted to such ancient timbers but its age was not that unusual. Of the four other Portsmouth-based ships detailed for Scotland, the *Happy Return*, which was Pepys's first choice of accommodation, was built in the same year as the *Gloucester*; the *Ruby* and the *Pearl* were both three years older, and the Dartmouth was only one year younger, having been finished in 1655. They all continued into the 1690s and beyond, and the *Ruby* was still afloat in 1707, when it was captured by the French.

Many of the Commonwealth-period vessels built in the early 1650s seem to have been particularly well constructed. Generally speaking, this was a tough and durable class of ship. It was not the age of the *Gloucester* that was the problem. What made it a very odd choice of ship to carry the heir to the throne was its career history over the previous ten years. A careful examination of Navy Board letters, frequently written by Pepys himself, reveal a huge question mark over its seaworthiness.

In the autumn of 1672, shortly after the Battle of Solebay, the *Gloucester* underwent a major refit but the quality of the work that was carried out at that time was soon being questioned. There was much controversy about leakiness in the bows. From 18 September to 17 October 1673, the *Gloucester* went back into dry dock at Woolwich and underwent further remedial work. This was overseen by the Master Shipwright Phineas Pett, one of the ubiquitous Pett family that dominates shipbuilding throughout the seventeenth century. Pett later gave a detailed account of the work he carried out:

> The ship being complained for a leak about her bows we did not only caulk her all over, fearing she might be faulty in other places, but we strictly searched her bows and hoodings ends, and that we might find out her defects in that place (there being no carpenter belonging to her he being some time before deceased) by the best light we could get we then proceeded, according to the most rational way, to strengthen her bows. We took off the cheeks of the lead under one of which we found a very great and dangerous leak for the scouring of which we shifted one of the harpins being defective at the end, and brought on for the more firm fastening her stem and bows together a pair of good

navel hoods without board and an excellent breasthook within board, bolted thereon and thereon into them to bind altogether, and there being no visible defect in the stem or head we proceeded to bring on the cheeks again all which being formed with some additional bolts and other strengthening works about her as knees and some standards upon the finishing the same we launched the ship as being put into a condition fit for the sea.[1]

It sounds like a thorough job, and Pett clearly considered it to be so. In December of that same year, the *Gloucester*, under Captain Sir William Jennens, was detailed to join Captain Rooth's fleet in the Downs and sail to the Straits of Gibraltar to carry out vital defence work. Sir Jennens wrote to Samuel Pepys, who was then Secretary at the Admiralty, requesting an urgent supply of victuals and 80–100 more men. But the *Gloucester* never got past Portsmouth. Once again it was proving very leaky about the bows and had to put into Portsmouth dockyard for yet further repairs. It was suspected that the main stem of the ship might be defective.

On 2 February 1674, despairing of the *Gloucester* ever being ready for sea service, Pepys wrote to Captain Rooth enclosing orders for him to take the *Nonsuch* 'in the room of the Gloucester'.[2] On 18 August 1674, Pepys wrote to the Navy Board, requesting them 'to enquire into the occasion of the leakiness of the Gloucester, whereby she was hindered of proceeding to the Southwest with Captain Rooth'.[3] He wanted to know why, when the ship had only just been repaired, it was already leaking again so profusely, and in particular why Mr Phineas Pett had not stripped the stem and examined it more carefully.

Pett replied, reasonably enough, 'that no workman into whose hands this ship should come to repair could presume (without great reflections upon those that rebuilt her) in the least to suspect any defect in the stem of that ship'.[4] He had not removed the main knee and head to examine the stem because frequent removal was 'a palpable bane and ruin to most ships'.[5] When she had been rebuilt, she had been completely stripped and a new head put in. Any defects in the stem should have been evident then, he argued. If there were not any defects at the time of rebuilding, then the *Gloucester* must have been damaged by storm some time in the interim. His defence was vigorous and detailed. He apologised for the 'tediousness' of his lengthy reply.

In dry dock in Portsmouth, the *Gloucester*'s stem was again stripped and pronounced to be sound. The cause of the renewed leakiness was blamed on a defect in the 'manger scuppers', a fault that had been concealed by 'a thin graven board' placed over them.[6] Pett rejected this explanation. He did not believe that a thinly graven board in such a place would have escaped the attention of his caulkers, and even if it had, 'a careful and skilful carpenter upon the ship would never have suffered such a thing to have spoyled her voyage'. He concluded ominously:

> I am glad to understand that your honours have an account from Portsmouth that her stem is good, but can not but humbly acquaint your honours with my opinion that the oftener stems are wounded with new bolts for new heads, it will require more than ordinary care to keep the ship from being leaky and furthermore I have been informed sometime since the ship went from here, that the deceased carpenter had been heard to express some fears of a defect in her stem which I can not in faithfulness omit to acquaint your honours that there may be more than ordinary scrutinous observation of the condition of the stem both within board and without now the lead is taken off.

Pepys writes sarcastically to the Navy Board 'that the miscarriage of the *Gloucester* was excused by the death of the old carpenter'.[7] The miscarriage being referred to here was, of course, the failure of her sailing with the rest of the fleet in 1673, and not her eventual foundering. It is, for all that, a most revealing and ominous phrase.

There the matter was left and apparently forgotten, but almost certainly not by Pepys, who had a prodigious memory for every last detail relating to naval ships. Forgotten or not, the *Gloucester* remained languishing 'in ordinary' in Portsmouth Harbour for the next eight years. It had no captain, no officers, just a skeleton crew of seven to nine men to keep it clean and tidy and look after the superficial fabric. On 20 December 1677 it is included among those ships 'greatly out of repair' that 'will require much time and charge to fit them for sea service'.[8] Then, extraordinarily, in April 1682, after more than eight years of rotting in harbour, it is selected as the ideal ship to convey James to Scotland and bring back his pregnant wife.

As if all this was not bad enough, there was another major issue relating to the *Gloucester*'s safety credentials that was similarly swept under the royal carpet at the time of its loss. The Restoration period was a time of great scientific experiment and advance, with new inventions the order of the day. Progressive men such as Pepys and his great friend Sir Anthony Deane, took a lively interest in all this modern rationalist thinking, which – it was confidently considered – would eventually solve many of man's problems. One of these problems, which particularly exercised the lively intelligence of Pepys, was the corrosive effect of shipworm and weed on a wooden hull. The traditional method of preservation was to grave the ship in dry dock and apply a mixture of rosin, whale oil and sulphur, and on occasion to sheath the hull with a thin layer of wooden boarding.

In the 1660s, the entrepreneur Sir Phillip Howard came up with the idea of using lead rather than wood for a far more durable result. The idea of lead sheathing was actually not a new one. The Romans had used it, as had the Spanish and Portuguese in the sixteenth century. The Englishman John Hawkins, a naval captain, administrator and the younger brother of Sir William, however, was not impressed, 'it is nothing durable but subject to many casualties',[9] was his terse comment, and so the Elizabethans did not copy their Iberian counterparts. Lead sheathing was not considered again for use on Royal Navy ships until Sir Phillip Howard revealed his new thinking on the subject to Anthony Deane and Samuel Pepys in 1669.

The novelty of Howard's approach was that the sheet lead was to be produced by milling and rolling rather than casting. This enabled a much thinner, more pliable and, most crucially, cheaper product to be created. Deane, who at the time was master shipwright at Portsmouth and so an influential player when it came to commissioning new products for the navy, was impressed by what he saw. In 1670, Howard formed a new company, which was granted rights to the sheathing of all Royal Navy ships, a monopoly protected by an Act of Parliament. Pepys's lifelong friend and protégé, William Hewer, with whom Pepys was later to share a house, was a major investor, owning one twelfth of the new company. It was no doubt anticipated that a fortune would be made in short order. It seems highly likely that Deane, and perhaps Pepys as well, were also investors. A fourth rate, the *Phoenix*, recently built by Anthony Deane, was selected to trial the new method.

Not everyone considered lead to be a cure all. There were those in Parliament, when the subject was debated, who criticised:

> … its excess in charge above the current method, its rough lying on a ship's sides to the prejudice of their sailing, its liableness to galling from the cables, and cracking when brought aground; its tediousness in bringing on or off; aptness to foul and difficulty in cleaning; lastly, its undurableness and doubtful efficacy in what was chiefly expected of it against the worm.[10]

But the doubters were not listened to. In 1673, the hull of the *Phoenix* was examined and the verdict was highly favourable. Before very long a number of His Majesty's ships were being sheathed in Howard's new lead product. Phineas Pett was an enthusiast and it was used in his repairs on the *Gloucester*, even though it was not one of the original twenty Royal Navy ships to be selected for sheathing.

The euphoria did not last long. In 1675, the *Henrietta*, which had also been recently sheathed in lead, had its rudder sheer off. The irons on the stern post had broken away. It could have been disastrous if Sir John Narborough, the captain, had not been able to ship a temporary rudder in its place. The following year the *Phoenix* reported a similar problem, 'we were coming home in a storm of wind, reeving our fore course when our rudder snapped off, the water's edge being worm eaten right through'.[11] Again emergency action had to be taken and the ship was lucky to survive. Soon other lead-sheathed ships were suffering from similar defects. As if this was not enough, an official report contained the following worrying observation from 1675:

> A new cry and of quite a different kind breaks out from abroad, of a quality discovered in our lead sheathing, tending (if not timely prevented) to the utter destruction of his Majesty's ships, namely that of eating into and wasting their rudder irons and bolts underwater, to such a degree and in so short a space of time, as had never been observed on any unsheathed or wood sheathed ship.[12]

Sir Phillip Howard argued that it was the fitting of the iron pintles that held the rudders in place that was at fault and that the lead sheathing was nothing to do with the problem. But by the end of the decade, most of the lead-sheathed ships were suffering from their iron work being eaten away; not just the rudder fastenings, but even the iron bolts and nails that held the ship's hull together.

In 1678 the Navy Board ordered that no more ships should be sheathed in lead until 'a more certain knowledge can be had of the true ground of the said evil'.[13] Howard and Deane continued to experiment with possible solutions to the difficulty but without success. What neither man understood was that the lead in contact with iron and seawater set up an electrolytic action that literally dissolved the ironwork.

The suspension of the experiment did not mean that those ships that had had lead sheathing were immediately stripped of it. The *Gloucester* was one of those still partly sheathed in lead when it set out for Scotland. It had shown no adverse effects because it had not been anywhere since the work had been carried out on it. Knowing about its lead sheathing, however, it no longer seems so surprising that when it struck the sandbank, its rudder immediately broke off, its seams came apart, and the ingress of water was rapid. If it had been a sounder ship it would doubtless have lasted much longer above water. Indeed, it might have come off the bank relatively unscathed.

In the summer of 1682, shortly after the *Gloucester* sinking, the Navy Board instituted an enquiry into the use of lead sheathing that nowhere mentioned the loss of the *Gloucester*, but the final report, dated 28 October 1682, decided against any further use of milled lead.

There is one further curious twist to this story of the *Gloucester's* structural weakness before it set sail on its final voyage. The most important and also the best paid of those men who were in charge of the *Gloucester* during the later years while it was laid up in Portsmouth Harbour was John Brookes, the carpenter. He had been in the navy since the Restoration, first starting out as a carpenter in the yard at Woolwich, then serving as ship's carpenter on both the frigate *Paul* and the *Royal Katherine* during the Dutch wars, before being appointed master carpenter on the *Assurance* in 1678, under Captain Stephen Akarman. He did not serve long under Akarman before he was transferred to the *Gloucester*. A few days after the *Gloucester* had been chosen to take James to Scotland, but before it actually set out, Brookes was dismissed from his position and summoned to Whitehall. Quite what misdemeanour Brookes had committed is unclear but a clue lies in a petition he sent to the Admiralty a few months beforehand, dated 30 December 1681. In this he writes:

> ... your petitioner came up from the ship in harbour at Portsmouth by leave to visit his family who lie in a sick condition and to dispatch some concerns in London, but your petitioner's leave being expired your petitioner would gladly by your honours favour have some time longer.[14]

Whether or not he took that extra time without permission or whether he was guilty of some other fault is not revealed in the scanty evidence that survives. He must have partially acquitted himself of whatever wrongdoing he was accused of in his interview, because he was subsequently reappointed to the *Gloucester*, but only as the second carpenter, James Ford being appointed above him. Brookes was, however, to retain his previous rate of pay.

To have two carpenters on full pay on one third-rate ship was most unusual. Perhaps it reflected a certain unease among some of the Admiralty commissioners about the former leakiness of the ship. In the circumstances they may have considered two carpenters to be better than one. Possibly they questioned Brookes about the *Gloucester*'s soundness, as well as examining him on the disciplinary charges, and decided that on balance his experience of the ship might be of value.

Whatever the explanation for the two carpenters, Ford was to drown when the *Gloucester* sank and Brookes was rescued. However, unlike most of the other skilled non-commissioned officers that survived the sinking, Brookes was not given another position. On the contrary, he spent the next several years petitioning for a new post and being refused repeatedly. The man who consistently blocked his reappointment was Samuel Pepys. Brookes supplied numerous character references. Richard Holden, vicar of Deptford Church, attested to the fact that he 'was, during his abode with us, a constant comer to Divine Service, and is well affected to his Majesty and the present government in both church and state'.[15] Brookes himself in his constant appeals made much of how he had 'lost all his clothes, tools and other things of considerable value in your Majesty's last voyage to Scotland'. He attached various sworn statements to the effect that he led 'a holy and sober life'. He referred bitterly to how the previous petitions he had sent had all been handed on to 'Mr Secretary Pepys, who hath ordered nothing for your petitioner'.

So what had Pepys got against the unfortunate Brookes? Part of the explanation may lie in a letter sent to Pepys by Captain Stephen Akarman dated January 1686, and written from Chatham. It is entitled by Akarman, 'An impartial account of the behaviour of John Brooke's'. He starts off by saying:

> As to his loyalty have nothing to say against him, as to his sobriety he would sometimes be in drinke and not fit for serving or able to commande himselfe. And as to his diligence and capacity have nothing to say for him but do believe he is not so capable as a carpenter as any one of his majesty's ships [carpenters] ought to be.[16]

Pretty damning stuff.

So, it seems that James was dispatched to Scotland on a ship that had been laid up for more than eight years, that was notorious for its leakiness in the bows, that had been subject to a disastrous experiment with a new kind of lead sheathing, and on which the carpenter, most recently responsible for its structural care before departure, was a negligent drunk. It was, of course, not Pepys's decision to select the *Gloucester* for the Scottish voyage; he had been out of office for the previous three years. But he, more than anyone alive, knew all about the *Gloucester*'s structural infirmities. He no doubt chose to stay silent because by the time he learnt of the *Gloucester*'s selection, there was little he could do to change the choice of ship. It was already far too late in the day to suggest an alternative. Besides, it was most unlikely that James, notorious for his physical recklessness, would have taken any notice of such fears even if Pepys had chosen to speak out. James believed his life was safeguarded by divine providence, not the precautions of men. So Pepys chose to stay silent and hope for the best. His privileged knowledge does, however, put a very different gloss on his otherwise strange determination to travel in a different vessel himself, and his vindictiveness to those he considered were to blame.

33

FISH STREET

Fish Street used to be situated just to the north of Old London Bridge, with the Sun Tavern at the lower end, close to the waterside. It was a favourite haunt of sea captains, ship builders, merchants and Navy Board employees. Pepys was a great enthusiast. On 6 November 1661, he went there straight from the office to eat pickled oysters and anchovies with Mr Furbisher and Mr Davenport and drink 'a great deal of wine'.[1] Two days later he was back again, this time to be 'very merry' with Sir J. Minnes, Sir William Batten, Captain Stoakes and Captain Clerke. Within a week he was there a third time to enjoy 'a most excellent dinner ... a pie of such pleasant variety of good things as in all my life I never tasted'.

During these years of Pepys's early visits, the Sun was owned by Thomas Pownall. He used to import his own clarets and he had the finer ones decanted into the heavy glass bottles that his smarter customers favoured. These were squat and onion-shaped, with flat bottoms and long necks. It was a very practical design, for the bottles did not topple over, either in the bustle of a busy inn or on board a rolling ship.

Glass had only recently come into fashion but it very quickly became the must-have container for a vintage wine. Pownall emblazoned his best bottles with a crest of the sun and his own initials 'TP' configured on either side. Vintners were fond of stamping their own insignia on their premium products; they understood the benefits of clever marketing. When the nearby Bombay Dock was dredged sometime last century, the shattered remains of just such a bottle were recovered from the mud, the remnants of some 350-year-old revelry. The shards are now preserved in the Museum of London.

Thomas Pownall was the landlord of the Sun Tavern from the days of the Civil War until his death in 1669. A few years later, Pepys's lifelong friend, and another habitué of the Sun, Sir Anthony Deane, enjoyed his visits there so much he decided to buy it.

Deane was a ship builder and designer best remembered for his *Doctrine of Naval Architecture*, which was dedicated to Pepys. For many years he was the commissioner in charge of the Portsmouth dockyards, where a number of new navy ships were built by him, but his business interests were not limited simply to navy contracts or building ships for the private sector. Like Pepys, he was also a member of the Royal Society and like so many of his contemporaries he saw himself as being something of a scientist. He invented a new cannon called the Punchinello. He was involved in Lord Howard's scheme for sheathing ships in lead. He had his finger in many different pies. He was also the commissioner in charge of the navy's victualling.

It was probably this last interest that prompted him to buy the Sun Tavern. It is highly likely, then, that the wine taken on board the *Gloucester* on its fatal voyage was supplied by Deane and, as it happens, in 2007, a bottle bearing the insignia of the Sun Tavern was discovered lying, perfectly intact, on the Leman and Ower sandbanks.

34

THE LEMAN AND OWER REVISITED

In early 2007, a group of shipwreck enthusiasts were diving the Leman and Ower sandbanks when they noticed some old timbers protruding from the sand. The banks themselves did not move more than a few centimetres a year but the sand waves that covered the seabed between the sandbanks could be shifted 2 or 3 metres in depth by a single storm, covering and uncovering old and long-forgotten artefacts. On this occasion the divers were lucky. The recent storms had revealed a wreck.

Since scuba diving became a popular mass sport in the early 1960s, there had been many searches for the wreck of the *Gloucester*. Most of them had been stimulated by the erroneous belief that James's lost strongbox had contained either his gold or the Crown jewels. In fact, the wreck contained historical artefacts of far greater value.

The early searches had concentrated on an area to the south and west of the western end of the Leman sandbank. This particular search area was not chosen randomly, it was based on the information supplied by John Berry in his 'Narrative', 'we run ashore upon the W. part of the Lemon … whilst our rudder held we bore away West'.[1]

As always, however, when it comes to searching for old wrecks, nothing is that simple. There are two problems with this search area. Firstly, it ignores the fact that the names Leman and Ower were interchangeable in the late seventeenth century. Berry refers to the Leman, but he may equally well have been referring to the

Ower. When he wrote his 'Narrative' the exact identity was not that important. Secondly, and more seriously, searching an area to the west and south of the Leman ignores the important clues contained in Wetwang's logbook and Gunman's journal.

After describing the saving of the shipwrecked people, Gunman made the following entry: 'at 7 oclock I set sail ... I steered away North West having the Lemon Ore my starboard side and another bank which broke on my larboard side about 4 miles asunder'.[2] The *Mary*, under Gunman's command, was anchored from half to a quarter of a mile west of the *Gloucester* shipwreck and in this statement Gunman is locating that position as lying between two parallel banks. It is also interesting that he calls one bank 'the Lemon Ore' and does not have a name for the other, suggesting that, so far as most of the navigators at this period were concerned, there was only one bank. The bank he names is the outer one, because he refers to it as being on his starboard side as he steers north-west. But he is quite definite that there was another bank to the 'larboard' of him. If the *Gloucester* came off the sandbank that it hit in a westerly direction, which it must have done, because all the eyewitnesses refer to a strong wind from the east or north-east, then the *Gloucester* must have hit the outer of the two sandbanks today called the Ower and not the inner one, today called the Leman.

Wetwang's logbook confirms Gunman's journal in locating the sinking and the rescue action as taking place between the two sandbanks. 'At half hower past eight oclock Captain came on board so I weigh'd and steard between the Lemmon and the Owrey WNW, NWbyW and NW and had from 16 to 14 fathoms, We saw both the sands breake being about 7 miles distanz one fro the other.'[3] When Wetwang remarks that the captain came on board at half past eight, he is referring to Captain Wyborne coming back to the *Happy Return* in the rescue boat with some of the survivors from the *Gloucester* wreck. Unlike Gunman, Wetwang realised that Leman and Ower were the names of the two separate sandbanks. On the other hand, he states that they were situated 7 miles distant from each other. Gunman's 4 miles distance apart is nearer the mark but it is possible that the places where Wetwang saw breaking water on the different banks was 7 miles apart.

Both these logbooks suggest that the *Gloucester* sank between the two sandbanks with a north-east or easterly wind blowing, and that the bank it actually struck must have been the outer one, today known as the Ower. This raises the question of how the *Mary*, *Gloucester* and *Happy Return* all managed to sail over the inner bank, or the Leman, without even noticing it, when they should have been taking sounding continuously. Gunman, on the *Mary*, mentions having 14 fathoms at 2 a.m. 'when we altered course from NNE to the N', and then mentions nothing further on the subject of soundings until at '5am oclocke I came into 7 fathoms of water', by which time it was already too late and the *Gloucester* was about to collide with the Ower bank. Berry, in his 'Narrative', states that just before striking they had 20 fathoms but that is all the information he gives relating to soundings. It is Lieutenant Wetwang on the *Happy Return* who provides the most detailed information: 'At 4 this morning steared N by W until 5 oclocke and had 15,7,9 and 18 fathoms the wind at East a stiff gale, at halph an hower past 5 the Glocester strocke upon the Lemmon.' This entry is very revealing. Wetwang's reference to soundings of 7 and 9 fathoms clearly suggests going over a sandbank at some time between 4 and 5 a.m. The most probable explanation is that it was the south-east end of the Leman sandbank that he was passing over when those soundings were taken.

The remarkable evidence of shallow soundings being recorded at least one hour before the *Gloucester* struck is clearly written down in Wetwang's log. So why did the *Happy Return* not fire off warning guns when it recorded standing into 7 fathoms? Perhaps the officer on watch, who could see three ships in front all safely past the bank and not firing guns, presumed there could be no danger. This does not explain, however, how it was that not one of the leading three ships, namely the *Gloucester*, the *Mary* and the *Charlotte*, appear to have been aware that they were passing over a bank at some time between 4 and 5 a.m. The *Charlotte* may perhaps be excused because as it was sailing on the *Gloucester*'s starboard bow it might just have passed to the east of the Leman sandbank and therefore might not have recorded any shallow soundings. It is difficult to see how the *Mary* and the *Gloucester*, on the other hand, could have avoided noticing it.

There are only two possible explanations. The first is that shallow soundings were recorded but those on board chose to ignore them. This seems most unlikely. We know that when the *Mary* stood into 7 fathoms at 5 a.m., it immediately bore away west and waved a Jack flag from the poop. The second explanation is that soundings were not being taken regularly enough in view of the considerable speed the ships were sailing at. This would be a very serious omission on the part of those officers in charge of both ships and it is difficult to understand why this question of soundings prior to 5 a.m. did not come up in the court martial. We do not know who was in charge of the *Gloucester*, although according to Pepys's testimony Captain Ayres had already retired to his bed. We know that William Sturgeon was the officer on watch on board the *Mary*, and we also know that he walked free from the court martial. It is surprising that Gunman, for all the flailing accusations he makes, never raises the issue. One can only presume that he knew nothing about the contents of Lieutenant Wetwang's logbook.

As already stated, it is clear from the surviving evidence that the *Gloucester* must have hit the outer bank, or the Ower. There remains the all-important question, however, for anyone trying to rediscover the wreck, as to just where along the bank it hit. The Ower bank is at least 12 miles long. However, when the draft of the *Gloucester* is factored in with what is known about the state of the tide, there are not so many places that it could have struck.

Wetwang records that it was 'just upon high water at a quarter past six oclock', when the *Gloucester* sank. This results in there being only one or two very limited stretches of the Ower bank where a ship of the *Gloucester*'s draught of 17ft 6in could have touched. They are those sections indicated on modern charts as the west and east elbows. All the various sources have the *Gloucester* beating along the bank in a westerly direction, coming off and then immediately sinking down into a depth of water somewhere between 15 and 18 fathoms. If it struck the eastern elbow it would then have had to flounder for almost 2 miles after coming off the bank in order to sink in such a depth of water. The western elbow fits much better with the available information. It is much steeper in its approaches from the south and south-east, and coming off the bank in a westerly direction one is in 15–18 fathoms within a quarter of a mile.

Nothing is ever certain when it comes to shipwrecks, but the divers scouring the seabed in 2007 were basing their search on the belief that the *Gloucester* wreck lay between the two banks and close to the western elbow of the Ower. The wooden ribs that were noticed just protruding from the sand indicated a large ship. It was also encouraging that what appeared to be the bows were facing towards the north-east. This is what was indicated by van de Velde's painting, and van de Velde usually got this kind of detail right.

A cannon was found close to the wreck, a thirty-two pounder. It was known that the *Gloucester* had carried thirty-two pounders on its lower deck. Better yet, the shaft of the cannon was marked with the broad arrow, indicating that it was a piece of ordnance once owned by the Royal Navy. Still, it was important not to get too excited. Warships of this period were forever stealing each other's cannon when they seized prize ships, and so the presence of English guns could as equally indicate a Dutch or a French ship as an English one. And even if it was an English warship, the *Gloucester* was not the only Royal Navy ship of the period to wreck on the Leman and Ower sands. The *Kent* had also wrecked there just ten years previously.

A Bellarmine jug was recovered that clearly tied the wreck to the second half of the seventeenth century. Again, it was promising. About a week later, a calabash was brought up. It probably originated from Africa and would have been used to hold drinking water or maybe some kind of dried food. It was the kind of object that would have been owned by an ordinary seaman. It had the initials 'GM' and the date 1671 crudely marked on it. West Africa was, of course, a common stopping off place for merchant seamen involved in the triangular trade of manufactured goods from Europe, slaves, gold and ivory from Africa to the Caribbean, and then sugar, hard woods, ivory and gold back to Europe. There was a George Miller on the *Gloucester*; perhaps it was his calabash. If so, he had been carrying it around for eleven years. Miller lived in the parish of St Botolph without Aldgate and left behind a widow 'in a deplorable condition' and two children, one almost 4 years old and the other just 12 weeks.[4] But again, the evidence was not conclusive; G and M are common enough initials.

Another object was found, this time from slightly higher up the social scale. This was a so-called slipped-in-the-stalk silver teaspoon, and it had the maker's touchmark on it: 'Daniel Barton'. Barton was a major English manufacturer of teaspoons of the period. This clearly suggested that the wreck was an English wreck. It also had the owner's initials 'TJ' engraved on it. It may have belonged to Thomas Jory, or Jewry. He was one of James's foot huntsmen, the man who is referred to in some accounts as 'a bold saucy fellow',[5] who hid himself under one of the seats in James's shallop just as the *Gloucester* was sinking. More importantly from the point of view of identifying the shipwreck, whoever was the owner of the spoon, the date on it was 1674. This ruled out any possibility that the wreck that had been found was the *Kent*, but it could well have been carried on the *Gloucester*.

It was soon evident that there were thousands of miscellaneous artefacts scattered around and miraculously preserved by the covering of sand. Part of a trumpet was recovered, which had surely been owned by one of James's four trumpeters on board. Then came a wine bottle, uncorked and empty but otherwise in perfect condition. The length of the neck and the position of the rim beneath the lip dated it to the last two decades of the seventeenth century. It was emblazoned with an image of the sun, the conventional circle of flames leaping from a sulky-faced cherub. As the new owner of the Sun Tavern and the man in charge of victualling the navy, what more natural than that Sir Anthony Deane should supply bottles of a very special wine, for a very special voyage, from his own cellars? The initials on either side of the sun were something of a puzzle; they were R.H. Deane's father-in-law had the initials R.H. and it is possible he had been installed as the Sun's new landlord. Deane himself was, of course, far too grand a figure to play that role. Alternatively, it is possible that the bottle was one of a small batch especially produced for RH, His Royal Highness the Duke of York, an ingratiating gift for the heir to the throne, who was once again in favour. What was for certain was that the shipwreck of the *Gloucester* had finally been found.

POSTSCRIPT

The *Gloucester* wreck contains a unique collection of artefacts representing the most extraordinarily diverse cross section of late Stuart society. There were on board at the time of sinking not just numerous members of the nobility but also scientists, musicians, businessmen, lawyers, priests, carpenters, gunners, huntsmen and many ordinary sailors. They all lost their most intimate and precious possessions.

Subclause 5 of Article 2 of the UNESCO Convention on the Protection of Underwater Cultural Heritage 2001 requires 'the preservation in situ' of all shipwreck material 'as the first option'. What this means in practical terms is that all shipwreck artefacts together with the hull structure must be left untouched on the seabed. The problem with this is that there is no government in the world that has sufficient financial resources to properly conserve and protect the millions of historic wrecks that exist. Around Britain's shorelines alone it has been calculated that there are upwards of 500,000 shipwrecks.[1]

The small group of enthusiasts who first found and identified the *Gloucester* wreck have been voluntarily and regularly monitoring the site in an attempt to safeguard it, although the threats are numerous. The wreck lies in relatively shallow water, easily accessible to sports divers, and so is constantly vulnerable to looting. This is particularly true of a shipwreck like the *Gloucester*, which had thousands of high-value artefacts on board.

Looting is not the only danger. The seabed is not a static environment; there is the constant erosion and shifting of the sand as a result of storms and longer-term geological movements. This is beginning to seriously threaten the integrity of the wooden hull and all that lies within and around it. Another threat is posed by trawling. Massive modern fishing gear can tear through and destroy a historic wreck site in a matter of minutes. Then there are the numerous and unavoidable perils posed by wind farms, pipelines, cabling, and all the complex seabed infrastructure of the modern world.

It is now urgent that all interested parties such as English Heritage, the Receiver of Wreck, the Ministry of Defence and the museum community get together and agree a way forward. The *Gloucester* wreck site is a place of immense national importance, deserving of careful and disciplined excavation and a permanent home in an appropriate museum. Only in this way can a vital part of Britain's maritime history be saved for the enjoyment and education of all.

PEOPLE ON BOARD
THE *GLOUCESTER*

(Please note this list is far from complete, particularly with reference to the seamen who survived and those who drowned with no dependents.)

PASSENGER SURVIVORS

ADAMS, Nathaniel | Chaplain
AYLESWORTH, Geoffrey | Musician
CAVANAGH, Edmund | Footman to his Majesty
CAVANAGH, John | Son of above
CHURCHILL, John (later 1st Duke of Marlborough)
CROFT, William | Page of the Backstairs to Mary of Modena
                       (fate unknown)
DICK, Sir James | Lord Provost
DRUMMOND, James, 4th Earl of Perth | Lord Justice of Scotland
FALCONER, Sir David | President of the Session
FARMER, Thomas | Musician
FASHION, Joseph | Musician, son of father of same name
FLOWER, Edward | Musician
FORTRY, James | Groom of Duke's Bedchamber
GORDON, Sir George (later 1st Earl of Aberdeen) |
   Lord Chancellor of Scotland
GRAHAM, James, 3rd Marquis of Montrose

GREETING, Edward | Musician
GRIFFIN, Edward, 1st Baron Griffin of Braybrooke |
   Treasurer of the Chamber
HULL, Daniel | Commander of the duke's barge
HUME, Sir Patrick, 1st Earl of Marchmont*
JACK, Patrick | Porterer to his Majesty
JEWRY, Thomas | Foothuntsman
LEAK, Richard | Chief Gunner of England and assistant to
   George Legge (fate unknown)
LEGGE, George, 1st Baron Darmouth | Master of Ordnance
MIDDLETON, Charles, 2nd Earl of Middleton
RONCHE, Father | Duchess's Almoner
SCARBOROUGH, Sir Charles | Royal Physician
SETON, George, 4th Earl of Winton
SPICER, William | Servant to Sir Charles Scarborough
STUART, Captain
STUART, James, Duke of York
TEDGE, Thomas | Assistant to George Legge
VAUX, Joseph | Servant to George Legge

PASSENGERS DROWNED

BEALE, Simon | Musician, trumpeter
CHILTON, Mr (see Roger Morrice's *Entring Book*) (could be Shelton)
CLIFTON, Mr
DEANE, Richard | Musician, trumpeter
DOUGLAS, Sir Joseph (John) | of Pompherton
FASHION, Joseph | Musician, father of son of same name
GORDON, Patrick | Lord Haddo's cousin
GREETING, Thomas | Musician, flageolet player
HOLLIS | Duke's Equerry
HOPE, John | Laird of Hopton
KER, Robert, 1st Earl of Roxburghe

* May not have been on board.

LEVINGTON (Leviston) | Physician
LITTLEDALE, Mr | Earl of Roxburghe's servant
OBRIAN, Donagh | Grandson to Henry O'Brien, 7th Earl of Thomond
PEASABLE, James | Musician, composer
PHILLIPS, Mr | (see Roger Morrice's *Entring Book*)
Servant | To Patrick Gordon
Servant | To James Dick
Servant | To Sir David Falconer
SHELTON | King's page
THOMPSON, Albion | Musician, trumpeter (probably drowned)
VANBRIGHT, Walter | Musician, kettle drummer

OFFICER SURVIVORS

BERRY, Captain Sir John
BERRY, Thomas | 1st lieutenant
HOLMES, Benjamin | Master

OFFICERS DROWNED

HYDE, James | 2nd lieutenant

SEAMEN SURVIVORS

ATKINS, John | Seaman
BROOKES, John | Carpenter
DURAMONT, Charles | Gunner
FRANCIS, John | Seaman
HOFORD, John | Assistant gunner
HULL, John | Boatswain
LAWRENCE, Harry | Assistant boatswain
THORN, Hugh | Assistant purser
WARD, Luke | Assistant carpenter

SEAMEN DROWNED WITH DEPENDANTS

ABBOTT, John | Carpenter's mate (married ten years, one child aged 2, wife pregnant, from Portsmouth)

ADAMS, John | Able Bodied (AB) (married, wife had two children by former husband girl aged 17 and boy aged 13, boy at sea, from Rochester)

ALISON, Magnus | AB (married, no children, from Wapping, Whitechapel)

AYMELL, Peter | AB (dependant mother aged 51, from Plymouth)

BALLING, Cornelius | Midshipman (married, one child aged 5, and another by a former husband aged 14, Stepney)

BENNING, James | AB (married, one child by a former husband)

BERRY, Rowland | AB (married, one child but no payment for it so probably by former husband, Shadwell)

BODMAN, Thomas | AB (married, no children, Shadwell)

BOULTON, Abraham | AB (married, no children, Portsmouth)

BROOKES, Gilbert | AB (widower, 32-year-old daughter, Dartmouth)

BROWNE, Robert | AB (married, Wapping)

BROWNE, Thomas | AB (married, one child 13 months, wife pregnant, Shadwell)

BROWNE, Thomas | AB (married, one child, disallowed as born out of wedlock, Tynemouth)

CADBURY, Robert | AB (married, but probably disallowed as unproven, probably Southwark)

CAREW, William | AB (married, three children)

CHAMPAIN, Thomas | AB (married, wife pregnant, Wapping)

CHEYNEY, Richard | Gunner (married, one child, Stepney)

CRANWELL, Francis | Cook (married, Greenwich)

DAVIS, Francis | AB (married, two children aged 10 and 4, wife pregnant, Wapping)

DAVIS, Henry | AB (married, wife over 60, one child 19 years old, Shadwell)

DEANE, John | Purser (married, four children aged between 8 and 4, Aldgate)

DRIVER, John | AB (married, wife had one child by former partner, Stepney)

DUKESBERRY, George | AB (married, dead not drowned, Hull)

DUNCAN, Patrick | AB (married, wife had two children by former husband, aged 7 and 4, Stepney)

EAVES, John | AB (married, one child 1, and wife pregnant, St Pancras)

ELLIOT, Thomas | AB (married, one child 16, Exmouth)

FORD, James | Carpenter (married, Deptford)

GALLASPY, John | AB (married, two children, 14 and 12, Fife, Scotland)

GARDNER, Peter | Midshipman (married, one child, wife pregnant, Covent Garden)

GARRETT, Martin | AB (married, Aldgate)

GIBSON, William | AB (married, three children, 19, 15, 13)

GODWIN, Thomas | AB (widower, eight children aged between 22 and 8. Two spinster daughters, Fareham)

GUILLE, Martin | AB (married, Whitechapel)

HILL, Richard | Gunner (married, three children aged between 16 and 11, Stepney)

HUNTER, John | AB (unmarried, widowed mother, Shadwell)

JARVIS, Humphrey | AB (married, two children by a previous wife aged 9 and 4, St Pancras)

JONES, | Surgeon (married, wife pregnant, one child aged 3, and another child aged 13 by previous husband, Stepney)

LAYTON, John | AB (married, one child 10 months, Fareham)

LLOYD, Samuel | AB (married, one child aged 1, and one child posthumous, Jersey)

MILLER, George | AB (married, two children, aged 4 and 12 weeks, an 11-year-old by previous marriage, Aldgate)

POORE, John | AB (married, two children aged 18 and 12, St Katherine's, Tower)

PRITCHARD, Walter | AB (married, child 16, Westminster)

RASSMUS, Thomas | Midshipman (married, wife pregnant, Stepney)

READ, John | AB (married, child 1 year, wife pregnant)

RICHMAN, Henry | AB (married, one child 1 year, East Greenwich)

RUTTER, William | AB (married, one child, Stepney)

RUTTLAND, Simon | Midshipman (married, two children, 12 and 10, Stepney)

SEYMOUR, John | Boatswain's mate (married, Wapping)

SHAND, John | AB (married, Wapping)

SHEFFIELD, John | AB (married, one child 7, Yarmouth)

SMITH, Thomas | Under swabber (married, Sandwich)

SOLOMAN, Richard | Midshipman (married, Stepney)

SPINCKES, Alex | AB (married)

SPURRIER, John | Gunner's mate (married, one child 11, Stepney)

STONE, William | Steward's mate (widowed mother)

STOWE, Robert | AB (married, three children 8, 6, 1, and wife pregnant, Wapping)

SWEETE, Robert | Quartermaster (married, Southwark)

SYMONDS, THOMAS | Quartermaster's mate (married, two children, 11 and 7, Bermondsey)

TEWKESBURY, John | AB (married, one child 6, St Katherine's, Tower)

THORNE, Allen | Quartermaster (married, one child 10, wife pregnant, Stepney)

TRUNNAMORE, Michael | AB (married, two children by former husband, Stepney)

WOOD, Robert | AB (married, one child 4, Southwark)

YOUNG, Walter | Cook's mate (married, wife pregnant, Wapping)

SEAMEN DROWNED WITHOUT DEPENDANTS

CARTER, John | Servant to Francis Cranwell, cook, East Greenwich

DEANE | John Deane's son, Aldgate

DEANE | John Deane's brother, Aldgate

OSSAN, James | Bachelor, Mariner, Shadwell

PHILLIPS, Thomas | Bachelor, Mariner, East Greenwich

ROWLESON, Roland | Bachelor, Mariner, Wapping

SEVEARNE, Thomas | Bachelor, Mariner, Stepney

APPENDIX 2

BOUNTY PAYMENTS

Very little is known about the social demographics of late seventeenth-century seamen. After the burning and sinking of the *London* in the River Thames in 1665, John Evelyn remarked that 300 men lost their lives and there were left fifty widows.[1] This suggests that the vast majority of seamen were unmarried, and Evelyn's figures have been taken as a rough benchmark by subsequent maritime historians such as N.A.M. Rodger in *The Wooden World*. One of the more interesting aspects of the bounty payments is that a careful study and analysis of them allows for a much more accurate understanding of the age and married status of the ordinary sailor.

When the *Gloucester* left Portsmouth for Scotland it was not being manned for home waters and peacetime duties. After the fetching of the Duchess of York, it was scheduled to be stationed off southern Ireland, which was classed as being 'abroad'. Also, technically, England was at war with the Algerines. The manning level, consequently, should have been for what was known as 'war abroad'. According to a manuscript to be found in the Pepys Library, the *Gloucester* was to be manned with 210 men in peacetime, 270 men during 'war abroad' and 340 men during 'war at home'.[2] Sir Anthony Deane, in his *Doctrine of Naval Architecture* of 1670, puts the number of men for war abroad at 250. James himself, who took a keen interest in all naval matters and was in a good position to know the answer with some accuracy, wrote to his son-in-law, William of Orange, on 9 May 1682, and mentions that the *Gloucester* had had a complement of 250 men on its final voyage.

In reality, and assuming that 250 was the administrative number being worked on by the Navy Board, it is unlikely that there were that many men actually on board. This would be because of the difficulties in recruiting sufficient numbers at such short notice. It is significant here that Thomas Smith was only signed on at Deal on 3 May. This was also still a period when 'dead pays' were an accepted practice, a system by which the captain would enter the names of a number of dead men on to a ship's books, the Navy Board would pay their wages, and the captain would take the extra money as a perk.

The exact number of seamen aboard will never be known, but it is interesting that in Roger Morrice's *Entring Book* there is the following remark for 12 May, 'Sir John [Berry] writ yesterday to town that there were in that vessel about 227 persons 150 of them yet missing.'[3] The total number of people on board the *Gloucester* must have been well in excess of 227 because there is a general consensus that there were at least eighty gentlemen and their servants, in addition to crew. It is, however, an unusually precise number and given the status of the source it could refer to the number of seamen originally on board, suggesting that dead pays and under-manning could have accounted for the missing twenty-three, a plausible number.

The data on the number of seamen drowned is similarly inconsistent. James, writing to Lord Hyde on 9 May, said, 'I have now had an account of the loss of the ship's company and find there were 110 lost, besides those who belonged to me, and those who came with me.'[4] This sounds fairly authoritative and it is roughly consistent with Gunman's remark in his letter to his wife, 'of all sorts above 150 men drowned'.[5] It seems likely that about forty of the passengers and their servants who were on board drowned, and so this leaves approximately 110 seamen.

Other reports put the total number of seamen lost as a bit higher. The *London Gazette* of 15–18 May mentions 130, and this figure is repeated by Luttrell in his entry for 13 May. At the top end of the estimates is Sir James Dick, who writes, 'There will be perished in this disaster above 200 persons for I reckon there was 250 seamen and I am sure there were 80 noblemen, gentlemen and their servants – my computation was that there were 330 in all, of which I can not learn that 130 are found alive.'[6] Pepys also does not distinguish between seamen and passengers, but in his letter to William Hewer of 8 May he states, 'many are lost I judge about 200 men'.[7] Other estimates can be found that vary from 100 persons drowned in the *Domestick Intelligence* of 11 May, to 250 lost in a letter from William Freeman of 14 June, but they are so wide of the general consensus they can most probably be safely ignored.

Looking at the above figures, a reasonable top estimate for numbers of seamen drowned would be 130. It is very unlikely to have been much more than this because in the middle of June 1682, Sir John Berry was appointed commander of the *Henrietta* warship and the first 100 places, when the muster books were opened, were to be reserved for surviving seamen from the *Gloucester*. This would suggest that well over 100 seamen must have survived as there would inevitably be some, for one reason or another, who would not wish to immediately sign on again.

There are several different lists of bounty payments and they are not all consistent with each other. Some have more names and some have names that do not appear on the other lists. The muddle is not helped by the fact that there is no consistency in the spelling of names. Despite these drawbacks, it is possible to identify sixty-three men who were sailors on the *Gloucester*, whose surviving dependents received a bounty payment. This is approximately 50 per cent of the total number drowned and so provides a good statistical basis for analysis. Of the sixty-three, fifty-eight had been married at the time of their drowning. A further two were widowers with daughters who were still dependent on them. The remaining three were included because although they were not married and never had been, they had dependent mothers. Assuming that those sailors who drowned were a representative cross section of all the sailors on board, it is clear that around 50 per cent of the sailors were married, a far higher proportion than the one in six suggested by Evelyn, which has up until now been taken as the benchmark.

The average age of the sailors is similarly surprising. There has traditionally been a presumption that most sailors of this period were young men signing up for some adventure. Unfortunately, the precise age of the seamen whose dependents received bounty payments is not given, but from the ages of their children and also the dates of their marriages it is evident that out of the sixty-three, twenty-eight were under 35, twenty-nine were aged between 35 and and 50, and six were older than 50. A presumption has been made when calculating these figures that if there is no clue as to age then the seaman was most probably in the youngest category. These figures would suggest that the men on the *Gloucester* were a lot older than may have been previously thought typical for a Royal Navy ship.

The extent of the towns the men came from is fairly limited, with a number originating from a scattering of far-flung port towns. Plymouth, Portsmouth, Dartmouth, Rochester, Tynemouth, Hull, Exmouth, Fife, Fareham, St Peter Port Guernsey, Yarmouth and Sandwich are all mentioned, but usually only one or occasionally two men from each place. The total number of men from these places is fifteen, and with the exception of Portsmouth and Sandwich, it is probable that most actually still travelled from London to sign on, even though their family home was elsewhere. Forty-five came from families who lived in London, and the most frequently cited parish was Stepney with twelve. The next most popular was Whitechapel with eleven, followed by Shadwell with five, Aldgate with three, and a scattering from St Pancras, St Katherine's by the Tower of London, Covent Garden and Westminster. Only eight of the forty-five came from south of the river from, predictably, the parishes of Southwark, Greenwich, Deptford and Bermondsey. For three of those whose dependents received bounty payments, a local parish is not given. It is also noticeable that the parish of Stepney did not just provide the most sailors, it also supplied the most experienced and qualified. They tended to be quartermasters, gunners, midshipmen and boatswains. Wapping and Shadwell provided the less experienced end of the crew.

Another surprising fact that emerges is that of the fifty-eight bereaved wives, no fewer than ten were pregnant and eight had children from a previous marriage. Even so the total number of children in each sailor family was relatively modest; seventeen of the widows had no children, nineteen had only one child, seven had two children, four had three children, and one had four children. This is excluding any children from a wife's previous marriage, because these children did not count for a bounty payment. Children from a husband's previous marriage did count, so long as they were still dependents. The state of dependency was not age related, so it can be found from the payment lists that a 32-year-old daughter who did not have a husband nor a job was still classed as a dependent, whereas a 13-year-old boy who was working at sea was no longer a dependent.

NOTES

CHAPTER 1

1 Foulness was a village to the east of Cromer in Norfolk that has now been lost to coastal erosion; London, 17 May: 'We hear the boats sent to careene off the mouth of the Humber, have taken up the dead bodies of several persons in the late wreck of the Glocester Frigate, amongst whom are some persons of quality'.
Yarmouth, 16 May: 'This morning two sailors were cast upon this shoare supposed to perish at the late dismal Wracke upon the Lemon-Ore, about 20 leagues from this place, and we hear that the bodies of several others have been taken up at other places, being by the tides left upon the sands', *The Domestick Intelligence.*
2 Daniel Defoe, *A Tour thro' the Whole Island of Great Britain* (London: Penguin, 1978).
3 When the *Association* was lost off the Isles of Scilly on 22 October 1707, the body of Admiral Sir Cloudesley Shovell, who was among those drowned, was discovered with the ring finger cleanly severed.
4 Prerogative Court of Canterbury Wills, Prob/11/370 TNA.
5 *Impartial Protestant Mercury*, 12 May 1682.
6 Calendars of State Papers Domestic (CSPD), E. Ridley to Sir Francis Radcliffe, Dilston.

CHAPTER 2

1 Samuel Pepys diary entry of 19 June 1666 in R. Latham and W. Matthews (eds), *The Diary of Samuel Pepys*, 10 vols (London: Bell & Hyman, 1970–83).
2 Pepys diary entry of 11 January 1668 in Latham and Matthews (eds), *The Diary of Samuel Pepys.*
3 John Scott was employed by the Duke of Buckingham and Lord Shaftesbury to dig up dirt on Pepys. Pepys was known to be a supporter of James, Duke of York, and so was in the opposing political camp to Shaftesbury.
4 *Survey of London*, Vol. 18, English Heritage. When Pepys finally returned to the Admiralty and a place of his own was more practical than continuing as a lodger, he only moved next door into No. 14.

5 Pepys diary entry of 7 October 1667 in Latham and Matthews (eds), *The Diary of Samuel Pepys.*
6 'There's a breach ready made, which still open hath bin,
   And thousands of thoughts to betray it within,
   If you once come to storme her, you're sure to get in,
   Then stand not off coldly,
   But venter on boldly
   With weapon in hand,
   If you do but approach her, she's not able to stand,
   With weapon in hand
   If you do charge her home she's not able to stand' etc. gives a feel of the song.
7 Pepys diary entry of 25 May 1668 in Latham and Matthews (eds), *The Diary of Samuel Pepys.*

CHAPTER 3

1 Arthur Hamilton Clark, *The History of Yachting* (London: G.P. Putnams and Sons, 1904).
2 Add. MS. 18447.
3 M. Haile, *Mary of Modena, Her Life and Letters* (London: Dent, 1905).
4 Ibid.

CHAPTER 4

1 W. D. Christie (ed.), *Letters addressed from London to Sir Joesph Williamson,* Vol. 2 (London: Camden Society, 1874), p.63.
2 Ibid., p.68.
3 Haile, *Mary of Modena.*
4 Ibid.
5 Sandra Sullivan, *Representations of Mary of Modena* (London: University of London, 2008).
6 Haile, *Mary of Modena.*
7 Ibid.
8 Ibid.
9 Ibid.
10 Ibid.
11 Ibid.
12 Ibid.
13 Ibid.
14 Duke of Rutland, *Manuscripts,* Vol. IV (London: Historical Manuscripts Commission, 1905).
15 Letter of 12 January 1679 in Haile, *Mary of Modena.*
16 Haile, *Mary of Modena.*
17 Ibid.
18 Ibid.
19 Add. MS. 18447.

20 Haile, *Mary of Modena.*
21 Ibid.

CHAPTER 5

1 Geoffrey Keynes (ed.), *Letters of Sir Thomas Browne* (London: Faber and Faber, 1946), p.251.
2 CSPD London, 16 March 1682, Newsletter to John Squier, Newcastle.
3 CSPD Newmarket, 10 March 1682, Earl of Conway to Secretary Jenkins.
4 A. Browning (ed.), *Memoirs of Sir John Reresby* (London: Royal Historical Society, 1991).
5 E. S. de Beer (ed.), *The Diary of John Evelyn*, 6 vols (Oxford: Oxford University Press, 1955).
6 Browning (ed.), *Memoirs of Sir John Reresby.*
7 CSPD, 7 March 1682, Earl of Conway to Secretary Jenkins.
8 CSPD, 9 March 1682, as above.
9 *True Protestant Mercury*, 6–10 May 1682.
10 Harold, Arthur and Viscount Dillon, 'Some familiar Letters of Charles II, and James Duke of York', *Archaeologie*, Vol. 58, Issue 1 (1902), p.168.

CHAPTER 6

1 CSPD, Newsletter to John Squier of Newcastle, 14 March 1682
2 Perry Gauci, *Politics and Society in Great Yarmouth* (Oxford: Clarendon Press, 1996), p.153; see Y/S1/4, pp.35–36.
3 Gauci, *Politics and Society*, p.135, see PL Paston to his wife, 19 May 1676.
4 CSPD, Francis Gwynn to Secretary Jenkins, 12 March 1682.
5 Samuel Pepys letter from Newmarket to James Houblon in London, 14 March 1682 in R.G. Howarth (ed.), *Letters and the Second Diary of Samuel Pepys* (London: J.M. Dent & Sons, 1932).
6 Samuel Pepys letter to William Viscount Brouncker, Newmarket, 13 March 1682 in Howarth (ed.), *Letters and the Second Diary of Samuel Pepys.*
7 Samuel Pepys letter to James Houblon, 14 March 1682 in Howarth (ed.), *Letters and the Second Diary of Samuel Pepys.*
8 CSPD Earl of Conway to Secretary Jenkins, 5 April 1682.

CHAPTER 7

1 T. Harris, *London Crowds in the Reign of King Charles II* (Cambridge: Cambridge University Press, 1987).
2 Diary entry of 20 June 1671 in de Beer (ed.), *The Diary of John Evelyn.*
3 Pepys diary entry of 15 August 1665 in Latham and Matthews (eds), *The Diary of Samuel Pepys.*
4 Thomas Thornton (ed.), *The Works of Thomas Otway* (London: F.C. & J. Rivington, 1813).

CHAPTER 8

1   A. Bryant, *Samuel Pepys, The Years of Peril* (Cambridge: Cambridge University Press, 1935), p.255.
2   Pepys diary entry of 1 May 1661 in Latham and Matthews (eds), *The Diary of Samuel Pepys.*
3   Portsmouth Record Series, 12 September 1655, D11A/16/2.
4   J.R. Tanner (ed), *Descriptive Catalogue of Naval Manuscripts in the Pepys Library, Cambridge*, 4 vols (Naval Records Society, 1903–23).
5   ADM 106/361.
6   Ibid.
7   ADM 51/4214.
8   ADM 106/359.
9   Ibid.
10 Ibid.
11 Ibid.
12 Ibid.
13 Ibid.
14 Ibid.

CHAPTER 9

1   In times of war, when the need for sailors increased dramatically, men could be either physically impounded as emergency labour, or bribed in a tavern with a few drinks. Merchant sailors between voyages or unemployed men in port towns were the most vulnerable to press gangs.
2   Pepys diary entry of 14 June 1667 in Latham and Matthews (eds), *The Diary of Samuel Pepys.*
3   Basil Lubbock, *Barlow's Journal of His Life at Sea in King's Ships, East & West Indiamen & Other Merchantmen From 1659 to 1703*, Vols 1–2 (Hurst and Blackett, 1934).
4   Sailors contributed 6*d* a month from their wages, which entitled the wounded and widows of those killed in action to receive some limited support.
5   Cesar de Saussure, *A Foreign View of England*, trans. Madam Van Muyden (London: John Murray, 1902).
6   de Saussure, *A Foreign View of England.*
7   ADM 106/3023.
8   PROB 11/370.

CHAPTER 10

1   S.W. Singer (ed.), *The Correspondence of Henry Hyde, Earl of Clarendon, and his Brother, Laurence Hyde, Earl of Rochester*, 2 Vols (London: Henry Colburn, 1818–28).
2   Ibid.
3   ADM 106/359.
4   Ibid.
5   ADM 106/361.

6   Ibid.
7   CSPD, 1 May 1682.
8   J.R. Tanner (ed.), *Samuel Pepys's Naval Minutes* (London: Naval Records Society, 1926).
9   Ibid.
10 F. Fox, *Great Ships* (London, Conway Maritime Press, 1980).
11 Daniel Defoe, *An Elegy on the Author of the True Born Englishman, together with an Essay on the Late Storm* (London, 1704).
12 Pepys diary entry of 30 April 1660 in Latham and Matthews (eds), *The Diary of Samuel Pepys.*
13 Ibid.

CHAPTER 11

1   Rutland, *Manuscripts.*
2   Ibid.
3   John Heneage Jesse, *Memoirs of the Court of England* (London: Richard Bently, 1843).
4   Count de Grammont, *Memoirs*, trans. H. Walpole and Mrs Jameson (London, *c.*1900).
5   CSPD, Newsletter to John Squier, Newcastle, 4 May 1682.

CHAPTER 12

1   Letter written by Colonel Atkins, 3 July 1666, from Castle Cornet, Guernsey, printed in the *London Gazette* of July 9–12, 1666.
2   JARVIS IX/1/A/2.
3   CSPD, Newsletter to John Squier, Newcastle, 4 May 1682.
4   T. Bruce Ailesbury, *Memoirs*, 2 Vols (London: Roxburghe Club, 1890).
5   Ibid.
6   Ibid.
7   Quoted in Bryant, *The Years of Peril*, p.377.
8   Ibid.
9   Ibid.
10 Pepys to W. Hewer, 8 May 1682, in Howarth (ed.), *Letters and the Second Diary of Samuel Pepys.*
11 *Impartial Protestant Mercury*, 16 January 1682.
12 Pepys to W. Hewer, 8 May 1682, in Howarth (ed.), *Letters and the Second Diary of Samuel Pepys.*

CHAPTER 13

1   Sir John Berry, 'Narrative', in S.W. Singer (ed.), *The Correspondence of Henry Hyde, Earl of Clarendon, and his Brother, Laurence Hyde, Earl of Rochester*, 2 Vols (London: Henry Colburn, 1818–28)
2   *Mary* logbook, JARVIS 1X/1/A/5.
3   Berry, 'Narrative', in Singer (ed.), *The Correspondence of Henry Hyde.*

4 Bevyl Higgons, *Historical Works*, 2 vols (London: 1736).
5 Berry, 'Narrative', in Singer (ed.), *The Correspondence of Henry Hyde*.
6 *Dartmouth* logbook, ADM 51/3819.
7 *Ruby* logbook, ADM 51/4322.
8 Pepys's Library, Magdalene College Cambridge, MS 2351.
9 Ibid.

CHAPTER 14

1 JARVIS 1X/1/A/5.
2 Berry, 'Narrative', in Singer (ed.), *The Correspondence of Henry Hyde*.
3 Ibid.
4 Ibid.
5 ADM 2/1726.
6 Tanner, *Samuel Pepys's Naval Minutes*.
7 E. Chappell (ed.), *The Tangier Papers of Samuel Pepys* (London: Naval Records Society, 1935).
8 Pepys to W. Hewer, 8 May 1682, in Howarth (ed.), *Letters and the Second Diary of Samuel Pepys*.
9 ADM 51/3932.
10 JARVIS 1X/1/A/5.
11 Ibid.
12 Berry, 'Narrative', in Singer (ed.), *The Correspondence of Henry Hyde*.
13 'Abstract of Gunman's Cause', Lincolnshire Archives, quoted in full in P.M. Cowburn, 'Christopher Gunman and the Wreck of the Gloucester Part II', *The Mariner's Mirror*, Vol. 42, Issue 3 (1956), pp.219–29.
14 E. Hallam Moorhouse, *Letters of the English Seamen* (London: Chapman & Hall, 1910).
15 Berry, 'Narrative', in Singer (ed.), *The Correspondence of Henry Hyde*.
16 Ibid.

CHAPTER 15

1 ADM 51/4214 Logbook of the *Happy Return*.
2 Berry, 'Narrative', in Singer (ed.), *The Correspondence of Henry Hyde*.
3 ADM 51/4214 Logbook of the *Happy Return*.
4 Ibid.
5 Berry, 'Narrative', in Singer (ed.), *The Correspondence of Henry Hyde*.
6 Ibid.
7 Add. MS. 5719.
8 Berry, 'Narrative', in Singer (ed.), *The Correspondence of Henry Hyde*.
9 Ibid.
10 Ibid.
11 Ibid.
12 Henry Ellis, *Original Letters*, Vol. IV (London: Harding, Triphook and Lepard, 1827).
13 ADM 51/4214 Logbook of the *Happy Return*.
14 JARVIS IX/1/A/5.

15 Pepys to W. Hewer, 8 May 1682, in Howarth (ed.), *Letters and the Second Diary of Samuel Pepys.*
16 Berry, 'Narrative', in Singer (ed.), *The Correspondence of Henry Hyde.*
17 Ibid.
18 Ellis, *Original Letters.*
19 Berry, 'Narrative', in Singer (ed.), *The Correspondence of Henry Hyde.*
20 Ellis, *Original Letters.*
21 ADM 51/4214 Logbook of the *Happy Return.*
22 Ibid.
23 Pepys to W. Hewer, 8 May 1682, in Howarth (ed.), *Letters and the Second Diary of Samuel Pepys.*
24 Moorhouse, *Letters of the English Seamen.*
25 Ellis, *Original Letters.*
26 Ibid.
27 Ibid.
28 Berry, 'Narrative', in Singer (ed.), *The Correspondence of Henry Hyde.*
29 Ellis, *Original Letters.*
30 Anon., *Life of James II* (London: 1702).
31 Tanner, *Samuel Pepys's Naval Minutes.*
32 Moorhouse, *Letters of the English Seamen.*
33 Ibid.
34 Berry, 'Narrative', in Singer (ed.), *The Correspondence of Henry Hyde.*
35 JARVIS IX/1/A/5.
36 ADM 51/3932 Logbook of the *Pearl.*
37 Ibid.
38 John Smith, *Advertisements for the Unexperienced* (London: 1631).

CHAPTER 16

1 JARVIS IX/1/A/5.
2 Ibid.
3 Singer (ed.), *The Correspondence of Henry Hyde.*
4 Ibid.
5 Agnes Strickland, *Lives of the Queens of England* (London: John Doran, 1855).
6 F.C. Turner, *James II* (London: Eyre and Spottiswoode, 1948).
7 James, Duke of York, to Prince William of Orange, 9 May 1682, in Groen van Prinsterer, *Archives de la Maison d'Orange-Nassau,* Vol. 5, 1650–88 (Utrecht: 1861).
8 Ibid.
9 Pepys to W. Hewer, 8 May 1682, in Howarth (ed.), *Letters and the Second Diary of Samuel Pepys.*
10 Ibid.
11 Ibid.
12 Ibid.
13 Add. MS. 5719.
14 Bundle 1160, Innes Ker Family Papers, NRA Scotland 1100.

CHAPTER 17

1 Pepys diary entry of 2 March 1669 in Latham and Matthews (eds), *The Diary of Samuel Pepys*.
2 Ibid.
3 Ibid.
4 Ibid.
5 Ibid.
6 Ibid.
7 Ibid.
8 Ibid.
9 Eric Halfpenny, 'Four Seventeenth Century British Trumpets', *The Galpin Society Journal*, Vol. 22 (1969), pp.51–57.
10 See page 124.
11 John Oldmixon, *History of England during the Reigns of the Royal House of Stuart* (London: J. Pemberton, 1730).

CHAPTER 18

1 Bundle 635, National Archives of Scotland, Roxburgh Family Papers held at Floors Castle.
2 Ibid.
3 Ibid.
4 *Domestick Intelligence*, 16 May 1682.
5 *Domestick Intelligence*, 17 May 1682.
6 Bundle 635, National Archives of Scotland, Roxburgh Family Papers held at Floors Castle.
7 Ibid.
8 Ibid.
9 Ellis, *Original Letters*.
10 Ailesbury, *Memoirs*.
11 Ibid.

CHAPTER 19

1 Pepys diary entry of 27 February 1663 in Latham and Matthews (eds), *The Diary of Samuel Pepys*.
2 Ibid.
3 Pepys diary entry of 24 May 1660 in Latham and Matthews (eds), *The Diary of Samuel Pepys*.
4 Pepys to W. Hewer, 8 May 1682, in Howarth (ed.), *Letters and the Second Diary of Samuel Pepys*.

CHAPTER 20

1   CSPD, Earl of Conway to Secretary Jenkins, 9 May 1682.
2   W. Hewer to Pepys, 13 May 1682, in Howarth (ed.), *Letters and the Second Diary of Samuel Pepys*.
3   Ibid.
4   James Houblon to S. Pepys, 13 May 1682, in Howarth (ed.), *Letters and the Second Diary of Samuel Pepys*.
5   Ibid.
6   Ibid.
7   William Bray (ed.), *Diary and Letters of John Evelyn*, 2nd edn (London: Henry Colburn, 1819).
8   Thomas Hill to Pepys, April 1673, in Margaret Willes, *The Curious World of Samuel Pepys and John Evelyn* (New Haven and London: Yale University Press, 2017), p.91.
9   Lady Mordaunt to Samuel Pepys, 13 May 1682, in Bryant, *The Years of Peril*, p.384.
10 M. Wood and H. Armet (eds), *Extracts from the records of the Burgh of Edinburgh* (Edinburgh: Oliver and Boyd, 1954).
11 Pepys at Berwick to W. Hewer, 19 May 1682, in Howarth (ed.), *Letters and the Second Diary of Samuel Pepys*.
12 Ibid.
13 Sir G. Fletcher to Sir D. Fleming, 29 May 1682, in Bryant, *The Years of Peril*, p.381.
14 Pepys to W. Hewer, 26 May 1682, in Howarth (ed.), *Letters and the Second Diary of Samuel Pepys*.
15 Pepys to W. Hewer, 19 May 1682, in Howarth (ed.), *Letters and the Second Diary of Samuel Pepys*.
16 W. Hewer to Pepys, 13 May 1682, in Howarth (ed.), *Letters and the Second Diary of Samuel Pepys*.
17 Pepys to W. Hewer, 26 May 1682, in Howarth (ed.), *Letters and the Second Diary of Samuel Pepys*.
18 W. Hewer to Pepys, 25 May 1682, in Howarth (ed.), *Letters and the Second Diary of Samuel Pepys*.
19 Quoted in Bryant, *The Years of Peril*, p.385.
20 Ibid.
21 Ibid.
22 Latham and Matthews (eds), *The Diary of Samuel Pepys*, Vol. 4, p.298.
23 M.J. Routh (ed.), *Bishop Burnet's History of His Own Time*, 2nd edn (Oxford: Oxford University Press, 1833).
24 Quoted in Bryant, *The Years of Peril*, p.386.

CHAPTER 21

1   Marquise Campana de Cavelli, *Les Derniers Stuarts a Saint Germain en Laye* (Paris: 1871).
2   MS Memorials of Mary D'Este, quoted in Strickland, *Lives of the Queens of England*, p.143.
3   ADM 51/4214 Logbook of the *Happy Return*.

4 JARVIS 1X/1/A/5, Gunman's Journal, 15 May 1682.
5 ADM 106/3023.
6 Ibid.
7 Ibid.
8 Ibid.
9 Ibid.
10 J.S. Clarke (ed.), *The Life of James the Second, King of England*, 2 vols, (London: Longman, 1816).
11 Walter Scott (ed.), *The Works of John Dryden*, Vol. 15 (Edinburgh: A Constable & Co., 1821).
12 Houblon to Pepys, 13 May 1682, in Howarth (ed.), *Letters and the Second Diary of Samuel Pepys.*

CHAPTER 22

1 Pepys diary entry of 4 June 1666 in Latham and Matthews (eds), *The Diary of Samuel Pepys.*
2 ADM 106/3023.
3 PROB 11/370.
4 Ibid.
5 Ibid.
6 Pepys to W. Hewer, 8 May 1682, in Howarth (ed.), *Letters and the Second Diary of Samuel Pepys.*
7 ADM 106/3540.
8 Ibid.
9 Ibid.
10 Ibid.
11 'Abstract of Gunman's Cause', quoted in in Cowburn, 'Christopher Gunman and the Wreck of the Gloucester Part II'.
12 Ibid.
13 Singer (ed.), *The Correspondence of Henry Hyde.*
14 James II to Prince William of Orange, 9 May 1682, in van Prinsterer, *Archives de la Maison d'Orange-Nassau.*
15 Pepys to W. Hewer, 8 May 1682, in Howarth (ed.), *Letters and the Second Diary of Samuel Pepys.*
16 Tanner, *Samuel Pepys's Naval Minutes.*
17 CSPD, Thomas Wheeler to the Navy Commissioners, 25 October 1672.
18 CSPD, John Butler to Secretary of State Williamson, 26 October 1672.
19 CSPD, John Butler to Secretary of State Williamson, 23 October 1672.
20 Ibid.
21 CSPD, Silas Taylor to Secretary of State Williamson, 26 October 1672.
22 CSPD, Thomas Wheeler to Samuel Pepys, 16 November 1672. An identical letter was also sent to Lord Brouncker.

CHAPTER 23

1 Clifford Dobb, 'London Prisons', in A. Nicoll (ed.), *Shakespeare in his Own Age: Volume 17* (Cambridge: Cambridge University Press, 1964), p.99.
2 ADM 106/3023.
3 CSPD, London, 13 May 1682, E. Ridley to Sir Francis Radcliffe of Dilston.

CHAPTER 24

1 29 September 1675, in William A. Shaw (ed.), *Calendar of Treasury Books, Volume 4, 1672–1675* (London: His Majesty's Stationery Office, 1909).
2 J. Evelyn, *Sylva* (London: 1664).
3 Pepys diary entry of 5 November 1665 in Latham and Matthews (eds), *The Diary of Samuel Pepys*.
4 'Abstract of Gunman's Cause', quoted in Cowburn, 'Christopher Gunman and the Wreck of the Gloucester Part II'.
5 Ibid.
6 Ibid.
7 Ibid.
8 Ibid.
9 Ibid.
10 ADM 106/3540.
11 'Abstract of Gunman's Cause', quoted in Cowburn, 'Christopher Gunman and the Wreck of the Gloucester Part II'.
12 Tanner, *Samuel Pepys's Naval Minutes*.
13 Ibid.
14 JARVIS IX/I/A/5, Gunman Journal, Lincolnshire Archives.
15 Ibid.
16 Ibid.
17 Scott (ed.), *The Works of John Dryden*, p.301.
18 Evelyn diary entry of 26 March 1685 in de Beer (ed.), *The Diary of John Evelyn*.
19 Scott (ed.), *The Works of John Dryden*, p.241.

CHAPTER 25

1 ADM 106/3023.
2 ADM 106/3023.
3 Pepys diary entry of 14 January 1666 in Latham and Matthews (eds), *The Diary of Samuel Pepys*.
4 Ibid.
5 ADM 106/3023.
6 Ibid.
7 Ibid.

CHAPTER 26

1 James II to Prince William of Orange, 9 May 1682, in Groen van Prinsterer, *Archives de la Maison d'Orange-Nassau.*
2 'Two Letters from Scotland', printed for John Morice (London: 1682).
3 John Stow, *Survey of London* (London: 1603).
4 Johann Wilhelm von Archenholz, *A Picture of England* (1789).
5 ADM 106/3023.
6 Ibid.
7 Pepys diary entry of 23 June 1662 in Latham and Matthews (eds), *The Diary of Samuel Pepys.*
8 John Seller, *Coasting Pilot* (London: 1671). Edition to be found in the University Library, Cambridge.
9 Ibid.
10 'Two Letters from Scotland', printed for John Morice.
11 Tanner, *Samuel Pepys's Naval Minutes.*
12 Ibid.
13 Ibid.
14 CSPD, 1681, p.328, quoted in Florence Dyer, 'The Journal of Grenvill Collins', *The Mariner's Mirror,* Vol. 14, Issue 3 (1928), pp.197–219.
15 Greenville Collins, *Great Britain's Coasting Pilot* (London: Freeman Collins, 1693).
16 Tanner, *Samuel Pepys's Naval Minutes.*

CHAPTER 27

1 *Impartial Protestant Mercury,* 12 May 1682.
2 George H. Chettle, *The History of the Queen's House to 1678* (London: Guild & School of Handicraft, 1937).
3 Berry, 'Narrative', in Singer (ed.), *The Correspondence of Henry Hyde.*
4 James Macpherson (ed.), *Original Papers containing the Secret History of Great Britain, from the Restoration to the accession of the House of Hanover to which are prefixed Extracts from the Life of James II, as written by himself,* 2 Vols (London: W. Strahan and T. Cadell, 1775).
5 J.S. Clarke (ed.), *The Life of James the Second, King of England.*
6 Harleian MSS 6922, *The Life of Lord Sothward, Bishop of Salisbury.*
7 ADM 20/31.
8 *Loyal Protestant,* 18 May 1682.

CHAPTER 28

1 Pepys diary entry of 2 April 1668 in Latham and Matthews (eds), *The Diary of Samuel Pepys.*
2 Hooke diary entry of 19 December 1676 in H.W. Robinson and W. Adams (eds), *The Diary of Robert Hooke* (Robinson and Adams, 1935).
3 George Sinclair, *Ars Nova et Magna Gravitatis et Levitatis* (Glasgow, 1669).
4 9 May 1682, in Moorhouse, *Letters of the English Seamen.*
5 'Two Letters from Scotland,' printed for John Morice (London: 1682).

6 ADM 2/1726.
7 Ibid.
8 ADM 3/278.
9 ADM 3/278.
10 ADM 1/5139.
11 Ibid.
12 ADM 106/361.
13 ADM 2/1726.
14 Ibid.

CHAPTER 29

1 Charnock, John, *Lives and Characters of Naval Officers of Great Britain*, 6 Vols (London: Robert Faulder, 1794–98).

CHAPTER 30

1 J. Churchill to James II, undated in W.S. Churchill, *Marlborough, His Life and Times*, Vol. 1 (London: Harrap, 1933).
2 Richard Holmes, *Marlborough* (London: Harper Press, 2008), p.150.

CHAPTER 31

1 Churchill, *Marlborough*.
2 See Chapter 25, where these numbers are gone into in some detail.
3 Churchill, *Marlborough*.
4 Ibid.
5 James Houblon to Samuel Pepys, 13 May 1682, in Howarth (ed.), *Letters and the Second Diary of Samuel Pepys*.
6 Singer (ed.), *The Correspondence of Henry Hyde*.
7 Gunman to his wife, 9 May 1682, in Moorhouse, *Letters of the English Seamen*.
8 Singer (ed.), *The Correspondence of Henry Hyde*.
9 Churchill, *Marlborough*.
10 Macpherson (ed.), *Original Papers*.
11 Ellis, *Original Letters*.
12 Pepys to W. Hewer, 8 May 1682, in Howarth (ed.), *Letters and the Second Diary of Samuel Pepys*.
13 ADM 51/4214.
14 Macpherson (ed.), *Original Papers*.
15 Singer (ed.), *The Correspondence of Henry Hyde*.
16 M.J. Routh (ed.), *Bishop Burnet's History of His Own Time*.
17 Singer (ed.), *The Correspondence of Henry Hyde*.
18 Pepys to W. Hewer, 8 May 1682, in Howarth (ed.), *Letters and the Second Diary of Samuel Pepys*.
19 Ellis, *Original Letters*.

20 Strickland, *Queens of England*, quoting Mary's Memoirs.
21 Singer (ed.), *The Correspondence of Henry Hyde*.
22 John Lauder, *Historical Observes, 1680–1686* (Edinburgh: Bannatyne Club, 1840).
23 Ailesbury, *Memoirs*.
24 Singer (ed.), *The Correspondence of Henry Hyde*.

CHAPTER 32

1 ADM 106/307 f 305.
2 C.S. Knighton, *Catalogue of the Pepys Library at Magdalene College, Cambridge: Census of printed books* (Woodbridge: 1981).
3 Ibid.
4 ADM 106/307.
5 Ibid.
6 Ibid.
7 Knighton, *Catalogue of the Pepys Library at Magdalene College*.
8 Knighton, *Catalogue of the Pepys Library at Magdalene College*, MS 2266, 20 December 1677.
9 C.R. Drinkwater Bethune (ed.), *The Observations of Sir Richard Hawkins in his Voyage into the South Sea in the Year 1593* (London: Hakluyt Society, 1847).
10 Add. MS. 11685.
11 Ibid.
12 Ibid.
13 Ibid.
14 ADM 106/3539.
15 Ibid.
16 Ibid.

CHAPTER 33

1 Pepys diary entry of 6 November 1661 in Latham and Matthews (eds), *The Diary of Samuel Pepys*.

CHAPTER 34

1 Berry, 'Narrative', in Singer (ed.), *The Correspondence of Henry Hyde*.
2 Jarvis IX/1/A/5.
3 ADM 51/4214.
4 ADM 106/3023.
5 Ailesbury, *Memoirs*.

POSTSCRIPT

1   This is a conservative estimate. The Board of Trade recorded that 1,115 ships were lost in 1852, the year that records began. While the total tonnage of shipping was probably higher in the nineteenth century than, say, the sixteenth century, the total number of ships was probably not very different and the incidence of wreck just as high if not higher. It is therefore reasonable to estimate that during the last 500 years, ships have been wrecked at the rate of 1,000 a year. However, 500,000 is still a vast underestimate considering the history of shipping around the coasts of Britain goes back at least 2,000 years.

APPENDIX 2

1   de Beer (ed.), *The Diary of John Evelyn*, Vol. 3, p.408.
2   Tanner (ed), *Descriptive Catalogue of Naval Manuscripts in the Pepys Library*, p.268.
3   Mark Goldie (ed.), *The Entring Book of Roger Morrice (1677–1691)* (Suffolk: Boydell & Brewer, 2007).
4   James, Duke of York, to Laurence Hyde, 9 May 1682, in Singer (ed.), *The Correspondence of Henry Hyde*.
5   Gunman to his wife, 9 May 1682, in Moorhouse, *Letters of the English Seamen*.
6   Singer (ed.), *The Correspondence of Henry Hyde*.
7   Pepys to W. Hewer, 8 May 1682, in Howarth (ed.), *Letters and the Second Diary of Samuel Pepys*.

BIBLIOGRAPHY

MANUSCRIPTS

BRITISH LIBRARY:

Add. MS.	5719	Original letters (James Dick)
Add. MS.	11685	Issues around lead sheathing
Add. MS.	15643	Committee of Intelligence 1679–82
Add. MS.	15892	Original letters (James, Berry, etc.)
Add. MS.	15896	York finances 1682–85
Add. MS.	18447	Letters of James II to George Legge 1679–89
Add. MS.	18958	Establishment in his RH Household, Michaelmas, 1682
Add. MS.	25364	Corr. Terriesi ff. 73–78
Add. MS.	37024	Rutter of England
Add. MS.	38863	Establishment of the Duke of York's household, Christmas 1677
Harl. MS.	6922	Life of Lord Sothward, Bishop of Salisbury, on the bravery of English seamen at the time of the sinking of the *Gloucester*

GUILDHALL LIBRARY, LONDON:

Commissary Court of London Original Wills 9172
Will of Francis Davis 1682, register 38, f. 105

THE NATIONAL ARCHIVES (TNA):

E 101/668 f32	Payments Navy 1681–83
E 351/2315	List of widows, etc. re. *Gloucester* bounty payments
E 351/2316	September 1682–December 1683
E 351/2461	Victualling 1681–82
LS 1/24	Lord Steward accounts
LS 8/18-19	As above
LS 9/24	Kitchen books
LS 13/7-8	Misc.
PC 2/69	1680–83

PRO 30/24/44/72	Royal Navy ships dimensions, guns, men, etc. Charles II.
PROB 4/23558	John Poore of the *Gloucester*, 18 July 1682
PROB 4/25166	James Ford of Portsmouth, Hants, 12 June 1682
PROB 4/32/21/2	Sir Donell Obrian, Knt, died at sea in the ship *Gloucester*, letters of administration
PROB 11/370	Image ref. 743, Will of Thomas Phillips
PROB 11/370	Image ref. 734, Will of James Ossan
PROB 11/370	Image ref. 568, Will of Banjamin Holly
PROB 11/370	Image ref. 684, Will of John Deane
PROB 11/370	Image ref. 629, Will of Thomas Sevearne
PROB 11/373	Image ref. 101, Will of Rowland Rowleson
SP 8/1	Letters and Papers 1681–84
SP 8/2	As above
SP 8/3	ff. 1–228 Letters from the Duke of York to William of Orange, February 1674–February 1685
SP 29/418	Charles II, January–April 1682
SP 29/419	Charles II, May–July 1682
SP 44/63	Military and Naval 1679–84, letters between Whitehall and Sir John Berry, etc.
SP 84/217	Holland, 1682–83
SP 94/67	Spain, 1682
T 38/581	Payment of the *Gloucester* company, plus bounty for *Gloucester* widows
T 48/10	Papers Royal Household 1674–91
T 48/12	Military and Naval 1678–1713
WO 55/1718	Survey of stores and arms 1681–83
ADM 1/3552	Navy Board letters, 1681–82
ADM 1/3555	f. 451 re. Sir Anthony Deane
ADM 1/5139	f. 650, 652, items 211, 212, re. new salvaging inventions and sharing of recovered goods
ADM 1/5253	ff. 25–26 Court martial, purser of the *Henry*
ADM 1/5246	f. 610 Petition of William Harrington, etc. re. new weighing and recovering wrecked ships invention
ADM 2/1726	*Mary* yacht voyages 1680–82, including *Mary* and *Katherine* yachts to Holland, March and April 1682 for collection of gold. Directions to Captain Crow re. escorting Herrington to site of *Gloucester* wreck
ADM 2/1740	Selections 1660–84
ADM 2/1746	Duke of York's private letter book, 1663–85
ADM 2/1750	Lords letters, Duke of York, January 1681–January 1684
ADM 2/1754	Secretary's letters, January 1682–May 1684 ff. 50–54 re. John Deane, gunman, bounty payments, etc.
ADM 3/278	Board minutes 1681–84, instructions to *Mary* and *Charlotte* yachts to find out *Gloucester* wreck, *Kitchin* yacht to take on diver, etc.

ADM 7/778	Sick seamen on *Gloucester*,1675
ADM 7/827	Duke of York orders
ADM 7/1009	General instructions 1660–1718
ADM 8/1	List books of ships 1673–89, includes manning levels for *Gloucester*, also *Gloucester* in docks Portsmouth 1673–82, etc.
ADM 16/1	Treasurer 1681–82
ADM 18/63	Bill books 1679–82, covers bounty payments re. *Gloucester*
ADM 18/64	Bill books 1683–85
ADM 20/31	Treasurer ledger 1681–82, includes list of widows, etc. re. *Gloucester* bounty payments
ADM 20/32	Treasurer ledger 1682–83, details of payments to crew on the *Gloucester* while in Portsmouth Ordinary
ADM 33/108	Muster books *Henrietta*, *Gloucester* Hulk, *Happy Return* and *Kitchen* yacht, etc.
ADM 33/110	Muster books *Ruby*
ADM 33/112	Muster books *Pearl*
ADM 33/119	Muster books *Mary* and *Charlotte* yachts, Dartmouth
ADM 33/125	Muster books *Mary*
ADM 51/42	Log of the *Ann* yacht 1681–84 (re. Grenville Collins)
ADM 51/3863	Logbook of *Henrietta*
ADM 51/3819	Logbook of *Dartmouth*
ADM 51/3932	Logbook of *Pearl*
ADM 51/4214	Logbook of *Happy Return*
ADM 51/4322	Logbook of *Ruby*
ADM 52/9	Payment of pensions 1682–85
ADM 106/51	Navy Board in letters 1682
ADM 106/52	Navy Board in letters 1682, including appt of John Hull, late boatswain of the *Gloucester*, and 100 ex-Gloucester men to be entered on the *Henrietta*
ADM 106/298	f. 210 re. poor quality of victuals on HMS *Advice*, 1674
ADM 106/307	ff. 361–370 re. defects of *Gloucester*
ADM 106/313	Report on men from the *Gloucester* 1675
ADM 106/359	Captains' Letters A–C 1682, Preparing of *Gloucester* for voyage 1682; f. 19 Johnathan Nevill's complaint against Captain Allin for beating him; f. 629 finding of boat belonging to *Katherine* yacht
ADM 106/360	Captains' Letters D–F 1682, Capt. Will Davies re. preparing *Katherine* yacht for sea; f. 208 list of works for the *Mary* yacht
ADM 106/361	Captains' Letters G–L 1682, Gunman letter re. trip to Foreland, 24 August 1682; f. 313 Herrington letter re. importance of going with Capt. Crow to the site of the *Gloucester* wreck
ADM 106/362	Captains' Letters M–S 1682, ff. 592, 596 re. lead sheathing
ADM 106/363	Captains' Letters T–Y 1682
ADM 106/319	f. 123 orders to receive nothing in warehouse except stores with king's mark

ADM 106/495	ff. 243–46, as above
ADM 106/2070	Abstract of letters from the Admiralty 1679–84, ff. 14–15 Letters Patent to Sir Anthony Deane, 30 April 1680, re. boatswain Hull, etc.
ADM 106/3023	Bounty papers
ADM 106/3074	Court martials 1679–1714
ADM 106/3538	Miscellaneous
ADM 106/3539	Miscellaneous musters and petitions including John Brookes, and petition of John Atkins
ADM 106/3540	Musters, also court martial of Captain Gunman and court martial on the burning of the *Henry*
ADM 106/3541	Misc. dockyard orders and petitions

ROXBURGHE FAMILY PAPERS HELD AT FLOORS CASTLE, KERSO:

BUNDLE 160	Misc. accounts, vouchers, etc., mainly relating to the personal affairs of the Earl of Roxburghe, 1676–88
BUNDLES 164–168	As above
BUNDLE 285	Compt book, debursements, for Robert, Earl of Roxburghe, by Harry Ker, 1680–82
BUNDLE 635	Accounts relating to attempts to retrieve the body of the Earl of Roxburghe, drowned in the wreck of the *Gloucester* off Yarmouth.
BUNDLE 989	Testamentary deeds, Robert Earl of Roxburgh, 31 December 1984
BUNDLE 991	Personal correspondence 1666–1711
BUNDLE 1160	List of debts due by earl, 1682

SETON PAPERS AND VARIOUS:

E 7/3	Treasury Register May–Dec, 1682
E 9/18	Warrants Treasury register May–Dec, 1682
E 661/109	Misc loose accounts, Winton 1675–88
E 661/124	Misc accounts 1681–87
E 661/130	Cost of the earl's stay in London 1687
E 661/135	Costs, discharge and legal papers 1680–88
E 661/136	Accounts due to George Seton's tailor 1682–86
E 661/137	Accounts for board and lodging 1673–87
E 661/144	Misc. loose papers 1680–88
E 661/145	As above 1682–83
E 661/151	Estate papers and vouchers 1682–83
E 661/152	As above
GD 1/441	Seton family papers
GD 1/1192	Seton Papers 1480–1922
GD 3/1/11/35	Seton family misc. 1620–1701
GD 3/13/4	Corr.
GD 16/34/237	Letter, 20 December 1683
GD 33/65/112/1	Haddo accounts

GD 44/33/14	Misc. papers 1648–1823
GD 73/1/6	Letters to Lord David Hay from Margaret Countess of Roxburgh 1689–1711
GD 137/2179	Diary of John Scrymgeor, 1670–1709
GD 150/3449/1-19	Middleton misc. letters
GD 160/193	Perth household and legal accounts
GD 160/354	Perth inventory of silver plate, etc.
GD 190/3/84	Perth corr.
GD 214/758	Notes on Buchanan's history of the Ker family
GD 220/5/750	Montrose letter, 14 March 1682
GD 331/30	Prestonfield business and personal corr.
GD 331/32	Prestonfield business and personal accounts
GD 331/63	Prestonfield business and personal corr.

MAGDALENE COLLEGE CAMBRIDGE, PEPYS LIBRARY:
MS 1490
MS 2265
MS 2266
MS 2351
MS 2873
MS 2899

NATIONAL MARITIME MUSEUM:
BRA 128/5B	Navy Board orders, relating to payments 1682–1770
DAR	George Legge papers
DAR/20	Lead sheathing
PLA P/1	Navy Board Orders 1682–1800
P47, G218:8/2	Bernard de Gomme, Channel Islands survey (1680)
SER 9	Navy Board letters covering 1682 and relating to the equipping of the Scottish fleet and relevant actions after loss of *Gloucester*
SER 103	Misc letters 1667–1703
SER 106	General account pay books of HM ships 1660–85
SER 107	List of officers 1688–97
SER 109	Guns and men 1677
SER 110	As above 1654–1732

EDINBURGH TOWN COUNCIL MINUTES:
SL1/1/30   1681–84

LINCOLNSHIRE ARCHIVES:
GUNMAN'S JOURNALS
JARVIS IX/1/A/1	1662–66	HMS *Oxford*
		Bonaventure
JARVIS IX/1/A/2	1666–71	*Orange*
/2a	1667-23-08	*Orange*
/3	1672	*Princess Royal*

/4   1675–79   *Anne* yacht
/5   1679–85   *Mary* yacht

PRIMARY PRINTED

NEWSPAPERS:
The Domestick Intelligence or News both from City and Country
The Impartial Protestant Mercury
The London Gazette
The Loyal Protestant & True Domestick Intelligence
The Observator in Dialogue
Pacquet of Advice from Rome
The Protestant Courant
The True Protestant Mercury

BROADSHEETS:
'True and Full Account of his Late Majesty together with several English Nobility
   being Surprised at Sea', printed for T. Tillier (London: 1689)
'Two Letters from Scotland', printed for John Morice (London: 1682)

BOOKS, ATLASES AND CHARTS:
Ailesbury, T. Bruce, *Memoirs*, 2 Vols (London: Roxburghe Club, 1890)
Anon., *Life of James 2nd* (London, 1702)
Anon., *A Collection for the Improvement of Husbandry and Trade* (London: 1693)
Archenholz, Johann Wilhelm von, *A Picture of England* (1789)
Beer, E.S. de (ed.), *The Diary of John Evelyn*, 6 Vols (Oxford: Oxford University Press,
   1955)
Benn, Aphra, *A Congratulatory Poem to Her Sacred Majesty Queen Mary, Upon Her
   Arrival in England* (London, 1689)
Blackburne Daniell, F.H. (ed.), *Calendar of State Papers Domestic: Charles II, 1672–3*
   (London: Her Majesty's Stationery Office, 1901)
Blackburne Daniell, F.H. (ed.), *Calendar of State Papers Domestic: Charles II, 1682*
   (London: His Majesty's Stationery Office, 1932)
Bodeyere, Guy de la (ed.), *Particular Friends: The Correspondence of Samuel Pepys and
   John Evelyn* (Woodbridge: Boydell Press, 2005)
Bray, William (ed.), *Diary and Letters of John Evelyn*, 2nd edn (London: Henry
   Colburn, 1819)
Browne, Sir Thomas, *Pseudoxia Epidemica* (1672)
Browning, A. (ed.), *Memoirs of Sir John Reresby* (London: Royal Historical Society, 1991)
Cartwright, Dr Thomas, *The Diary of Dr. Thomas Cartwright, Bishop of Chester*
   (London: Camden Society, 1843)
Chappel, E. (ed.), *Shorthand Letters of Samuel Pepys* (Cambridge: Cambridge
   University Press, 1933)
Chappell, E. (ed.), *The Tangier Papers of Samuel Pepys* (London: Naval Records Society,
   1935)

Charnock, John, *Lives and Characters of Naval Officers of Great Britain*, 6 Vols (London: R. Faulder, 1794–98)

Christie, W.D. (ed.), *Letters addressed from London to Sir Joesph Williamson*, 2 Vols (London: Camden Society, 1874)

Clarke, J.S. (ed.), *The Life of James the Second, King of England*, 2 Vols (London: Longman, 1816)

Collins, Greenville, *Great Britain's Coasting Pilot* (London: Freeman Collins, 1693)

Cowley, Abraham, *The Works of Mr Abraham Cowley*, 2 Vols (London: 1710)

Dalrymple, Sir John, *Memoirs of Great Britain and Ireland*, 3 Vols (London: 1790–91)

Defoe, Daniel, *An Elegy on the Author of the True Born Englishman, together with an Essay on the Late Storm* (London: 1704)

Defoe, Daniel, *A Tour thro' the Whole Island of Great Britain* (London: Penguin, 1978)

Drinkwater Bethune, C.R. (ed.), *The Observations of Sir Richard Hawkins in his Voyage into the South Sea in the Year 1593* (London: Hakluyt Society, 1847)

Echard, Laurence, *The History of England*, 3 Vols (London: Jacob Tonson, 1725)

Evelyn, J., *Sylva* (London, 1664)

Ellis, Henry, *Original Letters*, Vol. IV (London: Harding, Triphook and Lepard, 1827)

Foxcroft, H.C. (ed), *A Supplement to Burnet's History of My Own Time* (Oxford: Clarendon Press, 1902)

Fraser, Duncan, *Montrose before 1700* (Montrose: 1967)

Gadbury, John, *The Astrological Seaman ... unto which is added a diary of the weather for XXI years together, exactly observed in London* (London: 1710)

Gilbert, John Thomas (ed.), *The Manuscripts of the Marquis of Ormonde* (London: HMC, 1895–99)

Goldie, Mark (ed.), *The Entring Book of Roger Morrice (1677–1691)* (Suffolk: Boydell & Brewer, 2007)

Grammont, Count de, *Memoirs*, trans. by H. Walpole and Mrs Jameson (London, *c.*1900)

Hancock, David (ed.), *The Letters of William Freeman 1678–1685* (London: London Record Society, 2002)

Higgons, Bevyl, *Historical Works*, 2 Vols (London: 1736)

Hollond, John, *Two Discourses of the Navy* (London: Navy Records Society, 1896)

Howarth, R.G. (ed.), *Letters and the Second Diary of Samuel Pepys* (London: J.M. Dent & Sons, 1932)

Hume, David, *History of England*, 8 Vols (London: A. Millar, 1767)

Keynes, Geoffrey (ed.), *Letters of Sir Thomas Browne* (London: Faber and Faber, 1946)

Knighton, C.S., *Catalogue of the Pepys Library at Magdalene College, Cambridge: Census of Printed Books* (Woodbridge: 1981)

Latham, R. and W. Matthews (eds), *The Diary of Samuel Pepys*, 10 Vols (London: Bell & Hyman, 1970–1983)

Latham, R. (ed.), *Pepys's Navy White Book and Brooke House Papers* (Aldershot: Naval Records Society, 1995)

Lauder, Sir John, *Chronological Notes of Scottish Affairs, 1680–1701* (Edinburgh: 1822)

Lauder, Sir John, *Historical Observes, 1680–1686* (Edinburgh: Bannatyne Club, 1840)

Lauder, Sir John, *Historical Notices of Scottish Affairs*, 2 Vols (Edinburgh: Bannatyne Club, 1848)

Lavery, Brian (ed.), *Deane's Doctrine of Naval Architecture, 1670* (Naval Institute Press, 1981)

Lediard, Thomas, *Life of John Duke of Marlborough* (London: J. Wilcox, 1736)

Lee, N., *To the Duke on his Return* (London: 1682)

Legge, William, *Manuscripts of the Earl of Dartmouth*, 3 Vols (London: H.M.C, 1887)

Lubbock, Basil (ed.), *Barlow's Journal of His Life at Sea in King's Ships, East & West Indiamen & Other Merchantmen From 1659 to 1703*, Vols 1–2 (Hurst and Blackett, 1934)

Luttrell, Narcissus, *A Brief Historical Relation of State Affairs September 1678 to April 1714*, 6 Vols (Oxford: Oxford University Press, 1857)

Madan, Falconer (ed.), *Stuart Papers* (London: Roxburghe Club, 1889)

Mackerell, Benjamin, *Historie and Antiquities of Kings Linne* (Norfolk: 1738)

Macpherson, James (ed.), *Original Papers containing the Secret History of Great Britain, from the Restoration to the accession of the House of Hanover to which are prefixed Extracts from the Life of James II, as written by himself*, 2 Vols (London: W. Strahan and T. Cadell, 1775)

Manwaring, G.E. (ed.), *The Diary of Henry Teonge: Chaplain on Board H.M's Ships Assistance, Bristol and Royal Oak 1675–1679* (London: Routledge, 1927)

Martin, L.C. (ed.), *The Poems of Nathanial Wanley* (Oxford: Clarendon Press, 1928)

Middlebush, Frederick (ed.), *The Dispatches of Thomas Plott (1681–1681) and Thomas Chudleigh (1682–1685): English Envoys at the Hague* (1926)

Middleton, W.E.K. (ed.), *Lorenzo Magalotti at the Court of Charles II* (Waterloo: Wilfred Laurier University Press, 1980)

Moorhouse, Hallam E., *Letters of the English Seamen* (London: Chapman & Hall, 1910)

Mordaunt, Henry, *Succinct Genealogies* (London: 1685)

Oldmixon, John, *History of England during the Reigns of the Royal House of Stuart* (London: J. Pemberton, 1730)

Poynter, F.N.L. (ed.), *The Journal of James Yonge* (London: Longmans, 1963)

Prinsterer, Groen van, *Archives de la Maison d'Orange-Nassau, Vol 5, 1650–1688* (Utrecht: 1861)

Robinson, H.W. and W. Adams (eds), *The Diary of Robert Hooke* (Robinson and Adams, 1935)

Routh, M.J. (ed.), *Bishop Burnet's History of His Own Time*, 2nd edn (Oxford: Oxford University Press, 1833)

Roxburgh, Duke of, *Fourteenth Report, Appendix, Part III* (London: Historical Manuscripts Commission, 1894)

Rutland, Duke of, *Manuscripts*, Vol. IV (London: Historical Manuscripts Commission, 1905)

Saussure, Cesar de, *A Foreign View of England*, trans. Madam Van Muyden (London: John Murray, 1902)

Savile Foljambe, F.J., *Appendix to the 7th Report* (London: Historical Manuscripts Commission, 1879)

Scott, Walter (ed.), *The Works of John Dryden*, Vol. 15 (Edinburgh: A. Constable & Co., 1821)

Seller, John, *Coasting Pilot* (London: 1671)

Seller, John, *The English Pilot* (London: 1671)

Seller, John, *The North Navigation* (London: 1746)

Shaw, William A. (ed.), *Calendar of Treasury Books, Volume 4, 1672–1675* (London: His Majesty's Stationery Office, 1909)

Shaw, William A. (ed.), *Calendar of Treasury Books, Volume 7, 1681–1685* (London: His Majesty's Stationery Office, 1916)

Sinclair, George, *Ars Nova et Magna Gravitatis et Levitatis* (Glasgow: 1669)

Singer, S. W. (ed.), *The Correspondence of Henry Hyde, Earl of Clarendon, and his Brother, Laurence Hyde, Earl of Rochester*, 2 Vols (London: Henry Colburn, 1818–28)

Sprat, Thomas, *History of the Royal Society* (London: 1667)

Smith, John, *Advertisements for the Unexperienced* (London: 1631)

Stow, John, *Survey of London* (London: 1603)

Strype, John, *Survey of London* (1720)

Stuart Papers, Part 1, Vol. 51 (London: 1902)

Tanner J. R., *Descriptive Catalogue of Naval Manuscripts in the Pepys Library, Cambridge*, 4 Vols (Naval Records Society, 1903–23)

Tanner, J. R. (ed.), *Samuel Pepys's Naval Minutes* (London: Naval Records Society, 1926)

Tanner, J. R. (ed.), *Private Correspondence and Miscellaneous Papers of Samuel Pepys, 1679–1703*, 2 Vols (London: G. Bell & Sons, 1926)

Tanner, J. R. (ed.), *Further Correspondence, 1662–1679* (London: G. Bell & Sons, 1929)

The Marquis of Lansdowne (ed.), *The Petty-Southwell Corr., 1676–1687* (London: 1928)

Thornton, Thomas (ed.), *The Works of Thomas Otway* (London: F.C. & J. Rivington, 1813)

Wanley, Nathaniel, *Wonders of the Little World* (London: 1673)

Warburton, George (ed.), *A Memoir of Charles Mordaunt, Earl of Peterborough and Monmouth With Selections from His Correspondence* (London: Longmans, 1853)

Wood, M. and H. Armet (eds), *Extracts from the records of the burgh of Edinburgh* (Edinburgh: Oliver and Boyd, 1954)

SECONDARY PRINTED

BOOKS:

Anon., *An Impartial History of the Life and Death of James II* (London: 1746)

Archibald, E.H.H., *Dictionary of Sea Painters* (Woodbridge: 1980)

Barrett, C.R.B., *Trinity House* (London: Lawrence & Bullen, 1893)

Barbour, Reid, *Sir Thomas Browne – A Life* (Oxford: Oxford University Press, 2016)

Belloc, H., *James the Second* (London: Faber & Gwyer, 1928)

Bevan, Bryan, *I was James the Second's Queen* (London: Heinemann, 1963)

Birch, Thomas, *History of the Royal Society* (London: Royal Society, 1757)

Blomefield, Francis, *Topographical History of the County of Norfolk*, 10 vols (London: W. Miller, 1804)

Browning, A., *Thomas Osborne, Earl of Danby, 1632–1712*, 3 vols (Glasgow: Jackson Son & Co., 1951)

Bryant, A., *Samuel Pepys, The Man in the Making* (Cambridge: Cambridge University Press, 1933)

Bryant, A., *Samuel Pepys, The Saviour of the Navy* (Cambridge: Cambridge University Press, 1938)

Bryant, A., *Samuel Pepys, The Years of Peril* (Cambridge: Cambridge University Press, 1935)

Callow, John, *The Making of King James II: The Formative Years of a Fallen King* (Stroud: Sutton Publishing, 2000)

Cavelli, Marquise de Campana, *Les Derniers Stuarts a Saint-Germain en Laye* (Paris: 1871)

Chambers, William, *Story of the Setons* (Edinburgh: 1874)

Chettle, George H., *The History of the Queen's House to 1678* (London: Guild & School of Handicraft, 1937)

Churchill, W.S., *Marlborough, His Life and Times*, 4 Vols (London: Harrap, 1933)

Clark, Arthur Hamilton, *The History of Yachting* (London: G.P. Putnams and Sons, 1904)

Collinge, J.M., *Office Holders in Modern Britain, Vol 7, Navy Board Officials 1660–1832* (London: Institute of Historical Research, 1978)

Dobb, Clifford, 'London Prisons', in A. Nicoll (ed.), *Shakespeare in his Own Age: Volume 17* (Cambridge: Cambridge University Press 1964), 87–102

Douglas, Sir Robert, *The Peerage of Scotland*, 2nd edn edited by J.P. Wood, 2 Vols (1813)

Earle, P., *The Life and Times of James II* (London: Weidenfeld and Nicholson, 1972)

Earle, P., *A City Full of People* (London: Methuen, 1994)

Earle, P., *Sailors, English Merchant Seamen 1650–1775* (London: Methuen, 1998)

Fea, Allan, *James II and his Wives* (London: Methuen, 1908)

Fletcher, Reginald J. (ed.), *Pension Book of Gray's Inn*, Vol. 2 (London: Masters of the Bench, 1910)

Fontaine, H.C. de la, *The King's Musick* (London: 1909)

Fox, F., *Great Ships* (London: Conway Maritime Press, 1980)

Foxcroft, H.C., *Life and Letters of Sir George Savile* (London: Longmans, 1898)

Greaves, Richard L., *Secrets of the Kingdom* (Stanford: Stanford University Press, 1992)

Haile, M., *Mary of Modena, Her Life and Letters* (London: Dent, 1905)

Harris, T., *Politics Under the Later Stuarts* (London: Routledge, 1993)

Harris, T., *London Crowds in the Reign of King Charles II* (Cambridge: Cambridge University Press, 1987)

Hartmann C.H., *The King my Brother* (London: Heinemann, 1954)

Halswell, J., *James II, Soldier and Sailor* (London: History Book Club, 1972)

Heather, W., *Chart of the North Sea* (London: 1797)

Henning, B.D. (ed.), *History of Parliament, The House of Commons*, 3 Vols (London: Secker & Warburg, 1983)

Higham, F.M.G., *King James the Second* (London: Hamish Hamilton, 1934)

Holman, Peter, *Four and Twenty Fiddlers* (Oxford: Clarendon Press, 1993)

Hodson, D., *Portsmouth Record Series, Maps of Portsmouth before 1801* (Portsmouth: 1978)

Holmes, Richard, *Marlborough* (London: Harper Press, 2008)

Hopkirk, Mary, *Queen Over the Water* (London: John Murray, 1953)

Hornstein, S., *A Study in the Restoration Navy and English Foreign Trade 1674–1688* (London: Scolar Press, 1991)

Hunter, Michael, *Robert Hooke* (Woodbridge: Boydell, 1989)

Gauci, Perry, *Politics and Society in Great Yarmouth* (Oxford: Clarendon Press, 1996)

Gavin, C.M., *Royal Yachts* (London: Rich & Cowan Ltd, 1932)

Gater, G.H. (ed.), *Survey of London, Vol. 18* (London: 1937)

Grigsby, J.E., *Annals of our Royal Yachts* (London: George Harrup, 1953)

Jesse, John Heneage, *Memoirs of the Court of England* (London: Richard Bently, 1843)

Jones, G.H., *Life of Charles, 2nd Earl of Middleton* (London: Staples Press, 1957)

Jones, J.R., *The Politics of the Exclusion Crisis 1678–1683* (Oxford: Oxford University Press, 1961)

Kenyon, J.P., *The Stuarts, A Study in English Kingship* (London: Collins, 1972)

Knights, M., *Politics and Opinion in Crisis, 1678–1681* (Cambridge: Cambridge University Press, 1994)

Lipscomb, F.W., *Heritage of Sea Power, the Story of Portsmouth* (London: Hutchinson, 1967)

Longueville, T., *The Adventures of King James II of England* (London: Longmans, 1904)

Macaulay, T.B., *The History of England from the Accession of James the Second*, edited by C.H. Firth, 6 vols (London: 1913–15)

Maitland, Richard, *The History of the House of Seytoun* (Glasgow: 1830)

Manby G.W., *Great Yarmouth* (Yarmouth: Barber and Webster, 1806)

Manship, Henry, *History of Great Yarmouth*, edited by C.J. Palmer (Great Yarmouth: Louis Alfred Meall, 1854)

May, Peter, *The Changing Face of Newmarket 1600–1760* (Newmarket: Peter May Publications, 1984)

Middleton, Dorothy, *Charles Middleton* (London: Staples Press, 1957)

Miller, J., *James II, A Study in Kingship* (Hove: Wayland, 1978)

Muns, Jessica, *Restoration Politics and Drama, the Plays of Thomas Otway* (Delaware: The University of Delaware Press, 1995)

Nicholls, Sir George, *A History of the English Poor Law* (London: P.S. King & Son, 1854)

Norie, John, *Chart of the North Sea* (London: Norie, 1845)

Ollard, Richard, *Sir Robert Holmes and the Restoration Navy* (London: Hodder & Stoughton, 1969)

Oman, C., *Mary of Modena* (London: Hodder & Stoughton, 1962)

Pool, B, *Navy Board Contracts 1660–1832* (London: Longmans, 1966)

Prioleau, Betsy, *Seductress* (London: Penguin, 2004)

Roberts, David, *Thomas Betterton* (Cambridge: Cambridge University Press, 2010)

Robinson, A.W., *Marine Cartography in Britain* (Leicester: Leicester University Press, 1962)

Rodger N.A.M., *The Wooden World* (London: Collins, 1986)

Seton, George, *A History of the Family of Seton*, 2 Vols (Edinburgh: T. & A. Constable, 1896)

Slack, Paul, *The English Poor Law 1531–1782* (Cambridge: Cambridge University Press, 1990)

Strickland, Agnes, *Lives of the Queens of England* (London: John Doran, 1855)

Sullivan, Sandra, *Representations of Mary of Modena* (London: University of London, 2008)

Tanner, J.R., *Samuel Pepys and the Royal Navy* (Cambridge: Cambridge University Press, 1920)

Tedder A.W., *Navy of the Restoration* (London: Cornmarket Press, 1970)

Temple Patterson, A., *Portsmouth, A History* (Bradford on Avon: Moonraker Press, 1976)

Tomalin, Claire, *Samuel Pepys: The Unequalled Self* (London: Penguin, 2003)

Turner, F.C., *James II* (London: Eyre and Spottiswoode, 1948)

U.K. Hydrographic Off., *Admiralty Chart 105, North Sea*

White, Jerry, *Mansions of Misery* (London: Vintage Digital, 2016)

Willes, Margaret, *The Curious World of Samuel Pepys and John Evelyn* (New Haven and London: Yale University Press, 2017)

Willis, Arthur J. et al., *Portsmouth Record Series, Borough Session Papers 1653–1688* (London: Phillimore, 1971)

Wilson, Arnold, *Dictionary of British Marine Painters* (Leigh-on-Sea: F' Lewis, 1967)

Woodhead, J.R., *Rulers of London 1660–1689* (London: Middlesex Archaeological Society, 1966)

JOURNALS:

Caston, G.F., 'Potential gain and loss of sand by some sandbanks in the Southern Bight of the North Sea', *Marine Geology*, Vol. 41 (1981), pp.239–50

Caston, V.N.D., 'Linear Sandbanks in the Southern North Sea', *Sedimentology*, Vol. 18 (1972), pp.63–78

Chance, Bernard and Charles Scarborough, *Bulletin of the History of Medicine*, Vol. 12 (July 1942)

Cowburn, P.M., 'Christopher Gunman and the Wreck of the Gloucester Part I', *The Mariner's Mirror*, Vol. 42, Issue 2 (1956), pp.113–26

Cowburn, P.M., 'Christopher Gunman and the Wreck of the Gloucester Part II', *The Mariner's Mirror*, Vol. 42, Issue 3 (1956), pp.219–29

Cowburn, P.M., 'Charles II's Yachts', *History Today* (1962)

Davis, John and Christopher Daniel, 'John Seller: Instrument Maker and Plagiarist', *Bulletin of the Scientific Instrument Society*, 102 (2009), pp.6–11

Dyer, Florence, 'The Journal of Grenvill Collins', *The Mariner's Mirror*, Vol. 14, Issue 3 (1928), pp.197–219

Gregory, Robinson, 'The Casting Away of the Gloucester Frigate', *History Today* (1955)

Halfpenny, Eric, 'Four Seventeenth Century British Trumpets', *The Galpin Society Journal*, Vol. 22 (1969), pp.51–57

Harold, Arthur and Viscount Dillon, 'Some familiar Letters of Charles II, and James Duke of York', *Archaeologie*, Vol. 58, Issue 1 (1902), p.168.

Love, Harold, 'The Wreck of the Gloucester', *The Musical Times* (January 1984)

Power, Michael, *Shadwell, London Journal* (1978)

Tanner, J.R., 'Samuel Pepys and the Trinity House', *The English Historical Review*, Vol. 44, No. 176 (1929), pp.573–87

INTERNET

www.flageolets.com/biographies/greeting.php

www.historyofparliamentonline.org

PAINTINGS

Closterman, John, *John Churchill, 1st Duke of Marlborough* (c. 1685-90), National Portrait Gallery, London

Dahl, Michael, *Sir John Berry* (c. 1689), Philip Mould Ltd

Danckerts, Johan, *The Wreck of the 'Gloucester' off Yarmouth, 6 May 1682* (c. 1682), National Maritime Musuem, Greenwich, London

Lely, Sir Peter, *Catherine Sedley, Countess of Dorchester* (c. 1675) Lyme Park, Stockport

Lely, Sir Peter, *Mary of Modena* (1673)

Kneller, Sir Godfrey, *Sir Anthony Deane* (1690), National Portrait Gallery, London

Kneller, Sir Geoffrey, *King James II* (1684), National Portrait Gallery, London

Mignard, Pierre, *Duchess of Portsmouth* (1682), National Portrait Gallery, London

Monomy, Peter, *Wreck of the Gloucester*, National Maritime Musuem, Greenwich, London

Soest, Gerard, *Lady Margaret Hay, Countess of Roxburghe* (c. 1675), National Galleries Scotland

Unknown, *George Legge*, National Portrait Gallery, London

Unknown, *James* (1688), National Portrait Gallery, London

Unknown, *Captain Christopher Gunman* (c. 1670–75)

Unknown, *Charles Scarborough*, Royal College of Physicians Museum

Unknown, *George Gordon, 1st Earl of Aberdeen*, Haddo House, Aberdeenshire

Velde, Willem van de, the Younger, *Third Rate in a Storm*, Birmingham Museums and Art Gallery

Velde, Willem van de, the Younger, *Royal yacht Mary racing the Charlotte*, collection of Mr & Mrs David Wilson

Velde, Willem van de, the Younger, *The Gloucester Sinking*, National Maritime Musuem, Greenwich, London

Verelst, Simon, *Mary of Modena*

Wijck, Thomas, *York Watergate* (1670)

Wissing, Willem, *Mary of Modena in Coronation Dress* (1685), collection of John Wyndham

INDEX